THE YOUNG P
HANDBOOK

CENTRE FOR ECONOMIC & SOCIAL INCLUSION AND NEIL BATEMAN

FOURTH EDITION

Learning, work and financial support for 14-19 year olds

The Centre for Economic & Social Inclusion

This book has been produced by the Centre for Economic & Social Inclusion, an independent not-for-profit organisation dedicated to tackling disadvantage and promoting social justice. *Inclusion* offers research and policy services, tailored consultancy, bespoke and in-house training, and event management services.

Inclusion also produces the Welfare to Work Handbook. More information about this publication, and our other products and services, is available on our website at www.cesi.org.uk.

Neil Bateman

Neil Bateman is a nationally acclaimed author, trainer and consultant who specialises in welfare rights and social policy issues. He provides services to a wide range of organisations in the third sector. More details are at www.neilbateman.co.uk.

THE YOUNG PERSON'S HANDBOOK

Learning, work and financial support for young people aged 14 to 19

ISBN: 9 781870 563765
© 2009 Centre for Economic & Social Inclusion

First edition published in 2003
Second edition published 2004
Third edition published in 2007

Centre for Economic & Social Inclusion
3rd floor, 89 Albert Embankment, London SE1 7TP

Design: www.origin8creative.co.uk
Printing: Cromwell Press Group

Disclaimer

Every effort has been taken to ensure the accuracy of the advice in this handbook. However, we cannot guarantee the information is completely accurate. This is because guidance is constantly changing. Furthermore, partners can only endorse the contents of their own chapter(s). As far as the authors are aware, all chapters contain correct information at the time of writing.

THE YOUNG PERSON'S HANDBOOK

About this book

The Young Person's Handbook draws on the authors' expertise in benefits and welfare to work programmes to provide a reference guide for anyone seeking information on the support currently available to young people aged 14 to 19.

For information on financial support and welfare to work programmes available to adults of working age, *Inclusion* also publishes the **Welfare to Work Handbook**. For further information on this publication, please visit our website at **www.cesi.org.uk**.

Acknowledgements

We are grateful for the contributions of the following people in producing this handbook:

Neil Bateman for expertise in welfare rights and social policy

Gary Vaux for advice on benefits

Tracy Samuels of the Welsh Assembly Government for provider guidance

Ansar Rahman and **Tricia Farren** of Aspire-i Ltd for checking content on Connnexions

Isobel Brown of Careers Wales for checking content

Danny Logue of Skills Development Scotland for checking content

Martin McLaughlin of Careers Service NI for checking content

Lee Barbieri of Camden ITeC for advice on apprenticeships

Nancy Richardson of Keith Povey Editorial for copy-editing

Andy Mattock of origin8 creative for design and layout

Stuart King for indexing the handbook

We are also grateful for the contribution of the following *Inclusion* staff:

Erin Schwarz and **Rachel Fox** for researching and writing content, editing and proofreading

Polly Green for project management and proofreading

Paul Bivand for expertise on policy and programmes

Dr Fatima Husain for expertise on policy relating to young people

Rosanna Singler for researching and writing content

Dave Simmonds, **Jo Casebourne** and **Craig Watt** for advice and quality control

Jade Onofrio, for marketing, customer liaison and distribution

Thanks is due to former *Inclusion* employees: **Liz Britton, James Holyfield, John Prosser, Beejal Parmar, Nicola Smith, Danielle Mason, Justine Roberts, Cait Weston, Ken Wan** and **Becky Shah,** who contributed to previous editions of this handbook.

Contents

4

Chapter 4: Young People
Remaining in Learning Programmes   102

1 Introduction

Young people today are faced with a wide, and sometimes confusing, range of choices about their future. Those who need financial assistance from the government to make ends meet may find the benefits system complex and impenetrable, while those who are deciding what to do after compulsory education may not be aware of the full array of options available to them, from A-levels to baccalaureates and diplomas, from pre-employment programmes to apprenticeships and vocational qualifications. Others may simply not know where to turn for unbiased advice on the choices they encounter. The Young Person's Handbook sets out the options each young person is faced with, so that young people can make informed decisions that not only suit their circumstances, talents and interests now, but will also offer the chance to progress along a career pathway in the future. Primarily aimed at those who advise young people on the benefits, financial support, education and training opportunities that are open to them, the handbook should also be straightforward enough for a young person to read.

How to use this handbook

Some information in this handbook covers all nations in the United Kingdom, whereas other details apply to just one or two countries. Generally, information on government benefits and tax credits is applicable across the United Kingdom, while details of learning programmes and funding for learning programmes applies to specific areas. Readers can tell at a glance whether a section is relevant to

England, Wales, Scotland, Northern Ireland, or the whole United Kingdom by looking for the following symbols next to each section heading:

E ENGLAND

W WALES

S SCOTLAND

NI NORTHERN IRELAND

UK UNITED KINGDOM

Definition of 'young person'

For the purpose of this handbook, a 'young person' is defined as someone aged between 14 and 19, in line with the Learning and Skills Council's definition of a young person. Some of the careers services discussed in Chapter 2, such as Connexions, adopt a different understanding of the term 'young person,' offering a number of services to those who are aged under 14. In order to retain simplicity and consistency, this handbook presents only the options and services which are open to those aged 14 to 19. However, advisers dealing with people aged under 14 should be aware that some careers services can offer support.

What's changed since the last edition of the handbook?

The third edition of The Young Person's Handbook was published in 2007, and the intervening years have seen a number of changes to education and benefits for young people. The first and perhaps most significant of these changes is the government's plan to raise the school-leaving age in England to 17 in 2013 and 18 in 2015, keeping young people in compulsory education for longer. Second, the upper age limit for Income Support has been modified, so that those who are in full-time non-advanced education can now claim Income Support up to age 21, rather than age 20. Similarly, the age limit for Child Benefit has been altered so that a parent, guardian or carer can claim assistance for a person aged up to 21 (instead of 20), who is in full-time non-advanced education and started their course before turning 19. Finally, since the last edition of the handbook was published, Bridging Allowance has been abolished everywhere in the UK but Wales.

In terms of content, the fourth edition offers a vast deal more than previous editions. For the first time, The Young Person's Handbook covers options for young people across the whole United Kingdom, offering information on learning programmes and funding for education and training in Wales, Scotland and Northern Ireland, along with England. It is hoped that the handbook can now assist any young person with the choices that confront them, no matter where they live.

1

2 Careers Services for Young People

Whether or not you are currently in learning or work, if you are aged 14 to 19 and thinking about your learning and employment options, your local careers service should be your first port of call. A careers service will help you to explore your options and even support you while you are in work. There are different careers services for each area of the UK. They are:

- Connexions (England)
- Careers Wales
- Skills Development Scotland, and
- Careers Service NI.

This chapter will explain what you can expect from your careers service and how to access it.

Connexions

Recent changes to Connexions E

From 1 April 2008, local authorities (LAs) have been responsible for delivering Connexions. In the past, funding went to 47 Connexions Partnerships, but now it goes directly to all 150 LAs.[1]

This change does not mean that you will receive less support from Connexions – in fact, you may get more support than in the past. Since LAs have been running Connexions, young people have not only been able to get advice about their options once they turn 16, but have had more support if they are finding it hard to make a choice or if they are at risk of disengagement or facing extra barriers to staying in learning or work.

What is Connexions?

Connexions is a youth support service for all young people aged 14 to 19. The service mixes advice, guidance and support for personal development, with the aim of helping young people to move smoothly from education to working life.

From Connexions you can expect to receive:

- help to review your strengths and weaknesses, understand your situation, recognise your potential, and set goals
- advice and guidance on achieving your educational and life goals, including careers advice
- information and advice on health, lifestyle, housing, financial support and other personal issues, if you need it
- access to personal development opportunities, including volunteering, community service activities, sports, arts and recreational activities, and
- access to specialist advice and services (where needed), to remove barriers to learning and achievement.[2]

Connexions tries to make sure that each young person gets what they need. The service also provides access to specialist support, if it's required. For example, if you need help from a housing officer or social worker, then your Connexions adviser will get in touch with them. You should not simply be 'passed on' and allowed to 'slip through the net'.[3]

What can Connexions do to support you?

If you are aged 14 to 19, Connexions should provide you with:

- an introduction to Connexions, which explains what services are available and how you can access them
- information on education, training, leisure and cultural activities

- information on all kinds of support that teenagers and their parents might need, both locally and nationally
- advice and guidance on your next steps in learning and life (this should include information and guidance on career choices, and intensive face-to-face guidance from a personal adviser for those people who need it)
- reviews when you reach a main transition point (one of these points is the end of compulsory education)
- personal support, where needed to carry out the next steps, and
- the chance to give your view on the service you want and how it should be provided.[4]

Even though it is the role of Connexions to meet with you at key points in your life between the ages of 14 and 19 (such as when you leave school), you are under no obligation to receive the service. However, it is likely to be in your best interests to use Connexions.[5] Connexions can give you information about your other options, if you choose not to use the service.

Personal advisers

Personal advisers are a key part of the Connexions service.[6] They are there to help you to deal with things that you might find difficult in your life, and to make sure that you can take up opportunities available to you. They will try to get to know you and offer you advice and guidance. They should keep in close contact with you, if necessary, and offer you support as you make choices which affect your future.

You may have already come across a Connexions adviser at school, through Social Services or perhaps when taking part in activities during the summer holidays (such as Positive Activities for Young People[7]). Sometimes, personal advisers may come into your school to talk about your options when you leave. Every young person will have access to a personal adviser, though not all young people will need one. The adviser's role is to help you to:

- realise what you can achieve and support you in getting there, with advice on employment, training and further education

- build your strengths and tackle your weaknesses
- address any personal problems you might have
- explore positive and exciting new ways of developing your talents and interests (for example, by looking into volunteering, community projects, the arts and sport or leisure activities), and
- access specialist support services, if you need them.[8]

Personal advisers work in a range of settings, such as schools, colleges, one-stop shops and voluntary and community organisations. You can choose to see your personal adviser as much or as little as you like. The amount of contact you have will depend on your own needs and what is appropriate for you personally. In some cases, young people contact their adviser by phone or text message. You have the freedom to request another adviser if you are unhappy with the one you have been allocated. You should have a say in which adviser is appointed to work with you.[9]

Personal advisers should be aware of the boundaries between personal and professional life. This means that while your adviser will be supportive and caring, they will also maintain professional distance.

Young People's Charter

Every Connexions service should have a Young People's Charter which broadly sets out what you can expect from the service, and what you can do if those expectations are not met. You can request a copy of the Charter from your local Connexions service. In many cases, you will receive a copy of the Charter when you first come into contact with Connexions.

The Young People's Charter has been drawn up by young people for young people, and is based on the principles underpinning Article 12 of the United Nations Convention on the Rights of the Child.

There are two aspects to the Charter. One sets out what you can expect in a general way – for example, that you can expect to be treated with respect. The other should be more specific – for example, it should explain the meaning of treating you with respect, and how Connexions will make this work in reality.

The key points of the Charter are:

- respect (including equal opportunities and not being judged)
- having a voice and being heard
- having a choice (encouragement but no pressure)
- confidentiality (what will or won't be passed on)
- good advice, information and support
- getting help in convenient places at convenient times
- a personal adviser who is friendly, honest, well-trained and can be trusted
- a Connexions centre which is friendly and attractive to young people, with interesting things to do
- the chance for young people to get involved in the service, if they want to, and
- making it easy to give positive and negative feedback.

Confidentiality and data protection

Advisers may share information about you with other agencies, such as Social Services or Jobcentre Plus. Your adviser's role is to find anything which might stop you from taking part in learning, and in order to do this, your adviser might have to ask you for detailed information. They may then pass this information on to other agencies you are in touch with, so that these agencies can work more effectively to solve the problems you are facing. For instance, if you have been in care and are being re-housed, it may be useful for your social worker to know that you are about to start a course at a local college. That way, the social worker can try to re-house you somewhere closer to the college.

Personal advisers should always try to get your permission before passing information on to other agencies. Your consent should be given in writing, and your adviser is responsible for making sure that you understand:

- what is being proposed
- your right to withdraw consent, and
- the time period covered by the consent form.

Depending on the reason for your visit, when you first come into contact with a Connexions adviser they will normally ask you to sign a form. This form is for data protection. If you do not want Connexions to share any information about your circumstances with other agencies or services, you have the right to say so and the right not to sign the form. This does not mean that you cannot get help or guidance from the Connexions service.

Confidentiality and child protection

Confidentiality and child protection issues may arise in meetings between you and your personal adviser. The Children Act (2004) states that if there is evidence that you are at risk, or that others are at risk, then professionals must inform other agencies about the things that you tell them.

You have a right to see what is written in your file and your adviser should agree with you first before making entries about you.

Connexions cannot guarantee confidentiality in circumstances where:

- child protection issues are involved
- there is a significant threat to life
- you need urgent medical treatment
- potential or actual criminal offences are involved, or
- a breach of statutory provision is involved.[10]

Connexions and Work-Based Learning for Young People (E)

Connexions is responsible for placing you in Work-Based Learning for Young People (WBLYP), if you wish to take part in it. WBLYP is a scheme that can give you work-based training if you are aged 16 to 18. The scheme is made up of:

- apprenticeship programmes (see page 185)
- National Vocational Qualification training (see page 148)
- Entry to Employment (see page 277)
- the right to time off for study or training (see page 344).

Connexions is involved in WBLYP in several ways. The service is responsible for:

- placing you in suitable training
- holding regular reviews, particularly for those on Entry to Employment[11]
- negotiating with learning providers on your behalf, if problems come up
- finding you another suitable training course, should you leave training for any reason, and
- liaising with Jobcentre Plus, if you are applying for benefits.

During training, Connexions will stay in touch with you, check your progress and address any problems you may have. Towards the end of your course, Connexions will give you information and guidance on what to do next, if you need it. If Connexions helps you into WBLYP, it will make sure that you know how to keep in touch. Basic information about Connexions will be included in your Learning Agreement , which you will draw up with your training provider.

Connexions and employment

Connexions has links to employers and information about vacancies. However, if you are aged 16 or 17 and looking for work, it is not likely that Connexions will encourage you to take a job that docsn't include some kind of training.

If you are already in a job, you can still use the Connexions service. It will help you to find opportunities you might wish to take up in the future, which include leisure and recreational activities. Connexions can give you advice and guidance on personal development, or any other problems you might have (such as housing), as well as learning and employment opportunities.

If you are aged under 18 and in work, you are entitled to time off for study or training. Connexions will make sure that you can still access its service while you are in work.

Connexions and young people who are unemployed or unable to work

If you are aged 16 or 17 and you are unemployed or unable to work, then Connexions is responsible for giving you support; benefits are administered by Jobcentre Plus. Connexions advisers can still offer you support up to your 20th birthday, or up your 25th birthday if you have learning disabilities.[12]

Connexions Direct **E**

Connexions Direct is a helpline and online service which provides friendly, helpful advice about things such as learning, working, housing, health, drugs, relationships and money. If you call Connexions from a landline phone, the call will be free, but calls from a mobile phone are charged. However, if you phone or email Connexions Direct, they will call you back, so that you don't have to pay the entire cost of the call. You can also talk to an adviser online. Advisers are ready to listen to you and can give information on all kinds of different subjects. They are trained and have experience of helping young people. Connexions Direct is open from 8am to 2am every day, and the service is confidential (you do not have to give your name). Your call might be recorded to help train staff and to make sure that advisers handle calls properly.[13]

Accessing Connexions **E**

You can access Connexions in a number of different ways:

- visit www.connexions-direct.com
- phone Connexions Direct on 0808 001 3219
- text Connexions Direct on 0776 815 0850, or
- visit a drop-in centre.

To find out where your nearest Connexions service is, ask your school, college, or learning provider. You can also find out where Connexions is by using the telephone directory, or asking your LA.

Careers Wales

What is Careers Wales?

Careers Wales (CW) offers a range of support for young people, with the aim of encouraging them to pursue lifelong learning, training and career development by providing realistic careers information, advice and guidance. CW also provides a number of additional support services for young people, including:

- Education Business Partnerships (which prepare young people for the world of work)
- a vacancy service for people aged 16 to 19
- the Youth Gateway service
- help with CVs, application forms and interviews, and
- the Learndirect telephone helpline.

What can Careers Wales do to support you?

If you are in secondary school or college, you are entitled to a range of support from CW, including:

- specialist guidance through individual interviews, group activities and other related events from Year 9 onwards
- the information contained on the CW website, www.careerswales.com, which includes interactive tools to support you with your learning, from choosing Year 9 subjects through to post-16 options
- access to work experience, mentoring, business awareness and enterprise days through Education Business Partnerships, which will help prepare you for work
- access to a vacancy service if you are between 16 and 19 years old
- access to all post-16 learning opportunities across Wales through the 'Learning Choices Section' on www.careerswales.com (you can also telephone 0800 100 900 to access this information)
- access to the Youth Gateway programme, which provides extra help and support before choosing further education, employment or training
- help to produce a CV

- help to complete application forms, and
- help with jobseeking and interview skills.

Careers advisers

A careers adviser will help you make realistic, informed decisions by giving you impartial careers advice. Careers advisers have a professional qualification which they achieve 'on the job' (such as a Level 4 National Vocational Qualifications), or by attending a full-time course to get the Qualification in Careers Guidance.

A careers adviser from CW will be linked to your secondary school or further education college and will provide services in both English and Welsh. If you have a learning difficulty or disability, specialist careers advisers can give you extra support.

Careers advisers will not tell you what to do or what job you are best suited to, but they will:

- help you to work out and think about the choices available to you
- outline the different courses of action you could take, and
- help you set out plans which will lead to your goals (plans could include employment, training, education, or a mixture of these things).

They will usually help you by having one-to-one interviews with you, where you will talk about your abilities, preferences and priorities. You may sometimes work with an adviser in a group setting.[14]

Youth Gateway

Youth Gateway is an extra support service provided by CW especially for young people. It will you help to:

- build motivation
- make decisions
- boost your confidence
- make the most of yourself
- improve your team working skills

- develop job application, communication and interview skills, and
- make friends.[15]

Youth Gateway is a short programme run by CW's personal advisers. The programme will help you find out what your skills and abilities are, as well as barriers that are stopping you from moving forward. You will work one-to-one with your adviser, as well as in groups. You may also have the chance to do outdoor activities.

For more information on the Youth Gateway programme, contact your nearest Careers Centre or Shop.

Careers Wales and employment

CW works closely with employers and training providers to keep up to date with the jobs that are available locally. This means that the careers information you receive from them is realistic. CW also provides a service that matches you to any vacancies which come up, if you are aged 16 to 19. These vacancies are advertised in the Careers Centres and Shops as well as online at www.careerswales.com.

Careers Wales and young people
who are unemployed or unable to work

If you find yourself unemployed, CW will give you ongoing help, whatever your age and whatever the reason. This support includes help looking for a job, writing a CV and developing interview skills, as well as the chance to join a Youth Gateway programme and access vacancies.

Accessing Careers Wales

You can access CW in a number of different ways:

- talk to the careers adviser in your school or college
- call into your local Careers Centre or Careers Shop (these are open all year round)
- visit www.careerswales.com

- phone your local Careers Centre or Careers Shop (you can find your local number in the telephone directory)
- call the free Learning and Careers Advice helpline on 0800 100 900.

Skills Development Scotland

What is Skills Development Scotland?

Skills Development Scotland (SDS) provides services for people of all ages living in Scotland, giving unbiased, confidential career information, advice and guidance and employability services. SDS aims to help people in Scotland to:

- be well-informed and ready for work
- have the self-confidence and motivation to develop skills and take part in lifelong learning
- make sound career choices throughout life, beginning with the first step into the world for work, and
- have skills that meet the needs of employers, in order to succeed and make progress in the workplace.[16]

The kind of support you get from SDS depends on your individual needs. SDS aims to support young people who:

- are aged 12 and over, and in school (including young people who are about to make their first transition into employment)
- want to learn while working, or
- are not taking part in work or learning.

If you fall into one of the groups listed above, SDS will offer you advice and guidance. In particular, the service tries to offer the right support to young people who:

- face specific barriers to achieving their potential, or
- are at risk of becoming or staying disengaged from learning and work (including people who are looked after and accommodated, care leavers, people with disabilities or health problems, young carers, and young offenders).[17]

What can Skills Development Scotland do to support you? ⓢ

SDS offers support to all young people in education or care, and to those who have not yet found work, learning or training opportunities.[18] If you are aged 14 to 19, you are entitled to career guidance and employability services from SDS. This includes:

- detailed information about vocational learning and Skills for Work courses[19]

- help to develop your career planning skills and smooth your transition into work, learning or training

- one-to-one support, if you leave school at the earliest legal leaving date (this includes S4 summer and S5 winter leavers, and those who leave school at the end of S3)

- access to intensive employability help (for example, through Activate or other local initiatives) close to your school-leaving date from S4 onwards

- help from a SDS key worker before your official school-leaving date, if you are a vulnerable young person, and

- help to understand and access employment and learning, so that you can search for opportunities and access the 'hidden job market.'[20]

If you are aged 16 to 19, and you are having trouble finding (or staying in) employment, learning or training, SDS can offer you structured support that is tailored to your needs. This support could include:

- ongoing help from a careers adviser, who will be allocated to you if you need intensive support

- tailored help with employability, through a range of employability tools and intensive support (for example, Get Connected sessions and the WorkNet programme)

- access to the SDS key worker service, if you face extra barriers to achieving your aims, and

- access to the personal advisory service, if you are a Get Ready for Work trainee (see page 163).[21]

If you are at risk of becoming detached from work or learning, SDS will offer you more one-to-one support, to make sure that you achieve your career, work and learning goals. Young people at risk of becoming detached could include those who:

- are looked after or accommodated
- are care-leavers
- are disabled or have long-term health problems
- have mental health issues
- are from minority ethnic backgrounds
- have been excluded from school or are in alternative education
- are involved with the criminal justice system
- have caring responsibilities
- are being supported by social work departments, or
- have been referred to SDS by Joint Assessment, another agency or transition meetings.[22]

You may also get extra help from SDS if you are supported by youth workers, or if you are underachieving in S5 or S6.

SDS uses a range of methods to give you support and contact, including one-to-one help, online questionnaires, group sessions, Public Access Centres and online services. [23]

Personal advisers (S)

You will get one-to-one help from SDS in a number of situations. The person who helps you could be called a key worker or a personal adviser, depending on your situation. SDS offers one-to-one support in the following circumstances:

- If you leave school at the earliest legal leaving date (this includes S4 summer and S5 winter leavers, and those who leave school at the end of S3), you will get one-to-one help.
- If you are a vulnerable young person, you will get help from a key worker before your official school-leaving date.
- If you are aged 16 to 19 and having trouble finding (or staying in)

work or learning, you will get ongoing help from an adviser who will be allocated to you.

- If you face extra barriers to achieving your aims, you will have access to the key worker service.
- If you are a Get Ready for Work trainee (see page 163), you will have access to the personal advisory service.
- If you are at risk of becoming detached from work or learning, SDS will offer you extra one-to-one support.

Confidentiality and data protection

SDS will gather information about you from a number of sources, including:

- questionnaires or online forms you have filled out
- one-to-one discussions with you, and
- your school (your school should only give SDS information relevant to career planning, including information about your progress with school subjects, participation in careers-related activities and your particular strengths or abilities).

The personal information SDS collects from these sources should be treated with confidence. If you fill out any forms for SDS, they should contain information about how SDS will use your details to help your career choices, and your right to access the information. Some forms may also ask your permission to get a copy of your exam results from the Scottish Qualifications Authority.

Sometimes SDS might want to share your information with other organisations, such as your training provider or an organisation which supports your medical conditions. SDS should not share your information with other agencies or companies unless you have given consent, nor should information be passed on to your parents or carers without your consent.

When SDS no longer requires your information, your electronic files are deleted and your paper records disposed of in confidential waste.[24]

Confidentiality and child protection (S)

SDS aims to keep all of your personal information confidential. However, if issues of abuse come up during your contact with SDS, staff will have to share your personal information with other people or another agency. This is so that you can get the right kind of help for your situation. SDS has a Child Protection Policy which sets out strict guidelines for handling situations involving abuse (or suspected abuse). SDS staff are expected to handle your case with sensitivity, make you aware that they are going to share the information you have given them, and explain what kind of action will result. [25]

SDS staff have a duty to report any cases of abuse (or suspected abuse) against a child or vulnerable adult. A child is a person who is:

- aged under 16, or
- aged up to 18, and
    - subject to a Children's Hearing supervision, or
    - under local authority care by a court order.

A vulnerable adult is a person who is:

- aged 16 or over, and
- unable to safeguard his or her personal welfare, and
- in need of care and attention because of age or infirmity, or
- suffering from illness or mental disorder, or
- substantially handicapped by any disability.[26]

There are five different kinds of abuse that SDS staff must report. They are:

- physical injury, where your parent (or somebody else caring for you) physically hurts or injures you
- sexual abuse, where immature children or teenagers are involved in sexual activity they do not fully understand, and to which they are not able to give informed consent
- emotional abuse, where you are harmed by constant lack of love

or affection (this includes taunting, shouting, ridiculing, negative criticism, threats and verbal attacks)

- physical neglect, where your parents or carers fail to meet your basic needs (such as adequate food and clothing), or fail to make sure that you have appropriate supervision or medical treatment, and
- 'non-organic' failure to thrive, where you fail to thrive because of 'non-organic' reasons (such as inadequate diet or lack of emotional support).[27]

In general terms, an SDS staff member will take the following actions if they know or suspect that you are facing abuse:

- If you are in school or college when the SDS staff member finds out you are facing abuse, or suspects you are facing abuse, the staff member will talk to either the Child Protection Officer or a member of senior management at your school or college.
- If you are no longer in school or college when the staff member finds out you are facing abuse, or suspects you are facing abuse, the staff member will contact the SDS Child Protection Liaison Contact, who will give advice and support in dealing with the problem.[28]

Skills Development Scotland and pre-employment programmes

SDS runs two pre-employment programmes for young people. The programmes on offer are:

- Get Ready for Work (see page 163), and
- Skillseekers (see page 170).

If you are interested in joining one of these programmes, you can talk to an SDS adviser or your careers adviser at school.

SDS also runs the pre-employment programme Training for Work (see page 279), which is for people aged 18 or over. However, you cannot join Training for Work through SDS. Instead, you need to access the programme through Jobcentre Plus.

Skills Development Scotland and work-based learning

Skills Development Scotland is responsible for running apprenticeships in Scotland. If you aren't employed and you think an apprenticeship might be the right path for you, staff at SDS can advise you on the kinds of apprenticeships that are available and how you can get started on one. You can also talk to your careers adviser at school.

Skills Development Scotland and young people who are unemployed or unable to work

If you are aged 16 or 17 and you are unemployed or unable to work, then you can get support from SDS. Once you turn 18, you can get support from Jobcentre Plus, but you will still be able to get help from SDS, because it is a service for people of all ages.

Accessing Skills Development Scotland

You can access SDS (or Careers Scotland, which is run by SDS) in a number of ways:

- use the 'Contact Us' form at www.careers-scotland.org.uk to email your questions (you will get a response within five working days)
- phone Careers Scotland on 0845 850 2502, or SDS on 0141 225 6710
- find the address of your nearest centre online at www.careers-scotland.org.uk, if you would prefer to speak to someone face-to-face
- access a range of services online at www.careers-scotland.org.uk, including help with CVs, interview skills, planning your career and accessing job vacancies
- e-mail info@skillsdevelopmentscotland.co.uk, or
- visit www.skillsdevelopmentscotland.co.uk.

Careers Service Northern Ireland

What is Careers Service Northern Ireland?

Careers Service Northern Ireland (CSNI) is a careers information, advice and guidance service for people of all ages. The service is run by the Department for Employment and Learning, and helps young people (and adults) to make informed choices about their future career paths. Careers advisers from CSNI work in Jobcentres, Jobs and Benefits Offices and Careers Offices throughout Northern Ireland.[29]

Future changes to the Careers Service

In the next few years, big changes will be made to expand the support offered by CSNI and improve the service for young people. Planned changes include:

- increasing the number of careers advisers available to help Year 10 students, by September 2009[30]

- creating partnerships between CSNI and all post-primary schools, further education, training and apprenticeship providers (so that young people will get enough support to develop their career plans and decision-making skills), by September 2009[31]

- using labour market information 'champions', and training CSNI staff in labour market information (so that young people can access more of the right jobs, training opportunities and education)[32]

- developing the CSNI website into a 'Careers Information Hub' which gives help with career planning and offers up-to-date labour market information[33]

- creating a careers support package for parents (so that they can understand the choices young people face and help them in making decisions)[34]

- having more effective careers information, advice and guidance services for vulnerable young people,[35] and

- providing careers information, advice and guidance to match and support different people's needs.[36]

What can Careers Service Northern Ireland do to support you? (NI)

CSNI works together with your school, college or training organisation to make sure that you get enough support with your career choices. Your learning provider is responsible for giving you careers education, and CSNI is responsible for giving you impartial careers advice and guidance.[37] CSNI has negotiated partnership agreements between CSNI and the majority of post-primary schools, further education, training and apprenticeship providers, to make sure that you get quality careers information, advice and guidance, and develop your career decision-making skills.[38] So, if you are taking part in learning, CSNI could offer you:

- introductory class talks about the support you can get from CSNI
- presentations on career options, to help you make decisions
- advice sessions for groups of students
- one-to-one guidance interviews
- assessment (including psychometric assessment)
- information about the labour market, and
- attendance at careers events and parents' events.[39]

You can get individual support from CSNI at certain 'transition points' in your learning. This means:

- In Year 10, a careers adviser may visit your school and talk to your class about GCSE options and subject choice.[40]
- At the beginning of Year 12, a careers adviser will speak to your class and give you the chance to fill out a careers questionnaire, which will help you to plan your career choices.[41]
- In Year 12, you will have the chance of an individual interview with a careers adviser, who can give you advice and guidance on your options.[42]
- In Year 13 and 14, you will get advice on higher and further education choices.[43]

Future changes to the level and kind of help you can expect to get

CSNI has successfully piloted a new service where the level and type of support you get depends on your individual needs. After an assessment of your needs and your readiness to make career choices, you will be assigned to one of three general groups, each with a different level of support on offer, as follows:

- The self-help group is for people who have a career direction in mind. If you are in this group, you will be able to access information and guides in a careers centre or on a website, and get support from a careers adviser or careers support staff member when you need it.

- The brief staff-assisted group is for people who are moderately ready to make career choices. If you are in this group, you will have guidance from a careers adviser to help you access careers information and resources. You will have an individual learning plan to help you use careers resources and services and meet your goals. You will also be able to get help from a careers adviser or careers support staff member whenever you need it.

- The individual case-managed group is for people who are unsure which career to follow. If you are in this group, you will have one-to-one guidance from a careers adviser to help you explore career, learning or training opportunities that would suit you. You will also receive an individual learning plan, which will help you to achieve your goals.[44]

Young people with special support needs

CSNI works with schools, parents, young people and others to carry out transitions reviews for young people who are vulnerable or have special educational needs. The service also works with voluntary, community and legal organisations to make sure that young people with special support needs get the help necessary to support their career planning goals. In the future, CSNI will continue to build these partnerships and give a more tailored service to meet the careers information, advice and guidance needs of young people with special needs.[45]

Currently, CSNI offers specialist help to certain young people. If you are a young person with extra support needs, you can get specialist help from

CSNI if your career choices are affected by:

- a physical disability
- a medical condition
- a sensory impairment
- a general or specific learning difficulty, or
- emotional and behavioural difficulties.

You can get this specialist help from a careers adviser if you have extra support needs and you are:

- in full-time education at school or college until age 19
- thinking about doing training before your 22nd birthday
- already on a training programme, or
- unemployed

and you are thinking about:

- staying on at school or leaving school
- moving to a further or higher education college
- employment, or
- studying from home through a local further education college or a Learndirect Centre.[46]

Careers advisers

A careers adviser will give you help with:

- choosing subjects for GCSE, or other Level 2 subjects
- AS- and A-levels, or other Level 3 subjects
- further and higher education
- training and apprenticeships
- getting a job
- self-employment, and
- voluntary work.[47]

You can make an appointment with a careers adviser in your area for a one-to-one interview. Contact details are available at www.careersserviceni.com.

Careers Service Northern Ireland and employment

If you are in employment, CSNI is able to help you:

* improve your skills
* prepare for an interview
* write a CV, and
* research jobs.

Accessing Careers Service Northern Ireland

You can access CSNI in a number of ways:

* visit the CSNI website at www.careersserviceni.com, where you will find lots of information on careers and related areas[48]
* phone 0289 044 1781, or
* e-mail cssu.account@delni.gov.uk.

Endnotes

1   www.everychildmatters.gov.uk/youthmatters/connexions Accessed on
     3 February 2009

2   Connexions (2001) *Connexions for All*

3   Connexions (2002) *Connexions at a Glance*, p.5

4   Connexions, *Connexions Service Planning Guidance 2000*, Section G, para. 4

5   Connexions (2002) *The Connexions Youth Charter: Guidance for Connexions
     Partnerships*, Appendix 2

6   www.everychildmatters.gov.uk/youthmatters/connexions/personaladvisers/
     Accessed on 3 February 2009

7   www.c-world.co.uk/c-partners/payp.php Accessed on 3 February 2009

8   Connexions (2002) *Connexions at a Glance*, p.4

9   Connexions (2002) *Connexions at a Glance*, p.4

10   Connexions (2001) *The Connexions Framework for Assessment, Planning,
     Implementation and Review*, para. 2.43

11   www.connexions-direct.com/index.cfm?pid=79&catalogueContentID=158
     Accessed on 4 February 2009

12   Connexions (2001) *The Connexions Framework for Assessment, Planning,
     Implementation and Review*, para. 4.6

13   www.connexions-direct.com/ Accessed on 4 February 2009

14   new.careerswales.com/prof/server.php?show=nav.3016 Accessed on
     14 April 2009

15   www.careerswales.com/youngpeople/choices17/16to19_youth.asp Accessed on
     14 April 2009

16   www.careers-scotland.org.uk/AboutCS/WhatWeDo/WhatWeDo.asp Accessed on
     14 April 2009

17   Skills Development Scotland, *Operating Plan 2008–09*, p.12

18   Careers Scotland, *Careers Scotland (SE area) Contribution to Skills Development
     Scotland: Our Plans and Priorities for 2008–2009*, p.5

19   Careers Scotland, *Careers Scotland (SE area) Contribution to Skills Development
     Scotland: Our Plans and Priorities for 2008–2009*, p.6

20   Careers Scotland, *Careers Scotland (SE area) Contribution to Skills Development
     Scotland: Our Plans and Priorities for 2008–2009*, p.7

21   Careers Scotland, *Careers Scotland (SE area) Contribution to Skills Development
     Scotland: Our Plans and Priorities for 2008–2009*, p.7

[22] Careers Scotland, *Careers Scotland (SE area) Contribution to Skills Development Scotland: Our Plans and Priorities for 2008–2009*, p.6

[23] Skills Development Scotland, *Operating Plan 2008–09*, p.14

[24] www.careers-scotland.org.uk/AboutCS/WhatWeDo/Policies/DataProtectionPolicy.asp Accessed on 15 April 2009

[25] Careers Scotland (2005) *Child Protection Policy*, p.7

[26] Careers Scotland (2005) *Child Protection Policy*, p.5

[27] Careers Scotland (2005) *Child Protection Policy*, p.6

[28] Careers Scotland (2005) *Child Protection Policy*, p.5

[29] www.careersserviceni.com/Cultures/en-GB/CareerService/Promoting+the+Career+Service/ Accessed on 15 April 2009

[30] Department of Education and Department for Employment and Learning, *Preparing for Success: Careers Education, Information, Advice and Guidance*, para. 6.7.3

[31] Department of Education and Department for Employment and Learning, *Preparing for Success: Careers Education, Information, Advice and Guidance*, para. 6.7.4

[32] Department of Education and Department for Employment and Learning, *Preparing for Success: Careers Education, Information, Advice and Guidance*, para. 6.6.5

[33] Department of Education and Department for Employment and Learning, *Preparing for Success: Careers Education, Information, Advice and Guidance*, para. 6.6.6

[34] Department of Education and Department for Employment and Learning, *Preparing for Success: Careers Education, Information, Advice and Guidance*, para. 6.7.10

[35] Department of Education and Department for Employment and Learning, *Preparing for Success: Careers Education, Information, Advice and Guidance*, para. 6.7.12

[36] Department of Education and Department for Employment and Learning, *Preparing for Success: Careers Education, Information, Advice and Guidance*, para. 6.7.5

[37] Department of Education and Department for Employment and Learning, *Preparing for Success: Careers Education, Information, Advice and Guidance*, para. 6.7.2

[38] Department of Education and Department for Employment and Learning, *Preparing for Success: Careers Education, Information, Advice and Guidance*, para. 6.7.4

[39] Department of Education and Department for Employment and Learning, *Preparing for Success: Careers Education, Information, Advice and Guidance*, para. 6.7.2

[40] www.careersserviceni.com/Cultures/en-GB/CareerService/ Promoting+the+Career+Service/ Accessed on 15 April 2009

[41] www.careersserviceni.com/Cultures/en-GB/CareerService/ Promoting+the+Career+Service/ Accessed on 15 April 2009

[42] www.careersserviceni.com/Cultures/en-GB/CareerService/ Promoting+the+Career+Service/ Accessed on 15 April 2009

[43] Department of Education and Department for Employment and Learning, *Preparing for Success: Careers Education, Information, Advice and Guidance*, para. 6.7.3

[44] Department of Education and Department for Employment and Learning, *Preparing for Success: Careers Education, Information, Advice and Guidance*, para.6.7.5

[45] Department of Education and Department for Employment and Learning, *Preparing for Success: Careers Education, Information, Advice and Guidance*, para. 6.7.12

[46] www.careersserviceni.com/Cultures/en-GB/CareerService/ Promoting+the+Career+Service/ Accessed on 15 April 2009

[47] Department for Employment and Learning (2008) *Careers Service Northern Ireland leaflet 2945W*, p.2

[48] Department for Employment and Learning (2008) *Careers Service Northern Ireland leaflet 2945W*, p.3

3 Financial Support for those Outside Education, Training and Work

Aged 16 to 18 and unemployed 🇺🇰

If you are aged under 18 and you are unemployed, you can only get Jobseeker's Allowance (JSA) in certain circumstances. However, you may be able to get other benefits if you are a lone parent or a carer, or if you cannot work because of disability or ill health. For more information, see the sections about Income Support (page 52), Carer's Allowance and Employment and Support Allowance (page 305).

If you are unemployed, your parents or carers may get short-term payments (through extended Child Tax Credit and Child Benefit) while you are looking for a suitable government-funded training place or learning. This chapter explains the rules for claiming these payments.

The normal minimum age for claiming JSA is 18, but some people aged 16 and 17 can get JSA in certain circumstances, such as severe hardship. Jobcentre Plus should think about using its discretionary power to give you JSA on the grounds of severe hardship if you:

- make a claim for JSA, and
- have little or no money, and
- do not fall into the 'prescribed groups' (see page 59).

This chapter explains the rules for both Income Support (IS) and JSA.

You have a right to make a claim for JSA. Whether you are thinking about work, work-based learning or education, or you just don't know what to do, you should contact the Connexions Service (or the Careers Service if you live in Scotland, Wales or Northern Ireland), which will be able to advise you on your options (see page 16).

The benefits system for those aged 16 and 17 is complex and many advisers, as well as young people themselves, are unclear about entitlements. This chapter sets out the legislation and guidelines for making claims and giving payments.

Aged under 16 🇺🇰

You usually have to be aged at least 16 to be eligible for benefits. This means that the parent or carer you live with should claim benefits for you.

However, if you are aged under 16 and you are a parent, you can get Child Benefit, Healthy Start Vouchers and Health in Pregnancy Grant for your child. The rules for Child Tax Credit are different: you must be aged 16 or over to get Child Tax Credit for your child. If you live with your parents or carers, they may be able to claim Child Tax Credit for your child, if they can show that:

- your child normally lives with them, or
- they have the main responsibility for your child.[1]

Your parents or carers can also claim Child Benefit for you.

If you are aged under 16, you may be able to claim Housing Benefit in your own right (for example, if you had to take on rent liability for your accommodation).

If you have a disability, your parents or carers should claim Disability Living Allowance for you, but you can get this benefit in your own right once you turn 16.

segmentx
xxx
segmentxx

You may be able to claim the following benefits from the day when you turn 16:

- Income Support
- Employment and Support Allowance
- Carer's Allowance
- Industrial Injuries Disablement Benefit
- Tax Credits
- Guardian's Allowance
- Jobseeker's Allowance (but you can only claim this in certain circumstances if you're aged 16 or 17)

Child Benefit **UK**

Child Benefit (CB) is a payment of £20 per week for your eldest child, and £13.20 per week for all other children. If you only have one child, you will be paid £20 per week. Foster parents who have a child placed with them by a local authority cannot claim CB for that child.

CB is not a means-tested benefit. It is paid to people who are:

- responsible for a child aged under 16, or
- responsible for a young person aged under 21, who is in full-time, non-advanced education, and started their course before they turned 19 (this includes A-levels, most foundation degree courses, Level 3 National (or Scottish) Vocational Qualifications and government-funded work-based learning and training, such as Entry to Employment) (see page 155).

From November 2009, CB will not count as income for Housing Benefit and Council Tax Benefit.There are some circumstances where parents or guardians can get CB for young people who are older than 16 and younger than 21 and who are not in full-time non-advanced education.

Child Benefit is paid by Her Majesty's Revenue and Customs (HMRC) and you can make an online claim at www.hmrc.gov.uk.

Child Benefit Extension Period

If you are 16 or 17 and you live with your parents or guardians, they can claim CB for you until the 'terminal date' after you leave school (see table below), so long as you're not working. This is the rule for ordinary CB. However, your parents or guardians might be able to keep on claiming after the terminal date, for a longer time known as the Child Benefit Extension Period (CBEP). The CBEP starts on the Monday after you leave education or training and it lasts for up to 20 weeks. Your parents or guardian may also get Child Tax Credit during the CBEP. Your parents or guardians can only get CB during the extension period if they were eligible to claim CB before the extension period started. The amount of CB they get does not change during the extension period.

To get payments during the CBEP, you must:[2]

- be registered as available for work, education or training with your local Connexions or careers service (see page 16), and
- be unemployed, or working less than 24 hours per week, and
- not be getting Employment and Support Allowance, Income Support or Income-Based Jobseeker's Allowance, and
- not be in training or learning (your parents or guardians could claim ordinary CB and Child Tax Credit in such a case).

The following table explains the timeline for the CBEP:

Date of leaving education or unwaged training	Date CB stops (terminal date)	Date CBEP starts	Date CBEP stops
December – February	Last day in February	First Monday after leaving education	20 weeks after start of CBEP
March – May	Last day in May	First Monday after leaving education	20 weeks after start of CBEP

June – August	Last day in August	First Monday after leaving education	20 weeks after start of CBEP
September – November	Last day in November	First Monday after leaving education	20 weeks after start of CBEP

The following example may help to explain the CB rules:

Lauren is 17 and lives at home with her parent. She leaves an Entry to Employment course on 5 May. Her parent will get CB until the last day in May (the terminal date). If Lauren doesn't have a job or training place by 1 June, her parent can apply to have the CB extended, for a maximum of 20 weeks, counted from 5 May. The CB will stop whenever one of the following events happens, whichever comes first:

- Lauren turns 18 (she can then claim JSA in her own right)
- The 20 weeks of the CBEP are over
- Lauren gets a job

When can you legally leave school?

England and Wales

The school leaving date in England and Wales is the last Friday in June of the school year in which you turn 16 (from 2013 in England this will be the school year in which you turn 17 and from 2015 the one in which you turn 18).

Scotland

The school leaving dates are:

- 31 May, if you turn 16 between 1 March and 30 September (inclusive), or
- the first day of the Christmas holiday period, if you turn 16 between 1 October and the last day of February (inclusive)

Northern Ireland

The school leaving date is 30 June of the school year in which your 16th birthday occurs. If you leave school before the legal school-leaving date, you will be treated as if you had stayed on until that date.

How to claim extended Child Benefit

To claim extended CB, your parent or carer has to make a written request during the CBEP, within three months of the date when you stopped education or training.[3]

Some time before the date when you can legally leave school or non-advanced education, the Child Benefit Centre should automatically send your parents or guardians a letter (form CH298) to ask about your future plans. If your parents do not get this letter at the usual time (for example, because you leave school or non-advanced education earlier than intended), your parents or guardians can contact the Child Benefit Centre to ask about entitlement (contact details are on page 398). They can also notify the Child Benefit Centre about changes in circumstances online at www.hmrc.gov.uk.

On the form from the Child Benefit Centre, your parent or guardian has to give the date when you registered with the Connexions or careers service, and they have to sign the following declaration:

'I will let you know straight away if s/he starts paid work or a Work-Based Learning for Young People course, receives Income Support or Jobseeker's Allowance in her/his own right or starts a course of advanced education.'

Withdrawing extended Child Benefit

Extended CB should not be withdrawn if you refuse a job or a place on Work- Based Learning for Young People during the CBEP. Extended CB will end when one of the following happens, whichever comes first:

- You can claim Income Support, JSA or Employment and Support Allowance yourself
- You start a job where you work 24 hours or more per week

- You start a course of advanced education (for example, a university degree)
- You reach your 18th birthday (the last CB payment will be on the Monday before your birthday – after your birthday, you may be able to claim JSA)
- The CBEP ends[4]

Reclaiming Child Benefit and extended Child Benefit

If you leave school, but return to education before your 19th birthday, you can re-qualify for CB. You can also re-qualify for CB if you leave a job within the CBEP, whatever the reason for leaving. You will need to register for a job, education or a training place with the Connexions or careers service. If you left your job because of ill health, and you are too sick to go to the Connexions or careers service office, your parents can contact the local office (either in person or by phone) to confirm that you intend to find a training place when you are well again.

Your parents can then reclaim Child Benefit, normally by filling out form CH299, which they can get from the Child Benefit Centre.

Child Benefit when you are in education or training

If you are aged under 21 and you are in full-time, non-advanced education, or unwaged training which is funded by the government (known as 'approved training'), your parents can claim CB and Child Tax Credit for you. If you do not live with your parents or guardians, and no-one else is claiming CB for you, you may be able to claim Income Support in your own right (see page 52).

If you are aged 16 or over, but you are under 21, your parents can get CB if you:[5]

- attend a full-time course of non-advanced education at a recognised educational establishment, or
- attend a full-time course of non-advanced education elsewhere, so long as the Commissioners of Her Majesty's Revenue and Customs

agree that your course counts as education (home tuition may count, if you started it before you turned 16),[6] or

- are on approved training.

A 'recognised educational establishment' is a school or college, or somewhere similar.

When claiming CB, 'full-time' education means education for more than 12 hours per week, including tuition, exams, practical work and supervised study (such as homework or writing assignments). It does not include unsupervised study, private research or meal breaks.

'Non-advanced education' broadly means all qualifications up to and including A-levels, Level 3 National Vocational Qualifications or Scottish Vocational Qualifications, the Scottish Certificate of Education (Higher level), or the Scottish Certificate of Sixth Year Studies.[7] You will count as being in non-advanced education if you are between courses, so long as you have enrolled on the course you are waiting to start, or you are doing unwaged training between your courses.[8]

'Non-advanced education' is a level below advanced education. 'Advanced education' means a course which leads to a

- postgraduate degree or similar qualification
- first degree or similar qualification
- diploma of higher education
- Higher National Diploma
- teaching qualification
- any other course which is a level above an ordinary national diploma, a national diploma, a national certificate from Edexel, A-levels or Scottish Highers.

Approved training includes:

- Entry to Employment (often known as e2e) or Programme Led Pathways (in England)
- Skill Build and Foundation Modern Apprenticeships (in Wales)

- Get Ready for Work, Skillseekers or Modern Apprenticeships (in Scotland), and
- Access or Jobskills Traineeships (in Northern Ireland).

Your training must be funded by the government (for example, through Learning and Skills Councils, the Welsh National Council for Education and Training, the Scottish Executive, Scottish Enterprise, Highlands and Islands Enterprise or the Northern Ireland Department for Employment and Learning).[9]

If you are aged 19 or over, you will only qualify for CB if you started your course or training before you turned 19.[10] You will not qualify if you were aged 19 or over before 10 April 2006.[11]

You count as being in full-time, non-advanced education or approved training until the 'terminal date' after you leave. The four terminal dates are shown in the table on page 45.

CB is always paid on a Monday, and covers the week up to the following Sunday. When you leave education or training, CB should be paid up to and including the Sunday after your terminal date, unless you find a job before then. If you turn 18, or start working on or before a Monday, CB will stop from:

- the Monday following your 18th birthday (or the Monday of your 18th birthday, if you turn 18 on a Monday), or
- the Monday following the day when you start work or Work-Based Learning for Young People.

You can have a period of up to six months out of education or learning, if it is 'reasonable' (there is no legal definition for this). You can have a period longer than six months out of education or learning, if your time out is caused by illness or disability, and it is reasonable to ignore the break.[12] During a reasonable break, CB will still be paid. You could make the case that the rules about getting CB during breaks still apply after the terminal date and during the CBEP. Your parents or carers cannot get CB during a break if you start, or are likely to start, any of the following straight after the break:

- advanced education
- training which is not 'approved training', or
- education linked to employment or a position in an organisation.[13]

Child Benefit and other benefits

From November 2009, CB will not count as income for Housing Benefit and Council Tax Benefit. Until then, it counts as income and may reduce the amount of Housing Benefit or Council Tax Benefit you get, unless you qualify for the maximum amounts because you get Income Support, Income-Based Jobseeker's Allowance or Income Related Employment and Support Allowance.

If you get Child Tax Credit, then your CB does not count as income for Income Support and Income-Based Jobseeker's Allowance.

When the Child Benefit Extension Period ends

At the end of the CBEP, if you do not have a job or training place, or if you are not in full-time education, you may apply for discretionary JSA on the grounds of severe hardship (see page 42).

Child Tax Credit

Parents or carers can also get Child Tax Credit for you while you are in education or approved training. The rules about education and training for Child Tax Credit are the same as those for Child Benefit.[14]

Other benefits parents and carers can claim for young people

For some benefits, parents or carers can get extra amounts if they have dependent children or young people.

If your parent or carer claims Incapacity Benefit or Widowed Parent's Allowance, and they have been getting an extra amount for a dependent

Financial Support for those Outside Education, Training and Work

child since before 6 April 2003, they can keep on getting this extra amount if you meet the CB rules about education or training.

If your parent or carer claims Income Support or Income-Based Jobseeker's Allowance, they can get extra amounts if they have not made a claim for Child Tax Credit as long as they were in receipt of them before September 2005. The CB rules about education and training apply.

Housing and Council Tax Benefits are worked out with extra amounts for children, whether or not your parents or carers get Child Tax Credit. If your parents or carers qualify for CB because you are in education or training, these CB amount should be included when working out their Housing and Council Tax Benefits.

Carers can be treated as a parent for Working Tax Credit, which may increase their entitlement to Working Tax Credit.

Income Support and Jobseeker's Allowance

In general, if you are unable to work because of caring responsibilities or because you are in education and estranged from your parents, you should claim Income Support (IS), and if you are unable to work because of a disability or ill-health, you should claim Employment and Support Allowance (ESA). If you are able to work and you have not yet found work, education or training, you should claim Jobseeker's Allowance (JSA) while you look for a job, education or training. The rules for IS and JSA are described in more detail below.

What is Income Support?

IS paid to certain people who don't have to be available for work (for example, because they have caring responsibilities). IS can be paid on its own or to top up other benefits or earnings from part-time work.

Remember, if you claim IS in your own right, your parents or carers will no longer be able to get CB and Child Tax Credit for you. If you are living with your parents or carers, this may mean that the family income as a whole will be less, so it is important to get advice before you claim IS. This is especially true if you are disabled, because the Child Tax Credit your parents or carers get should already include extra amounts for your disability. This extra money could be lost if you claim IS in your own right.

Who is entitled to Income Support?

In general, the following people can claim IS:

- anyone aged 16 or over who is unable to work or take up training or education (for example, because of caring responsibilities)
- certain people aged 16 to 21 who are on a training course[15]
- certain people aged 16 to 21 who are in education, including those estranged and who have to live away from parents or carers.

There are more detailed rules that you will have to meet to claim IS, and these are given in the following sections. As well as meeting these rules, your income and capital will need to be low enough for you to qualify. For more details, see the Welfare Benefits and Tax Credits Handbook by the Child Poverty Action Group.

Young people who can't do work or training

You can claim IS if you are aged 16 or 17 and you can't do work or training because you are:[16]

- a lone parent
- a single foster parent
- looking after a child aged under 16 because the child's parent (or the person who usually looks after the child) is ill or temporarily away
- looking after a member of your family who is temporarily ill
- receiving Carer's Allowance
- regularly caring for someone who has claimed or receives Attendance Allowance or high- or middle-rate Disability Living Allowance
- expecting a baby in 11 weeks or less (but not if you are in relevant education (see page 54), unless you fall under another category)

- gave birth seven weeks ago or less (but not if you are in relevant education (see page 54), unless you fall under another category)
- a person from abroad who can get benefits in limited circumstances, under the urgent cases regulations
- a refugee learning English on a course (the course must run for more than 15 hours per week, and you must start the course within a year of coming to Britain) – you will be able to get IS for up to nine months
- part of a couple looking after a child aged under 16 while your partner is temporarily out of the UK
- required to attend court (for example, as a witness or a defendant)

If you can't do work or training because of ill-health, you should claim Employment and Support Allowance rather than IS.

Young people in relevant education or on approved training

If you are aged 16 or 17 and you are in relevant education or approved training (see page 54), and you also fall under one of the following categories, then you can claim IS:[17]

- You are a parent responsible for a child who lives in your household
- You are an orphan with no-one acting in place of your parents
- You are living away from your parents (or anyone acting in their place) of necessity, and they cannot support you because they are:
  - chronically sick, or
  - mentally or physically disabled, or
  - in prison, or
  - unable to come to Britain because of immigration laws
- You have refugee status and in order to get a job, you have started to learn English (on a course or courses which run for more than 15 hours per week and which you started during your first year in Britain) – you will be able to get IS for up to nine months
- You are a student from abroad with limited leave to stay in the UK, and you do not have recourse to public funds (if you are temporarily without funds, you may get IS for up to six weeks)

- Of necessity, you are living away from your parents (or anyone acting in their place) because:
    - you are in physical or moral danger, or
    - you are 'estranged' from your parents (or anyone acting in their place), or
    - there is serious risk to your physical or mental health
- You used to be in the local authority's care, and you are living away from your parents (or anyone acting in their place) of necessity (if you are covered by the support for care-leavers, you will not qualify (see page 319)). You will not have to show estrangement.

If you are aged 19 or over, you must have started, enrolled or been accepted on your course or training before your 19th birthday to qualify for IS. You count as being in education until the terminal date (see the table on page 45). So, if you leave training, or full-time education during the summer term, you can claim IS until the last day of August. Then, in September you may be able to get JSA (see page 52) if you don't fit into one of the IS categories for people outside education.

If you are disabled, you should claim Employment and Support Allowance instead of IS.

If you are aged 16 or 17 and you are in local authority care, or you are covered by the support for care-leavers, you can only get IS in very limited circumstances (such as being a parent or disabled (see page 53)).

Definition of terms

This section explains some of the key terms used to work out whether you can claim IS. Jobcentre Plus staff follow guidance on the use of these terms.

A person acting in the place of your parents

To decide that someone is acting in the place of your parents, Jobcentre Plus staff will look at whether that person:[18]

- provides supervision and financial, social, moral or other care and guidance, and

- provides shelter, food and clothing, and
- is responsible for any necessary disciplinary action that is appropriate for someone your age.

A person acting in the place of your parents also includes:

- foster parents, and
- a local authority or voluntary organisation that looks after you, no matter whether they are paid to look after you.[19]

If someone other than your parent is claiming CB or a different benefit for you, this is strong evidence that they are acting in place of your parents.[20]

In physical or moral danger

This covers physical or moral danger that could happen if you live at home. The danger does not have to come from your parents. If you (or your representative) give evidence that you could be in physical or moral danger, this should be accepted unless there is stronger evidence that goes against your case. You will not count as being in physical or moral danger unless you can show that you have to live away from home because of it.[21] Legally, you do not have to have a history of harm to count as being in danger now.[22] Physical and moral danger can include situations where you have to live away from your parents because of political problems in another country.[23]

Estranged

For this term, Jobcentre Plus uses the same meaning as the dictionary: 'alienated in feeling or affection'.[24] This means that you are estranged from your parents if:

- you have neither the intention nor the wish to live with them, and you have no wish for prolonged physical or emotional association with them, or
- your parents have neither the intention nor the wish to live with you, and they have no wish for prolonged physical or emotional association with you.[25]

You can be estranged even when your parents are giving you some financial support. You must show that you have to live away from your parents because of the estrangement.[26] According to case law, you can still be estranged even if you have contact with your parents, as long as there is emotional disharmony.[27] Your can have polite contact with your parents or carers, and still be legally estranged.[28]

Your own evidence of estrangement will usually be accepted, and Jobcentre Plus will only look for extra evidence if they doubt yours. No-one should contact your parents without your permission and only if your evidence is contradictory or improbable. Contacting your parents must only happen with your consent, and you should not be put under pressure to give consent.[29] A third party (like a social worker or youth worker) can provide evidence of estrangement.

Serious risk to physical or mental health

This term means that there must be a serious risk to your physical or mental health – the fact that there may be a risk is not enough. For example, this term could apply if you suffer from chronic bronchitis which is made worse by the damp conditions in your parents' home, or if you have a history of mental illness which is made worse by your parents' attitude towards you. Actual harmful events do not need to have happened, but you must identify the risk[30] and show that you have to live away from home because of it.[31]

How to claim Income Support UK

To claim IS, you can go to your local Jobcentre Plus office or contact them by phone. You should tell them that you want to claim IS as someone who qualifies while in education, and you should not be put off from making a claim. You can also download a form online from www.dwp.gov.uk.

You should fill out the form and return it within one month of first contacting the Jobcentre Plus office or longer when it is reasonable to do so. Your claim will then be accepted from the date you first contacted

Jobcentre Plus. If you delay returning your form, you may lose some of your benefit. If you return the form after the normal one-month deadline, you should explain why it is late and ask for your claim to be dated from when you made first contact. It is best to get the form back to Jobcentre Plus within one month to avoid problems. A Decision Maker will decide if you can get IS. You will get a letter to tell you their decision.

You may be interviewed as part of the claim process. You should attend the interview (and let the Jobcentre Plus office know if you can't attend, so that they can arrange a different time). It is helpful to have someone come with you to the interview, especially if you are claiming IS while in education under the 'estrangement' or 'risk' categories.

The standard letter at Appendix 1 may be helpful if you have someone who is helping you with your claim.

If you are refused Income Support

If your IS claim is refused, you have the right to appeal to an independent tribunal. Appeals are often successful, especially if you can get help from an independent advice agency.

Income Support amounts

The IS personal allowance for people aged 16 or 17 is £50.95 per week (2009-10 rates). This is the only rate available to young people.

IS is normally paid into a bank or building society account (or a Post Office Card Account), though in exceptional circumstances you can be paid by cheque.

Types of Jobseeker's Allowance

There are two types of JSA:

- Contributory JSA
- Income-Based JSA

Contributory JSA is paid to people who have worked and paid enough National Insurance contributions, so it is not likely that someone aged 16 or 17 will qualify. This section is about Income-Based JSA.

Who is entitled to Jobseeker's Allowance?

Usually, you can only claim JSA if you're aged 18 or above, but some people aged 16 or 17 can get it. If you think you might be eligible, you should not be turned away from making a claim, and you should be referred to a specialist adviser for people aged 16 or 17 at Jobcentre Plus. The adviser should get in touch with you within four hours from the time when you first contacted Jobcentre Plus. They will work out whether or not you can get JSA.[32]

There are four different ways you could be entitled to JSA:

- entitled to JSA during the CBEP
- entitled to JSA for a limited time
- entitled to JSA at any time, or
- able to claim JSA on grounds of severe hardship.

Prescribed groups

If you are entitled to JSA, you will fall into a 'prescribed group'. The group you are in could affect the amount of JSA you are paid, or the obligations that you have. The different groups are listed below.

Couples

If you are married or have a Registered Civil Partnership, and you are living with your partner in the same household, you will claim JSA as a couple, and you will get the couples rate. The amount you get depends on a combination of your age and the benefit your partner is claiming.

You will be treated as a couple if you are living together in the same household as though you are husband and wife (if you are a same-sex couple, you will be treated as though you are civil partners). If your partner has a different home, you will not be treated as a couple just because you spend time together (which includes having a physical relationship).[33] If you are not sure whether you are a couple, or if you have been classed as a couple when you feel that you shouldn't have been, it is important to get independent advice.

If you are part of a couple, and you are both unemployed and aged under 18, you must each qualify for JSA in order to get the couple rate. If only one of you qualifies for JSA, then as a couple, you will only get a single person's allowance (which takes into account the age of the person who claims). If you are a couple and you are both aged under 18, and one of you is ill, disabled or has a child, then your partner should be able to get JSA for you both.

If one of you is aged over 18, then that person will get JSA at a single person's rate, unless the other member of the couple also qualifies for JSA or IS.

Joint claims

Some couples have to make a joint claim for JSA. This means that both people must attend interviews and meet the rules for JSA (for example, the rules about being available for, and actively seeking, work, and the rule about having a Jobseeker's Agreement).

You need to make a joint claim for JSA if you are both aged at least 18, unless:

- you have a child (or children)
- one of you works for at least 16 hours per week
- one of you meets the basic rules for Income Support or Employment and Support Allowance (for example, you have caring responsibilities or ill-health)
- your parents or carers can get Child Benefit for one of you, or
- one of you cannot get Income-Based Jobseeker's Allowance because of immigration or residence restrictions.

If one of you is aged under 18, you will have to make a joint claim if the person aged under 18:

- is claiming JSA on the grounds of severe hardship, or
- qualifies for JSA in other circumstances.[34]

Couples where both are aged under 18 do not need to make a joint claim for JSA,[35] but to get the couples rate, you must both be eligible for JSA.

Claiming Jobseeker's Allowance during the Child Benefit Extension Period

You may be able to get JSA if you are in your CBEP and you have to live away from the parental home (or the home of any person acting in the place of your parents) because you:[36]

- are estranged, or
- were in custody immediately before the age of 16, or
- were placed away from home as part of a programme of rehabilitation or resettlement, under the supervision of a probation officer or social worker, or
- have suffered physical or sexual abuse, physical or moral danger, or there is a serious risk to your mental health or physical health
- have a physical or mental handicap or illness, and need special accommodation, or
- cannot get support from your parents because they are in custody, chronically sick, have a mental or physical disability or can't enter or re-enter the country, or
- have no parents or someone to act as your parent.

If you are married or have a Registered Civil Partnership (or if you live with a partner as though you are husband and wife, or as though you are civil partners), you may qualify for JSA if your partner is:

- 18 or over, or
- aged 16 or 17 and registered for Work-Based Learning for Young People, or

- a young person who is responsible for a child in the household, or
- a young person who is eligible for JSA, Income Support or Employment and Support Allowance, or
- a young person who is laid off or on short time for up to 13 weeks, and who is available for employment, or
- a young person who is temporarily away from the UK because they are taking their child abroad for treatment, or
- a young person who cannot do work and training because of severe mental or physical disability, or because of a disease which a medical professional says is unlikely to end within 12 months

Claiming Jobseeker's Allowance outside the Child Benefit Extension Period

In some circumstances, you can get JSA for up to eight weeks. This is the case if you:[37]

- have been discharged from prison or custody after the CBEP and you meet any of the above rules for claiming JSA during the CBEP, or
- have stopped living in local authority care and are forced to live away from your parents (however, most young people aged under 18 who have been in local authority care cannot get JSA (see page 59)).

Claiming Jobseeker's Allowance at any time

You can get Income-Based JSA at any time if you:[38]

- have been temporarily laid off work or put on short-time (you can get JSA for a maximum of 13 weeks). 'Laid off' means that you have not been made redundant, so you are still employed, but because of a work shortage, you are working reduced hours
- are a member of a couple which is responsible for a child who lives in the same household
- are entitled to claim IS, but decide to claim Income-Based JSA instead (an adult might claim Income-Based JSA in order to get National Insurance contribution credits, but there is no obvious advantage for a young person to claim Income-Based JSA instead of IS)
- have accepted a firm job offer in the armed forces and:

- were not in employment or training at the time of the offer, and
- have never had your Income-Based JSA reduced because of an employment or training sanction (except for a Jobseeker's Direction), and
- have accepted an enlistment date which is within eight weeks from when the offer was made.

Claiming Jobseeker's Allowance on the grounds of severe hardship

If you don't fall into any of the above groups, and you have little or no money, you can still make a claim for JSA. JSA should be paid if severe hardship would result from you not getting the benefit.[39]

In theory, the decision to pay JSA on the grounds of severe hardship is made at the discretion of the Secretary of State. In practice, decisions are made on behalf of the Secretary of State by either the Jobcentre Plus office, or the Under-18s Support Team (UEST) in Sheffield. You will be considered for severe hardship payments of JSA only if you cannot get IS, Employment and Support Allowance or JSA in any other way (see page 42).

How to claim Jobseeker's Allowance

Although most young people cannot claim JSA, Jobcentre Plus staff should not refuse to let you make a claim.

To claim JSA (including making a claim on the grounds of severe hardship), you must be registered for both employment and training with Connexions. However, if you go to the Jobcentre first, they should contact Connexions or the Careers Service for you.[40] Connexions or the Careers Service will give you an ES9 or ES11 referral form to take to the Jobcentre Plus office, where you will be interviewed. It is often easier to go to Connexions or the Careers Service first.

There are a couple of exceptions to the rule about being registered with Connexions or the Careers Service. You do not have to be registered if you:

- are claiming JSA under special rules for people who are laid off or on short time working

- have enlisted in the armed forces
- could not register because of an emergency at Connexions, such as a fire, or
- would suffer hardship because of the extra time it takes to go to Connexions and register.

If either the third or fourth bullets apply, you can register at Jobcentre Plus on a temporary basis for up to five working days.[41] The date when you first contact Connexions, the Careers Service or Jobcentre Plus should be treated as the date of your claim, so long as you contact Connexions, the Careers Service or Jobcentre Plus within five days (this is very important because you could miss out on money that you are entitled to; check this happens).[42]

If you do not contact Connexions or the Careers Service after going to Jobcentre Plus, your JSA claim can be stopped.[43]

You must actively look for education, work and training while you get JSA. You will have to wait for three days after you claim JSA to receive a payment, unless you are claiming JSA on the grounds of severe hardship.

Jobseeker's Interview

What should you take to the interview?

When you make a claim for JSA, you will have a Jobseeker's Interview. Before your interview, Jobcentre Plus should give you the JSA claim forms and booklet (JSA1 and ES6). You should complete the forms before your interview, if you have time. You should also be given a form (ES9JP or ES11JP) by Connexions or your Careers Service to confirm that you have registered with them. You should bring these forms with you.[44] If you do not bring the forms, or if you have trouble completing the forms, you can get help when the forms are checked before your interview starts.[45]

You will also need to take the following things with you to the Jobcentre Plus office:

- Your National Insurance number, if you have one
- Some evidence of your identity and address

- The P45 form from your last job, if you have one

If you don't have a National Insurance number, your claim should not be put off while you wait to get one, and you can get benefits on an interim basis.[46]

If you don't have evidence of identity, you should explain why not. By law, you may still get benefits even if you don't have evidence of identity. This is the case when:

- the evidence does not exist
- your health or disability stops you from getting the evidence, and no-one else can reasonably get it for you
- it is not practical to get the evidence from a third party, or
- there is a serious risk to your physical or mental health if you get the evidence.[47]

The interview

Your interviews should be carried out by an adviser who has good interview skills and can handle sensitive issues. The adviser should also have a good understanding of the labour market and benefit rules for getting JSA, particularly:

- where the rules are different to the rules for adults, and
- the roles of the different people and agencies involved with young people.[48]

The adviser should also check to see whether you meet any of the rules for young people who can get Income Support.

You can bring along someone such as an adviser, youth worker, relative or friend to your interview, and it is usually a good idea to do so.[49]

Jobseeker's Agreement UK

Young people have a special Jobseeker's Agreement (form ES7). This agreement deals with training in a different way to adult agreements. Your adviser should draw up your Jobseeker's Agreement together with you.

The Jobseeker's Agreement lists:

- your availability for work, including any restrictions
- the type of work and training you are looking for
- the activities you will carry out each week to look for work and training and improve your chances of finding them
- what the Jobcentre Plus office will do to help you, and
- brief information about sanctions and disallowances.

You will keep a copy of your Jobseeker's Agreement.[50]

Labour market concessions

If you have never been 'sanctioned', you have certain 'labour market concessions'. This means you can restrict your availability to jobs with suitable training.[51] You can refuse jobs which do not offer the right kind of training. Young people who have not been sanctioned have 'good cause' for refusing a job where the training content is not suitable, or where no training is offered.

If you have labour market concessions you are expected to actively seek work and training as a minimum requirement for your benefit.
You can also take steps to find full-time education in your weekly search activities. You must take at least one step each week to find work and one step each week to find training.[52] If it is reasonable to take only one step in a given week, your step can be either to find work or to find training.[53]

If you have been sanctioned

If you have been sanctioned, you will lose your labour market concessions. This means you cannot restrict your availability to jobs with suitable training, and you cannot refuse jobs that don't offer suitable training. To get your benefit, you must actively seek work. You cannot seek training as an alternative to work. However, you can look for training as a step to finding a job.[54]

Jobseeker's Direction

A Jobseeker's Direction is a written statement which tells you what you must do to improve your chance of getting a job. If you do not follow a Jobseeker's Direction, and you cannot show that you had a good reason for not following it, then you may lose your JSA.

If you have 'labour market concessions' (for example, the right to refuse a job that does not provide suitable training), then you cannot be given a Direction to do something which goes against the concession. If you do not follow a Jobseeker's Direction, this will not affect your labour market concessions. Jobcentre Plus staff are told to take care before giving a Jobseeker's Directions to someone aged under 18 who has labour market concessions.[55]

Sanctions for Jobseeker's Allowance

If your JSA is 'sanctioned', this means that you will not get the benefit at all, or you will get it at a lower rate. There are various circumstances when your JSA could be sanctioned. If your JSA is sanctioned, it is very important to get independent advice and submit a written appeal, because appeals against sanctions are often successful.

Sanctions and reductions of JSA differ depending on:

- whether you were in work or training before claiming JSA
- whether you get JSA as a member of a prescribed group or on the grounds of severe hardship
- whether you are a new jobseeker
- the action (or lack of action) which led to the sanction.

Sanction rules for new jobseekers

When you first leave full-time education, you are classed as a 'new jobseeker'. You stop being a new jobseeker if you:[56]

- become employed or self-employed for 16 or more hours per week
- complete a course of training
- give up a training place without good cause, or
- lose a training place through misconduct .

As a new jobseeker, you can turn down one training place without good cause and not be sanctioned. This one time, you count as having 'automatic good cause'.[57] 'Turning down' means that you have:

- failed to apply for a training place
- failed to accept a training place
- refused a training place
- failed to attend a training place
- failed to pursue a training place
- neglected to avail yourself of a training place, or
- left a training place.

If you turn down a training place with good cause, then you are still a new jobseeker, and you will keep your right to turn down one training place without being sanctioned.

If you use your automatic good cause, and then you either turn down training again or lose your training place because of misconduct, your JSA will be sanctioned.

Good cause

Training

If you turn down unwaged training, Jobcentre Plus staff must think about whether you had good cause for your decision. 'Good cause' is not defined in law, but Jobcentre Plus will look at certain things to decide whether you had good cause. You may have good cause if you:

- have a disease or physical or mental disability which affects your ability to attend training, or puts your health or the health of others at risk. (The Decision Maker should first decide whether your disease or disability means that you cannot work, but you do not need to be incapable of work in order to have good cause for turning down training)[58]

- have a sincerely-held religious or conscientious objection
- must travel more than an hour to and from training either way (if there is no learning provider within one hour of where you live, this is relevant)
- were attending court as a witness or party to proceedings
- have caring responsibilities, and no other household member or close relative of the person being cared for could take over your duties, and it is not practical for you to make different care arrangements
- were arranging or attending a funeral (if the deceased is a close relative or friend)
- had to deal with a domestic emergency (Jobcentre Plus will look at the nature of the emergency and may question your availability for work, or whether you are actively seeking work)
- had to perform duties for the benefit of others in an emergency
- risk your health and safety by participating
- will breach a Community Order or Disposal or Anti-Social Behaviour Order by attending training, or[59]
- could not attend training because it disrupted your part-time study.[60]

This list is not exhaustive and it does not carry legal force, so even if your circumstances are not covered by the above, you may still be able to argue that you had good cause.[61]

You could also show good cause if you stopped doing training because it was unsuitable,[62] but you should usually try to use the complaints procedure before leaving. Decision Makers know that your age and lack of experience could mean that you are not familiar with complaints procedures, or you are too frightened to use these procedures, so you may still have good cause even if you did not make a complaint.[63] You will have good cause if a Connexions or careers service adviser told you that the training was unsuitable and advised you to leave, or not attend or apply for it.[64]

The rules about good cause for turning down employment are the same as the rules for turning down training.[65]

Sanctions if you are not a new jobseeker

If you are not a new jobseeker, a Decision Maker can sanction your JSA if, without good cause, you have:[66]

- lost employment or a place on a training programme through misconduct
- left employment voluntarily
- refused, failed to apply for, or failed to accept employment
- neglected a reasonable opportunity of employment
- refused or failed to carry out any reasonable Jobseeker's Direction
- given up a place on a training scheme or employment programme
- failed to attend a training scheme or employment programme
- refused or failed to apply for or accept a place on a training scheme or employment programme, or
- neglected a reasonable opportunity of a place on a training scheme or employment programme.

For examples of what counts as good cause, see page 68.

Leaving employment

If you leave employment (including employed-status apprenticeships) voluntarily and without just cause, or because of misconduct, you will be sanctioned in the same way as an adult who gets JSA. Your case will be referred to a Decision Maker in the same way as an adult case. Your JSA will not be stopped while you wait for the decision, but if the Decision Maker decides against you, then your JSA can be stopped for between one and 26 weeks.

There is a lot of case law which can help you to challenge a sanction based on employment. You can also appeal the length of the sanction – it is quite common to get a full 26-week sanction when a shorter period would be more appropriate. When deciding the length of your sanction, the Decision Maker must take into account:

- if your job was due to last more than 26 weeks, how long it would have lasted for

- if you are going to be re-engaged by the same employer, the date you will be re-engaged
- if your job was for less than 16 hours per week, your rate of pay and hours of work, and
- any physical or mental stress connected with the job.

Case law says that Decision Makers should take into account all of your circumstances and the justice and merits of your case when deciding the length of your sanction.[67]

If you were unemployed for 13 weeks and then you take a job where you work for at least 16 hours per week, there is a trial period from the fifth to the twelfth week of your job. During the trial period, you can leave your job for any reason other than misconduct, without being sanctioned.[68] This is called Employment on Trial.

If you leave non-employed status training voluntarily and without good cause, and you then claim JSA as a member of a prescribed group (see page 59) or on the grounds of severe hardship, you will be sanctioned. You will have your JSA reduced to 60 per cent of the normal amount for a set period of two weeks. It will be reduced to 80 per cent if you or a family member you claim for is seriously ill or pregnant.

If you are sanctioned, you can apply for payments under the JSA hardship rules in certain circumstances (see page 79). Don't confuse JSA hardship payments (paid when you are sanctioned) with JSA paid to people aged 16 or 17 on the grounds of severe hardship.

Refusing to take up employment

If you refuse employment, or neglect to avail yourself of employment (including employed-status training), you can be sanctioned unless you still have your labour market concession. (The labour market concession is a right to refuse jobs which do not offer suitable training. You will usually have the concession if you have not been sanctioned in the past (see page 66).) Your JSA will be reduced for two weeks, or until your 18th birthday (if your birthday is sooner). To be sanctioned for refusing to take up employment, the job you refused must have been offered to you by Jobcentre Plus or Connexions in England.

If you refuse to take up non-employed status training, and you are claiming JSA as a member of a prescribed group, then your JSA can be reduced to 60 or 80 per cent of the normal amount for two weeks. If you refuse training and you are claiming JSA on grounds of severe hardship, then your benefit can be revoked (stopped). If you make a new JSA claim, your payments will be reduced to 60 or 80 per cent of the usual amount for the first two weeks.

Connexions and careers service staff are legally required to tell Jobcentre Plus promptly if they think you have refused employment or training, or if they think you have neglected to avail yourself of a suitable employment or training opportunity. They will tell Jobcentre Plus by using form ES22 or ES95N.[69]

Rules about leaving or refusing training or employment for prescribed groups

If you are in a prescribed group and you refuse or leave training or employment, or if you leave training because of misconduct, a Decision Maker will handle your case. If you leave a place, Jobcentre Plus will give you form ES86Y so that you can state the reasons why you left. If you left because of misconduct, the learning provider will be asked to give information.

Rules about leaving or refusing training or employment for severe hardship claimants

If you are claiming JSA on grounds of severe hardship, and you leave training or employment, your case will not be handled by a Decision Maker. Instead, the Jobcentre Plus office adviser (on behalf of the Secretary of State) decides whether you had good cause to leave.[70] If you had good cause to leave training, you will get a certificate of good cause.

If you refuse a training place, Connexions or the careers service will tell Jobcentre Plus. Jobcentre Plus will check its evidence against your evidence for good cause. If more evidence is needed, you will be asked to explain your refusal at an interview as soon as possible. If you do not attend the interview, Jobcentre Plus will assume you don't want to comment (but this is not in the law).

If the Jobcentre Plus adviser doesn't think you had good cause for refusing a training place, then your payment is automatically reduced for the first two weeks of your new JSA claim.

If you fail to complete a training course, the Jobcentre Plus office adviser will decide if you had good cause, after looking at evidence from Connexions (or careers services in Wales, Scotland and Northern Ireland) and from you. If they decide that you had good cause, you will be given a good cause certificate. You will get a good cause certificate no matter whether your good cause was 'actual' or 'automatic' (you have 'automatic good cause' for turning down one training opportunity if you are a new jobseeker). See page 72 to find out what you should do if you leave a training course because you believe it is sub-standard.

If the Jobcentre Plus office adviser decides that you did not have good cause, or if you showed misconduct, you will get Decision Certificate ES91 and your JSA payments will be reduced to 60 or 80 per cent of the usual amount for two weeks.

Misconduct

What is misconduct?

Case law says that misconduct is being blameworthy and behaving wrongly in direct or indirect connection to your activities on the training course or job.[71] Simply being inefficient, breaking minor rules, or doing something which you did not know was wrong will not usually amount to misconduct, even if it gives your employer or training provider grounds to dismiss you.[72] Misconduct can happen outside work (for example, being convicted of theft outside work, which means that your employer cannot let you work with valuables,[73] or losing your licence because of driving offences, when driving is an essential part of your job).

The following things may count as misconduct:

- willfully disobeying a reasonable order (unless you had a good reason)
- actions outside the training place which affect your suitability for the training

- failure to follow regulations (for example, safety rules)
- refusing to do appropriate work
- refusing to work overtime (this only counts if overtime is mentioned in your learning agreement and you were given enough notice about having to work overtime)
- negligent or inefficient work (a lot of factors are taken into account before a decision can be based on this, including the seriousness of your omission, the extent to which you are to blame, and the level of skill and responsibility expected of you)
- offensive behaviour, arguing and fighting, and
- dishonesty.

The following things do not count as misconduct:

- refusing to do work that is not part of your learning agreement
- refusing to work overtime if it is not mentioned in your learning agreement, or if the request to work overtime is unreasonable, or if you are not given enough notice to work overtime
- inefficiency, if you were doing your best (inefficiency counts as misconduct only if you are failing to meet standards that you are capable of meeting)
- being a naturally slow worker
- cases where there is medical proof that you were not responsible for your actions because of mental illness
- breaking workplace rules which you were not aware of
- cases where you have been dismissed for absence but have obeyed all the rules about notification
- failing to obey an instruction because of a misunderstanding
- refusing to perform tasks because of a genuine religious or conscientious belief, and
- work as a self-employed person which you decided to end.

Misconduct is not the same as reasonable cause for dismissal. For example, in some cases it might be reasonable to dismiss you for inefficiency, but inefficiency is not usually misconduct, and your benefit should not be sanctioned.

Proving misconduct

The person who says that you lost your job or training place because you acted with misconduct must prove it (this is usually the learning provider). Jobcentre Plus staff will decide that you acted with misconduct if it is more likely than not that the allegations are true. Before a decision is made, you will have a chance to comment on statements made against you by the provider or witnesses. It is important to comment, and if you don't take the chance to do so within a week, Jobcentre Plus staff will think about a sanction.[74] If Jobcentre Plus staff ask you to provide evidence and information within seven days, you should try to do this but if you can't, you can ask for longer if it is reasonable – there is no legal time limit on how long this can be.

What is leaving employment voluntarily without just cause?

You should only be classed as leaving work voluntarily if you left of your own free will, without any coercion, and if leaving was something you brought upon yourself.[75] If you volunteer for redundancy when your employer is planning to stop trading or wants to lose jobs,[76] this does not count as leaving voluntarily. If you leave because your employer changes your terms and conditions of employment without your agreement,[77] this also does not count as leaving voluntarily, so long as you tried to change matters. You must show that what you did was reasonable and that you took steps to resolve problems and look for other work before claiming JSA.

You may have just cause for leaving voluntarily if:[78]

- you were not aware of the terms and conditions of the job when you agreed to take it
- you have pressing or urgent domestic or personal circumstances
- you have a genuine grievance about the job, but have been unable to resolve it

- you were not suited to the type of work and thought it was better to leave than be dismissed
- you were asked to do work outside your normal or contractual duties
- the work conflicted with a sincerely-held religious or conscientious belief
- you left because you got a better job and that second job fell through
- you left to do study or training
- the job was affecting your health or safety, or it was beyond your capabilities
- you had to live away from home for long periods.

These are just examples.

Summary of sanctions for Jobseeker's Allowance

The rules about sanctions are very complicated. The main rules for people who are claiming JSA as part of a prescribed group (and not on severe hardship grounds) are summed up here. Look up the reason for your sanction in the table below, then check what the sanction is. For sanctions of JSA which is paid on the grounds of severe hardship, see page 71.

Sanction Type	Period of Sanctions (weeks)	Decision Method	Effect on Payment
Misconduct (employment)	1–26	Sector Decision Maker (SDM)	Hardship – by application, not automatic
Misconduct (training)	2	SDM	Automatic reduced rate of JSA

Leaving training early	2	SDM	Automatic reduced rate of JSA
Neglect to avail	2 *	SDM	Automatic reduced rate of JSA
Refusal of training	2	SDM	Automatic reduced rate of JSA
Jobseeker's Direction	2	SDM	Hardship – by application, not automatic

*Sector Decision Makers may give sanctions that last for 1–26 weeks. However, your JSA is only reduced for a maximum of two weeks.

If you are sanctioned, your benefit will be reduced by either 40 per cent or 20 per cent. Your benefit will normally be reduced by 40 per cent unless you (or a member or your family) are pregnant or seriously ill.

Jobseeker's Allowance hardship payments

Hardship payments are not the same as JSA which is paid on the grounds of severe hardship. Hardship payments are JSA paid at a reduced rate, in certain circumstances, to people in hardship. You can apply for hardship payments if your JSA has been stopped, or if you are waiting for a decision.

If you are claiming JSA on grounds of severe hardship, and you are waiting for a decision or have received a benefit penalty, you can apply for hardship payments. You do not have to prove that you will suffer hardship, because you have already proved severe hardship. But you cannot get hardship payments if you have failed to meet labour market conditions (see page 66).

For all the situations listed below, if you are claiming JSA as part of a prescribed group (see page 59), you must show that you (or a member of your family) would suffer hardship if you do not get hardship payments. You can apply for hardship payments in the following situations:[79]

a) Your JSA has been refused because you do not satisfy labour market conditions

You can claim hardship payments if your JSA was refused because you are not available for work, not actively seeking work and training, or will not draw up and sign a satisfactory Jobseeker's Agreement.

If you are claiming JSA on grounds of severe hardship, and you do not satisfy labour market conditions, you cannot get hardship payments.

b) You have been sanctioned

Most sanctions last for two weeks. You will automatically get a reduced rate of JSA without needing to apply for hardship payments. But for some sanctions, your JSA will be stopped (not reduced) from one to 26 weeks. You won't get any payment unless you claim hardship.

c) You are waiting for a decision on whether you satisfy certain labour market conditions at the start of your claim, so your claim has not been processed

These conditions are being available for work, actively seeking work and training, and drawing up and signing a Jobseeker's Agreement.

d) Your JSA has been suspended until a decision is made on whether you satisfy certain labour market conditions

These are the same conditions as in c).

Hardship payment amounts

The amount of your hardship payment will be your normal amount of JSA reduced to 60 per cent, or reduced to 80 per cent if you (or a member of your family) are pregnant or seriously ill.

If you are paying rent, you will still be able to get Housing Benefit even when your JSA is stopped or paid at a reduced rate.

How to claim hardship payments

To claim hardship payments, you will have to attend an interview at Jobcentre Plus and fill in a form. Jobcentre Plus staff should not put you off from applying for hardship payments.

JSA hardship payments are usually paid two weeks in arrears. You can apply for a Social Fund crisis loan to cover the time before the first hardship payment is due (see page 91), but the loan will be repaid by reducing your benefit.

You will have to attend an interview at Jobcentre Plus every two weeks before you get your payments.

If you are claiming hardship payments by post, special rules apply. In this case, the claim form must be requested, filled in and returned to the Jobcentre Plus office. You must give your contact details in case of any queries. Jobcentre Plus will then make a decision about whether you meet the hardship criteria without interviewing you.

Behavioural problems

Connexions advisers are told that if you are on JSA and your behaviour makes it difficult for you to look for, or stay in, training or work, then you may have a medical condition (physical or mental) which makes you unable to work.[80] Connexions and Careers Service staff should tell Jobcentre Plus about this and to help you to make a claim for Employment and Support Allowance.

The severe hardship rules for Jobseeker's Allowance UK

What is 'severe hardship'?

According to the law, the Secretary of State can decide to pay JSA to someone who would suffer severe hardship if they did not get the benefit.[81]

Severe hardship is not defined in the law and there are no published rules. However, Jobcentre Plus guidance says that every claim of severe hardship will be looked at on its own merits, and that all of your circumstances will be taken into account.[82] This means that Jobcentre Plus staff must not use blanket rules about what does or does not make severe hardship (for example, they cannot say that you must be living away from home or be homeless).

Some of the things which Jobcentre Plus will take into account are:

- your accommodation, and the risk of eviction if you don't get JSA
- sources of income and capital
- health and personal circumstances, and
- whether you can afford food or accommodation without JSA.[83]

These are only guidelines and examples. Whatever your situation, if you think you are suffering severe hardship, you should apply for JSA. You shouldn't be barred from applying or turned away without having the chance to make a claim. Try to take with you as much evidence of your hardship as possible, and be ready to fully explain why you think that you are suffering hardship.

All cases are looked at individually, and you should mention all the things which you think are relevant to your case. As examples, payments have been paid to young people who:

- live with parents and could not find a Work-Based Learning for Young People place by the end of their Child Benefit Extension Period (CBEP)
- live with family or friends who cannot or will not support them financially (for example, because relationships have broken down or the family and friends are on benefits or in low-paid work), and
- have been getting Income Support on the grounds of estrangement while in education, and have then moved on to JSA during the CBEP, and have no income when the CBEP ends.

The difference between 'hardship' and 'severe hardship'

Along with severe hardship payments of JSA, there are also hardship payments of JSA. Hardship payments are made if you have been sanctioned for refusing a job or training place. They are paid at a reduced rate, so you should make sure you know whether you are being paid because of hardship or severe hardship.

Who makes the decision about severe hardship?

Local Jobcentre Plus staff make the decision to pay JSA on the grounds of severe hardship. If the decision is likely to be negative, then your case may be given to the Under-18s Support Team (UEST). The person who decides your case must have done Severe Hardship Direction training and have a Certificate of Authority from the UEST in Sheffield.

If no-one with this certificate is available at your local Jobcentre Plus office, your case can be referred to the UEST. Refusals ('nil decisions') and partner cases must always be referred to the UEST. The staff at the Jobcentre Plus office can decide to pay you JSA on the grounds of severe hardship, but they cannot decide to refuse JSA – only the UEST can make a decision to refuse the benefit.

The person who decides your case is responsible for:

- deciding if you would suffer severe hardship without JSA
- making directions to pay JSA
- deciding on the length of the direction
- referring cases to UEST, and
- certain backdating cases.

The following things must be referred to UEST:

- likely refusals (nil decisions)
- likely revocations for example in cases where a young person has failed to pursue a training course or neglected to avail themselves of a reasonable opportunity of training without good cause
- couple cases
- decisions on whether it is inappropriate to make payments from the date of claim
- decisions on whether or not backdating is appropriate
- cases where severe hardship payments have been made for 24 weeks
- all cases where an 'authorised officer' is unavailable in the local Jobcentre Plus office

- cases where permission to contact parents or third parties is refused without good reason, and
- cases of alleged abuse where a referral to social services is refused without good reason.

The Decision Maker in the Jobcentre Plus office decides:

- the date of your claim
- whether you qualify for JSA under a prescribed group, and
- if your entitlement is affected because you have been sanctioned for not complying with the labour market rules.

Appealing the decision about severe hardship

You can appeal against decisions made by Decision Makers. You cannot appeal against discretionary decisions made by the Secretary of State (including decisions that you will not suffer severe hardship), but can ask for these decisions to be reviewed, and you can make a formal complaint to Jobcentre Plus. In some cases, if your complaint is not solved, you may be able to take a kind of legal action called judicial review, or you can complain to the Parliamentary and Health Service Ombudsman.

The standard letter at Appendix 1 may be helpful if someone is helping you with your claim.

Backdating Jobseeker's Allowance on the grounds of severe hardship

Your claim for JSA on the grounds of severe hardship can be backdated if it is reasonable, or if you have good cause and your labour market conditions are straightforward.[84] If you want to backdate your claim, you should say this on your JSA5 form. The usual reason for refusing to backdate a claim is that you have so far 'survived' without the JSA so you can't have been in severe hardship. The local Jobcentre Plus office can backdate your claim for up to four weeks, but if you want to backdate it for a longer time, your case must go to the UEST.[85]

Severe hardship interviews

If you claim JSA under the severe hardship rules, you will have to attend an interview to give information about your circumstances.

The interviewer should record your details on a form known as an ESYP2JP, and if you are refused a severe hardship payment, you should ask for a copy of this form. The interviewer has a list of information that they need to get from you. The box shows the information they need to get.

Information collected at severe hardship interviews

Claim details

Date of claim, name, address, date of birth, National Insurance number, date you left relevant education. Details of partner, if any. What you have been doing since leaving school or full-time education, or since your last benefit claim. Details of last employment and earnings, including what you spent it on, if you spent it. Are you supported by relatives or friends? Have you ever been in custody? Other benefit payments for example, Disability Living Allowance. Have you ever been in care, and are you still the subject of a care order? Are you living with parents or guardians? If yes, why can't they support you? If no, why aren't you living with them? When did you leave home? Can you return home? Can you return home and be supported financially?

Accommodation details

Type of accommodation and cost. Do you have access to cooking facilities? Have you applied for Housing Benefit? Will you have to pay any money to the landlord over and above Housing Benefit? Is there any risk of eviction if JSA is not paid? If living with parents or carers, what are their financial circumstances? Do parents receive any benefits for you?

Financial circumstances

Do you or your partner have any other income? Do you have any savings? How much? Any debts? Type? How much? Any deductions from benefit payable at present? Any relatives or friends who can help?

Health matters

Are you or your partner pregnant? If yes, expected date of birth? Do you or your partner have any health problems?

Miscellaneous

Are you represented by a third party? If so, type of representative (for example, social worker, friend, relative)? Why do you think you are in hardship?

Third party evidence

Usually, Jobcentre Plus staff must not ask your parents or carers to confirm that you cannot live with them or be supported by them. They should accept your own evidence, and only look for extra evidence if they doubt your evidence. No-one should contact your parents or a third party unless what you say is contradictory or improbable.[86] The third party they contact doesn't have to be a parent – it could be someone else who knows your situation.

If Jobcentre Plus staff feel that they need evidence from a third party, they must ask your consent before making contact, and you must sign a statement to give permission.[87] They must get your consent voluntarily and not because of threats or inducements.[88] You must not be put under undue pressure to give your consent.[89] In cases where Jobcentre Plus needs to contact your parents or carers, you can refuse permission, but it is important to explain the reasons why.

You can ask a third party (for example, a relative, youth worker, social worker, Connexions or careers service adviser, or a voluntary organisation worker) to give extra evidence or confirm your circumstances – such information may help your case.

If a third party goes with you to the interview, the Jobcentre Plus officer may ask them to confirm your evidence.[90] Jobcentre Plus can also get information from a third party by telephone or letter. If there is doubt about your evidence, or if you don't give enough evidence to convince the adviser that you will suffer severe hardship, and it is necessary to contact a third party, then Jobcentre Plus should think about giving you a severe hardship payment for a short time while they are getting the extra evidence.[91]

The standard letter at Appendix 1 may be helpful if someone is helping you with your claim.

Allegations of abuse[92]

Abuse is a sensitive issue, and Jobcentre Plus staff are reminded of this. If you make allegations of abuse, Jobcentre Plus should record:

- the general nature of the abuse

- if the abuse was at home, whether there are any other children or young people living there
- whether your Connexions or careers service worker is aware of the abuse, and
- whether or not a social worker is helping you.

The Jobcentre Plus staff will ask you whether or not you are happy to be referred to Social Services. The Jobcentre Plus staff will try and arrange an appointment with Social Services, but they must not put undue pressure on you. However, if you refuse a referral, or if you do not attend a meeting with Social Services, Jobcentre Plus will think about whether there is still enough evidence of hardship to pay you JSA. According to Jobcentre guidance, if you fail to seek or accept further help, this is not enough to cast doubt on paying you JSA.[93]

Jobcentre Plus may decide to notify the Police and/or Social Services themselves.[94]

Payments of Jobseeker's Allowance on grounds of severe hardship

JSA which is paid on grounds of severe hardship is the same as the amount for people aged under 25 (£50.95 per week in 2009-10).

You will be given JSA for a certain length of time, depending on your circumstances, but the law does not set a limit on payments. Jobcentre Plus guidance says that severe hardships directions are usually for up to eight weeks at a time.[95] However, you can get a direction for up to 16 weeks if any of the following things will apply to you in that time:

- you will turn 18
- if you are pregnant, you will reach the 11th week before you are expected to give birth
- you will start a training course, further education or a job

Payments for shorter periods can be made when:

- you will start a job or training
- you will have capital available
- supporting evidence is not readily available, or
- you have no fixed address.

Stopping your payments of Jobseeker's Allowance for severe hardship[96]

Your JSA payments can be stopped early (revoked) if:

- your circumstances have changed so you are no longer at risk of severe hardship
- without good cause, you have failed to follow up a training opportunity, or you have rejected an offer of training
- the original severe hardship decision was based on a mistake of fact, or ignorance of a material fact
- you return to education or approved training (you may then qualify for Education Maintenance Allowance and/or Income Support – see pages 221 and 52)
- you fail to sign on (if you sign on again within five working days and you have a good cause for signing on late, your JSA claim should not be broken)[97], or
- you go on holiday (but there are exceptions).

If you stop meeting the rules for labour market conditions (such as attending Jobcentre Plus as required, and being available for and actively seeking work or training), you may stop being entitled to JSA. This decision is made locally by a Decision Maker, and you have a right of appeal.

Your JSA cannot be stopped early/revoked if it has already been stopped because you did not meet rules about labour market conditions or because you signed off.

Sanctions for Jobseeker's Allowance claimed on the grounds of severe hardship

The rules about sanctions are very complicated. The main rules for people who are claiming JSA on the grounds of severe hardship are summed up here. Look up the reason for your sanction in the table below, then check what the sanction is.

Sanction Type	Period of Sanctions (weeks)	Decision Method	Effect on Payment
Misconduct (employment)	1–26	Sector Decision Maker	Hardship – by application, not automatic
Failure to complete training (including misconduct)	2 (imposed from start of next Direction)	Adviser	Automatic reduced rate of JSA
Rejecting an offer/ failing to pursue an opportunity of training	2 (imposed from start of next Direction)	Adviser	Automatic reduced rate of JSA
Neglect to avail	2 *	SDM	Automatic reduced rate of JSA
Jobseeker's Direction	2	SDM	Hardship – by application, not automatic

*Sector Decision Makers may give sanctions that last for 1–26 weeks. However, your benefit is only reduced for a maximum of two weeks.

If you are sanctioned, your benefit will be reduced by either 40 per cent or 20 per cent. Your benefit will normally be reduced by 40 per cent unless you (or a member or your family) are pregnant or seriously ill.

How do you re-claim Jobseeker's Allowance on grounds of severe hardship?

Severe hardship payments are given for fixed periods only. At the end of these periods, your JSA stops automatically and you must re-apply.

The Jobcentre Plus office will interview you again, to review your circumstances. Connexions and other careers services in Scotland, Wales and Northern Ireland will be asked to give the same information they gave at the time of your first claim.

Young Person's Guarantee

If you are aged between 18 and 24, through the Young Person's Guarantee you are promised an offer of a job, work-focused training, or other meaningful activity before you reach the 12-month stage of your Jobseeker's Allowance (JSA) claim.

The Guarantee is being rolled out nationally from early 2010, but parts of it will start in some areas from as early as October 2009 (for example, the Future Jobs Fund will start in some places in October 2009 – see below for further details).

The Guarantee will provide you with one of the following four options:

• support to take an existing job in a key employment sector with funding for sector-specific training, recruitment subsidies and training on the job

• a work-focused training place, lasting up to six months, which should lead to a job after the training has finished

• a place on the Community Task Force – this is unpaid work experience focused on improving your employability through jobs which benefit local communities (you will continue to receive JSA in this period)

• a new job supported by the Future Jobs Fund (see below).

To decide which of these options to take part in, you will have a discussion with your Jobcentre Plus adviser as you approach the 12-month stage of your JSA claim. Participation in one of the options is compulsory if you want to continue to get JSA after 12 months.[98]

Community Task Force

Where a subsidised job or training is unavailable or unsuitable, and you have been claiming JSA for nearly 12 months, you may be required to take part in the Community Task Force option as part of the Young

Person's Guarantee. This is a work experience placement designed to increase your employability and benefit the wider community. The placement is offered alongside training and will last for up to six months.[99] You will receive a Training Allowance worth the same amount as your benefit, plus a top-up of £15.38.[100] The Community Task Force option will be voluntary from January 2010, and mandatory from spring 2010.[101] It is possible that you could be fast-tracked on to the Community Task Force part of the Young Person's Guarantee. This decision is made by your personal adviser, if they feel it would benefit you to be fast-tracked.[102]

The work experience you gain while taking part in the Community Task Force should show that you can carry out tasks similar to those in a normal working environment. The tasks should give you work-related skills and increase your chances of finding paid employment.[103]

If you do not find work at the end of the placement, you will go back to claiming JSA, returning to the point at which you left the claims process.[104] If you choose to end your work experience through the Community Task Force and stop claiming JSA, but you then return to re-claim JSA within 28 days of leaving, the usual linking rules will apply, and you will return to the stage of the process you were at when you left the benefit. If the break is longer than 28 days, you will return to the start of the process.[105]

While taking part in the Community Task Force option, you are still subject to sanctions as you would be if you were on New Deal (see page 67).[106]

Future Jobs Fund

Starting from October 2009,[107] if you are aged 18 to 24 and have been claiming JSA for between 10 and 12 months,[108] you will be eligible for a six-month paid job supported by the Future Jobs Fund. The job should be for 25 hours per week or more, and you will be paid at least the National Minimum Wage.[109] [110]

If your JSA claim is fast-tracked because you were not in education, training or employment prior to making your claim, you may be able to apply for a job through the Future Jobs Fund after claiming JSA for six months, rather than 12 months. Jobs supported by the Future Jobs Fund are not limited to people claiming JSA, but can be available to those on Income Support, Incapacity Benefit, or Employment and Support Allowance as well. However, you will have to claim one of these benefits for 12 months before you become eligible to access the fund.[111] It is up to your Jobcentre Plus personal adviser to decide whether or not you can apply for a job supported by the Future Jobs Fund.[112]

Jobs are designed to improve the local community. You will be referred to potential jobs following discussions with your personal adviser, who will decide which jobs you are likely to be eligible for.[113] The type of work on offer could include sports coaching, crime prevention, social care, hospitality, tourism, working with children, and jobs which improve the environment.[114]

Once you have started your job, you should receive extra help from your employer to get any training and support you need in the workplace, and you may also be eligible for Train to Gain funding to help pay for training. Plus, you should get help with finding employment once your job is over.[115] Future Jobs Fund jobs could also potentially form the first six months of an apprenticeship. As with other jobs through the Fund, if you're doing a job as part of your apprenticeship, you should be working for at least 25 hours per week and you should receive at least the minimum wage. Apprenticeships will normally continue beyond six months and are subject to different rules (see page 185).

Future Jobs Fund employers should offer an exit interview to assess your experience of the job, and provide you with a reference that details your performance, attendance record and any skills that you have developed while in work.[116]

If you think that you may need some training before starting a Future Jobs Fund job, then you should discuss this with your personal adviser at Jobcentre Plus, since they can authorise up to eight weeks of full-time training for people on JSA in these circumstances.[117]

You may not be on Flexible New Deal (or any New Deal options) at the same time you are doing a job through the Future Jobs Fund.[118]

Young Person's Bridging Allowance

In Wales the Young Person's Bridging Allowance is available for certain young people who are in between training or work. It is a payment of £15 per week. The Young Person's Bridging Allowance no longer exists outside Wales.

Social Fund Payments

The Social Fund is a system of grants and loans to help with one-off costs. The regulated Social Fund gives payments for maternity, funerals and cold weather, while the discretionary Social Fund gives loans and grants out of a budget held by each local Jobcentre Plus office.

Grants do not have to be repaid but loans do.

Sure Start Maternity Grant[119]

This is a grant of £500 per baby. You can get the Sure Start Maternity Grant if you are expecting a baby in the next 11 weeks, if you have given birth within the last 3 months, or if you are adopting a baby less than 12 months old. To get the grant, a healthcare professional (such as a midwife or health visitor) must give written confirmation that you got advice about the baby's health and welfare (or that you got advice on maternal health, if you claim the grant before your baby is born). The written confirmation can be given on your claim form.

To get the grant, you (or your partner) must also be getting one of the following benefits in the week that you make your claim:

- Income Support
- Income-Based Jobseeker's Allowance
- Income Related Employment and Support Allowance
- Tax Credits (but only if you get more than the family element of Child Tax Credit, or if you get a disability or severe disability element in Working Tax Credit)

Your savings do not affect the grant. You will need to make a claim for the grant, because it is not paid automatically.

Health in Pregnancy Grant

The Health in Pregnancy Grant (HPG) is a grant which was introduced in April 2009. It is a payment of £190 to all pregnant woman who have reached 25 weeks in their pregnancy, and who have gone to ante-natal appointments with a healthcare professional (such as a midwife, obstetrician or General Practitioner). You can be any age to get the HPG. It is not means-tested and you don't need to be on benefits or a low income to qualify. You should claim the HPG from HMRC within 31 days of getting advice from a healthcare professional.[120]

You can be paid a Sure Start Maternity Grant on top of the HPG.

Funeral payments

You can get help with funeral costs if:

• you or your partner are getting Income Support, Income-Based Jobseeker's Allowance, Income Related Employment and Support Allowance, Housing Benefit or Council Tax Benefit, Child Tax Credit paid at a rate which exceeds the family element, Working Tax Credit, which includes the disability or severe disability element pension credit, and

• you are the nearest relative of the person who died, or have to arrange the funeral.

You can make a claim on form SF200.

Cold Weather Payment

You can get an automatic payment of £25 per week if you:

• are claiming Income Support, Income-Based Jobseeker's Allowance or Income Related Employment and Support Allowance, and

• you are disabled, or you have a disabled child, or you have a child aged under 5.

Community Care Grants UK

You can get a Community Care Grant if you claim Income Support, Income-Based Jobseeker's Allowance, or Income Related Employment and Support Allowance. This includes people who are in hospital, prison or similar accommodation, and who may claim any of those benefits within the next six weeks. If you have capital above £500, this will reduce the amount of your grant. You must show that the grant will do at least one of the following:[121]

- help you (or someone you claim benefit for) to get set up in the community after being in institutional or residential care (for example, after being in prison, hospital, a care home, or living with foster parents)
- help you (or someone you claim for) to remain in the community rather than risk going into institutional care
- ease exceptional pressure on you and your family (for example, pressure from meeting the extra one-off costs of having a disabled child)
- help you to set up home as part of a resettlement plan after being homeless
- help with travel and reasonable overnight costs to visit someone in hospital or residential care
- allow you to care for a prisoner who has been released on temporary licence

People setting themselves up in their own accommodation should give a list of all the things that they need to the Social Fund Officer. The list should include prices taken from something like an Argos catalogue. The normal grant amount is around £500–£700, but the amount isn't fixed in law and you could get more if you can show that the items you need are essential.

If you are leaving care, you can usually get a grant from the local council that looked after you, but that doesn't stop you from also getting a Community Care Grant, if you meet the rules above and you still need essential items.

Because these grants are discretionary, it often helps to have evidence and letters to support your claim. Don't be put off from claiming. If you are refused, you can ask a Social Fund Inspector to review your case.

Crisis Loans[122] UK

You may be able to get a crisis loan if you don't have enough money to meet your immediate short-term needs, and you need help because of an emergency or a disaster. You can get a crisis loan especially if it is the only way to stop serious damage or risk to your health. The most common crisis loan payment is to cover the first few weeks of a Jobseeker's Allowance or Income Support claim, when it is taking a while to get your normal weekly benefit sorted out. But remember, if you get a crisis loan, this is money has to be paid back out of your benefit later. If you are getting a Community Care Grant after being in institutional care, and you have to pay rent in advance to a private landlord, you can also get a crisis loan to help.

If your crisis loan application shows that you may also qualify for a Community Care Grant, the DWP officer who deals with your claim should think about whether or not you should get a Community Care Grant.[123] However, you cannot always rely on this being done.

If you have had a JSA sanction (see page 67), you can only get a crisis loan in certain circumstances.

There is a list of items that you can't get either a Community Care Grant or a crisis loan for. These include:

• education or training needs (including school clothing or uniforms)
• medical, surgical or dental items or services
• debts to government departments, and
• work-related expenses.

In addition, crisis loans cannot be made for:

• telephone costs
• mobility needs

- holidays
- television or radio costs, or
- motor vehicle expenses (except travel costs).

You can apply for a crisis loan by telephone. If you are at a DWP office, staff should not send you home to make a phone call,[124] and if you have trouble with being understood on the phone, or if English is not your first language, you should be offered an immediate interview in the office.[125] If you apply by phone, the call is on a freephone number, but it will cost money if you call from a mobile. Because an application can easily take 30 or 40 minutes, you should ask the Social Fund office to call you back. In some areas, the government has imposed a limit of no more than three crisis loans per person every 12 months.

Budgeting Loans UK

To get a budgeting loan, you must have been claiming Income Support, Income Related Employment and Support Allowance, or Income-Based Jobseeker's Allowance for at least 26 weeks. If you have capital over £1000, this will reduce the amount of your loan.

To get the loan, you must need help with one of the following:

- Furniture and household equipment
- Clothing and footwear
- Rent in advance and/or removal costs
- Home improvements, maintenance and repairs
- Travel costs
- Expenses to do with looking for or taking up work
- Debts for any of the above

If your loan is refused, you can ask a Social Fund Inspector to review your case. You will have to repay both crisis and budgeting loans, but you can have the repayment amount coming out of your benefit reduced so that you repay the loan over a longer period. DWP can waive recovery of the loan, particularly if your circumstances change for the worse after you apply for the loan.[126] However, they may resist waiving recovery, and in this case, you should get advice. Both budgeting and crisis loans are interest-free.

When deciding whether or not to make a discretionary Social Fund loan or grant, DWP officials must think about the following:

- The nature, extent and urgency of your need
- Whether you have other resources to meet the need
- The possibility that some other person or group may wholly or partly meet your need
- The likelihood of repayment, and the likely time-frame for repayment
- The total amount of the local Social Fund budget[127]

You can be refused a crisis or a budgeting loan on the grounds that you are unlikely to be able to repay it. So, if you need a crisis loan because your benefit has not yet been paid, you can either ask for an interim payment of the benefit,[128] or you can argue that you are more likely than not to get the benefit, and you will then be able to repay.[129]

You should apply for a Community Care Grant in preference to a loan, though you are allowed to apply for both.

Endnotes

1   S 8 (2) Tax Credits Act 2002 & Reg. 3 (1) Child Tax Credit Regulations 2002

2   Reg. 5 The Child Benefit (General) Regulations 2006

3   Reg. 5 (2) (f) The Child Benefit (General) Regulations 2006

4   Reg. 3 The Child Benefit (General) Regulations 2006

5   S 141 Social Security Contributions and Benefits Act 1992 as amended by S 1 Child Benefit Act 2005

6   Reg. 3 The Child Benefit (General) Regulations 2006

7   Reg. 1 (3) The Child Benefit (General) Regulations 2006

8   Reg. 3 (2) The Child Benefit (General) Regulations 2006

9   Reg. 1 (3) The Child Benefit (General) Regulations 2006

10 Reg. 3 (4) The Child Benefit (General) Regulations 2006

11 Reg. 2 (5) The Child Benefit (General) Regulations 2006

12 Reg. 6 (3) The Child Benefit (General) Regulations 2006

13 Reg. 6 (4) The Child Benefit (General) Regulations 2006

14 S 8 (4) Tax Credits Act 2002, Regs 2 and 5(1) – (3A) Child Tax Credit Regulations

15 This increased to age 21 in April 2009.

16 Reg. 4 ZA & sch. 1B Income Support (General) Regulations 1987

17 Regs 13 (2) (a) – (e) Income Support (General) Regulations 1987 (as amended from 10 April 2006)

18 Decision Makers Guide, Vol. 4, para. 20668

19 Decision Makers Guide, Vol. 4, para. 20670 – 20675 and Reg. 13(3) (a) Income Support (General) Regulations 1987

20 Decision Makers Guide, Vol. 4, para. 20669

21 Decision Makers Guide, Vol. 4, para. 20693

22 Kelly v Monklands District Council 1866 SLT 169

23 R(IS) 9/94

24 R(SB) 2/87

25 CIS/4096/2005

26 Decision Makers Guide, Vol. 4, para.20690

27 R(SB) 2/87

28 CH/3777/2007

[29] IS Bulletin 04–07 Estranged Young People aged 16 - 19 claiming Income Support.

[30] R(IS) 9/94

[31] Decision Makers Guide, Vol. 4, para. 20694

[32] Jobcentre Plus JSA for 16-17 year olds Guidance. Initial contact section, paras 2–3.

[33] R(SB) 8/85 & R(SB) 4/83

[34] S 3A(1) (e) Jobseekers Act 1995

[35] S 3A (1) (d) Jobseekers Act 1995

[36] Reg. 57 (2) Jobseeker's Allowance Regulations 1996

[37] Reg. 60 Jobseeker's Allowance Regulations 1996

[38] Reg. 61 Jobseeker's Allowance Regulations 1996

[39] S 16 (1) Jobseeker's Act 1995

[40] Jobcentre Plus internal staff guidance on Jobseeker's Allowance for 16/17 year olds ("JSA Guidance") : Initial Contact

[41] JSA Guidance: Initial contact para. 35

[42] JSA Guidance: Initial contact para.6

[43] JSA Guidance: Initial contact para. 28

[44] JSA Guidance: New Jobseeker Interview para. 1

[45] JSA Guidance: New Jobseeker Interview para. 7

[46] Reg. 2 Social Security (Payments on Account, Overpayments and Recovery) Regulations 1988

[47] Reg. 4(1) (b) Social Security (Claims and Payments) Regulations 1988

[48] JSA Guidance: New Jobseeker Interview para. 25

[49] JSA Guidance: New Jobseeker Interview para. 23

[50] JSA Guidance: New Jobseeker Interview para. 65

[51] Reg. 64 (2) & (3) Jobseeker's Allowance Regulations 1996

[52] Reg. 65 Jobseeker's Allowance Regulations 1996

[53] Reg. 65 (2) Jobseeker's Allowance Regulations 1996

[54] Reg. 65 (5) Jobseeker's Allowance Regulations 1996

[55] JSA Guidance: Labour Market Issues: para. 84

[56] Reg. 67 (3) Jobseeker's Allowance Regulations 1996

[57] Reg. 67 (1) & (2) Jobseeker's Allowance Regulations 1996

[58] DWP Decision Maker's Guide Vol. 6, para. 34769

[59] DWP Decision Maker's Guide Vol. 6, para. 34780

[60] DWP Decision Maker's Guide Vol. 6, para. 34811

[61] JSA Guidance: Labour market issues: paras 123 –125. Also see DWP Decision Maker's Guide Vol. 6 para. 34766 et seq.

[62] JSA Guidance: Labour market issues: para. 125

[63] DWP Decision Maker's Guide Vol.6,para. 34797

[64] DWP Decision Maker's Guide Vol. 6, para 34799

[65] DWP Decision Maker's Guide Vol 6, para. 34757

[66] Summarised in DWP Decision Maker's Guide Vol. 6, para. 34002 and reflecting several pieces of legislation

[67] R (U) 8/74

[68] S 20(3) Jobseekers Act 1995 & Reg. 74 Jobseeker's Allowance Regulations 1996

[69] Para. 155 et seq. Benefits Liaison Instructions and Good Practice Guidelines for Connexions Services DfES

[70] S16 (2) (b) Jobseekers Act 1995

[71] R (U) 2/77

[72] DWP Decision Maker's Guide Vol. 6 para. 34106

[73] R (U) 10/53

[74] JSA Guidance: Labour market issues: para. 53

[75] R (U) 3/81

[76] Reg. 71 Jobseeker's Allowance Regulations 1996

[77] R (U) 25/52

[78] DWP Decision Maker's Guide Vol. 6, para. 34278 et seq.

[79] DWP Decision Maker's Guide Vol. 6, Chapter 35.

[80] Para.139 et seq. Benefits Liaison Instructions and Good Practice Guidelines for Connexions Services DfES.

[81] S 16 (1) (a) Jobseekers Act 1995

[82] JSA Guidance: Making a severe hardship decision: para.208

[83] JSA Guidance: Making a severe hardship decision: paras 209–210

[84] JSA Guidance: Making a severe hardship decision: para. 83

[85] JSA Guidance: Making a severe hardship decision: para. 87

[86] JSA Guidance: Making a severe hardship decision: para. 5

[87] JSA Guidance: Making a severe hardship decision: paras 6–8

[88] JSA Guidance: Making a severe hardship decision: para. 11

[89] JSA Guidance: Making a severe hardship decision: para.10

[90] JSA Guidance: Making a severe hardship decision: para. 18

[91] JSA Guidance: Making a severe hardship decision: paras 29 & 36

[92] JSA Guidance: Conducting a severe hardship interview: paras 43–53

[93] JSA Guidance: Conducting a severe hardship interview: para. 59

[94] JSA Guidance: Conducting a severe hardship interview: paras 60–79

[95] JSA Guidance: Making a severe hardship decision: paras 127–134

[96] JSA Guidance: Making a severe hardship decision: paras. 33–100

[97] Reg. 27 Jobseeker's Allowance Regulations 1996

[98] www.dwp.gov.uk/docs/ctf-pqq-events-qa.pdf

[99] www.dwp.gov.uk/supplying-dwp/what-we-buy/welfare-to-work-services/opportunities-to-tender/communitytaskforce.shtml Accessed on 29 July 2009

[100] www.dwp.gov.uk/docs/ctf-pqq-events-qa.pdf Accessed on 29 July 2009

[101] www.dwp.gov.uk/docs/ctf-pqq-events-qa.pdf Accessed on 29 July 2009

[102] www.dwp.gov.uk/docs/ctf-pqq-events-qa.pdf Accessed on 29 July 2009

[103] www.dwp.gov.uk/docs/ctf-pqq-events-qa.pdf Accessed on 29 July 2009

[104] www.dwp.gov.uk/supplying-dwp/what-we-buy/welfare-to-work-services/opportunities-to-tender/communitytaskforce.shtml Accessed on 29 July 2009

[105] www.dwp.gov.uk/docs/ctf-pqq-events-qa.pdf Accessed on 29 July 2009

[106] www.dwp.gov.uk/docs/ctf-pqq-events-qa.pdf Accessed on 29 July 2009

[107] http://research.dwp.gov.uk/campaigns/futurejobsfund/pdf/fjf-guide.pdf Accessed on 29 July 2009

[108] http://research.dwp.gov.uk/campaigns/futurejobsfund/pdf/fjf-guide.pdf Accessed on 29 July 2009

[109] http://research.dwp.gov.uk/campaigns/futurejobsfund/pdf/fjf-guide.pdf Accessed on 29 July 2009

[110] http://research.dwp.gov.uk/campaigns/futurejobsfund/ Accessed on 29 July 2009

[111] http://research.dwp.gov.uk/campaigns/futurejobsfund/ Accessed on 29 July 2009

[112] http://research.dwp.gov.uk/campaigns/futurejobsfund/ Accessed on 29 July 2009

[113] http://research.dwp.gov.uk/campaigns/futurejobsfund/pdf/fjf-guide.pdf Accessed on 29 July 2009

[114] http://research.dwp.gov.uk/campaigns/futurejobsfund/ Accessed on 29 July 2009

[115] http://research.dwp.gov.uk/campaigns/futurejobsfund/pdf/fjf-guide.pdf Accessed on 29 July 2009

[116] http://research.dwp.gov.uk/campaigns/futurejobsfund/pdf/fjf-guide.pdf Accessed on 29 July 2009

[117] http://research.dwp.gov.uk/campaigns/futurejobsfund/faq.asp Accessed on 29 July 2009

[118] http://research.dwp.gov.uk/campaigns/futurejobsfund/faq.asp Accessed on 29 July 2009

[119] Reg. 5 Social Fund Maternity and Funeral Expenses (General) Regulations 1987

[120] The Health in Pregnancy Grant (Entitlement and Amount) Regulations 2008

[121] Social Fund Directions: Direction 4.

[122] Social Fund Directions Nos. 23 & 29

[123] Social Fund Directions: No. 49

[124] DWP staff guidance on Crisis Loans: para. 29

[125] DWP staff guidance on Crisis Loans: para. 24

[126] See use of the word 'repayable' in S.139 (3) Social Security Contributions and Benefits Act 1992 & Social Fund Direction No. 5

[127] S140 (1) Social Security Contributions and Benefits Act 1992

[128] Reg. 2 Social Security (Payments on Account, etc) Regulations 1988

[129] Social Fund Commissioner's Advice on Amounts to Award: (Living Expenses) Effective from 04/02/02

4 Young People Remaining in Learning Programmes

Your choices

This chapter describes what you can do when you reach the current school leaving age of 16. (In England, the leaving age will be raised to 17 in 2013 and to 18 in 2015.)[1] Broadly speaking, you have the choice of:

- staying in learning as a full-time student
- learning as you earn, in a work-based programme such as an apprenticeship, or
- getting a job.

Why stay in learning?

If you decide to stay in learning after you turn 16, you will have the chance to gain valuable skills and qualifications. Your skills and qualifications will affect the kind of work you can do (and the amount of money you can earn) now and in the future. Generally, people who have few qualifications have more trouble finding work, and a lower earning potential, than those with qualifications.

Most people leaving school at age 16 in England, Wales or Northern Ireland are qualified to Level 2 on the National Qualifications Framework (see page 109). This means they have five GCSEs graded at A–C. Nearly all people leaving school at age 16 in Scotland are qualified to Level 4 on the Scottish Credit and Qualifications Framework (see page 200). This means they have seven or eight Standard Grades graded at 1–7. So, if you are planning to leave school at age 16 and get a job, you may find it difficult because employers will often look for qualifications above Level 2 or Level 4. It is likely that:

• you will find it hard to get a job

• your choice of jobs will be very limited, or

• you will be on a low wage with little opportunity for change.

There is a lot of evidence that leaving compulsory education without any qualifications at all can make getting a well-paid job more difficult.

Once you have passed the age of 19, the government will not fund you to get qualifications above Level 2, except in special circumstances. With the financial help available for young people in learning, you and your family will usually be better off if you stay in learning.

Overview of different learning choices

Staying in full-time learning as a student

If you decide to stay in learning as a full-time student, you have the choice of:

• re-taking your GCSEs or Standard Grades

• switching to vocational GCSEs or Standard Grades

• studying academic or vocational subjects for your General Certificate of Education, commonly known as AS- or A-levels (England, Wales and Northern Ireland)

• studying academic or vocational subjects for Highers or Advanced Highers qualifications (Scotland)

• doing a Skills for Work course at Access 3, Intermediate or Highers level (Scotland)

• studying for a 14–19 Diploma (England)

• studying for a Welsh Baccalaureate or a Scottish Baccalaureate

• doing a Work-Based Learning Pathway (Wales), or

- working towards a vocational qualification, such as a BTEC, OCR National, or City and Guilds qualification.

Depending on the path you choose, you could have the chance to progress to a higher education qualification, such as a bachelor's degree, Foundation Degree, Higher National Diploma or Higher National Certificate, once you have left school or college.

Starting an apprenticeship

If you want to continue learning, but would prefer to follow a vocational path, you could consider starting an apprenticeship. Apprenticeships give you the chance to earn money and learn at the same time, and you can enrol on an apprenticeship programme at a further education college or with a work-based learning provider. Depending on your ability and where you live, you could enrol on:

- a Foundation Apprenticeship programme (England and Wales)
- an Advanced Apprenticeship programme (England)
- a Modern Apprenticeship programme (Scotland and Wales), or
- a Level 2 or Level 3 ApprenticeshipsNI programme (Northern Ireland).

As an apprentice, you will learn through hands-on work and training courses, build up your knowledge and skills, gain qualifications and earn money. Apprenticeships are designed to give you the skills and experience you need to climb your chosen career ladder.

Joining a pre-employment programme

If you're not sure what you want to do, or you're not ready for an apprenticeship, think about joining a pre-employment programme. A pre-employment programme may also be a good choice if you're trying to overcome a barrier in your personal life that stops you from getting a job. There are a number of pre-employment programmes running in the UK, including:

- New Deal for Young People and Flexible New Deal (UK)
- Entry to Employment (England)

- Skill Build (Wales)
- Get Ready for Work (Scotland)
- Skillseekers (Scotland)
- Training for Work (Scotland)
- Training for Success (Northern Ireland), and
- Bridge to Employment (Northern Ireland).

These programmes aim to give you the confidence and skills you need to enter the world of work. Each programme covers a range of activities that will help get you ready for work: you may go on a work placement and get vocational training, or you may work as part of a small group and get one-to-one attention to improve your skills and help you overcome barriers. Depending on your programme, you could get a weekly training allowance and help with expenses.

Getting a job and training

If you decide to find a job, you could:

- do voluntary work
- go abroad to work
- get a job where training is provided
- get a job where training is not provided, or
- become self-employed.

You might be keen to start earning money, but make sure you don't forget your long-term future in your hurry to earn cash now. It is really important to get a job with training opportunities – especially opportunities that will lead to nationally recognised qualifications. This is because jobs for people with low skills and no qualifications are disappearing, and you might earn less money in the long run if you don't do formal training.

If you choose to get a job without training opportunities, you could still improve your knowledge and skills if your employer allows you time off to study for a vocational qualification at a local college. You should be aware that if you do choose to get a job, you have the right to time off for study or training, which is explained in the next section.

Your right to time off for study or training

No matter where you live, you have the right to paid time off work to study or train for approved qualifications if you:

- are an employee, and
- are aged 16 or 17, and
- are not in full-time education, and
- have no (or few) qualifications.

Time off for study or training helps young employees to get the skills and qualifications they need, which in turn helps businesses to be more competitive.

You can do your study or training in the workplace, in a further education college, or through open or distance learning. The amount of time you spend on study or training has to be reasonable, after considering the requirements of your course or training programme and the effect you might have on your employer's business by taking time off work.

You are entitled to be paid at your normal hourly rate for the time you spend on training. If your employer unreasonably refuses to give you time off, or fails to pay what you are entitled to, you can complain to an Employment Tribunal (see page 345).

Getting careers advice

As you can see from the list of options above, you have a wide range of choices after you turn 16. Doing an apprenticeship may appeal to you, or perhaps you would like to carry on studying for academic qualifications. But before you make a choice, you should talk to an adviser at your local careers service, because they can give you more information about your options. Your adviser will tell you what qualifications or skills you need to get onto the learning programme of your choice, and what you will get out of taking this particular route.

To find out more about careers services, and how they can help you, turn to Chapter 2.

Making decisions for the right reason

Whatever you decide to do, the choice you make should be based on your abilities and interests. This is important because many young people start a learning programme that does not suit them, and they end up leaving the programme. All sorts of pressures can force you into doing something that you do not really want to do. Remember that some young people are better at academic study than others. If you find studying traditional academic subjects difficult, then you could try more practical subjects. Tell your careers adviser what you want to do, and talk about your strengths and weaknesses. It is essential that you join a programme which suits the way you like to learn. Also think about where you want to learn. Some people are more suited to a further education college than others.

The following sections contain more detailed information about the different learning programmes described in this overview of your choices. It should help you to decide which type of learning programme would suit you best.

Where can you study as a full-time student?

Staying in school

If you choose to do your A-levels, Highers or Advanced Highers, you can stay on at school. For many, the good thing about staying in school is that you can continue to learn in familiar surroundings, with teachers and peers you already know. You could think about moving to another school if you're looking for a change.

The subject choices on offer at your school will depend partly on how many people are in your year level and partly on whether your school has arrangements with other local schools or colleges to give you a wider choice.

Going to a college

In England, Wales and Northern Ireland, you can continue your studies in a sixth-form college, where you are likely to be offered a large range of A-levels. If you want a change from your school environment and the chance to meet new people and make new friends, going to college might be a good option for you.

In Scotland, you can choose to do your Advanced Highers (and also your Highers, in some cases) at a college.

Going to a further education college

Further education colleges can cater for either academic or vocational learning, or both. What your local further education college provides will depend on what else is offered in your area. For example, if most local schools have sixth forms, or if there are local sixth-form colleges, your further education college may specialise in vocational courses that meet the needs of commerce and industry. In other areas, where a further education college is the main (or only) option after you have turned 16, the college will offer everything you could get in a school or sixth-form college.

All further education colleges have part-time and mature students, and some colleges may be spread over more than one site. A number of colleges also have separate sixth-form centres where you can do A-levels as well as other vocational subjects.

Qualification Levels

The qualifications discussed in this chapter are often described as different 'levels' of education (for example, A-levels are described as Level 3 qualifications). In England, Wales and Northern Ireland, the National Qualifications Framework (NQF) sorts qualifications into levels, and in Scotland, the Scottish Credit and Qualifications Framework (SCQF) does the same thing. The two frameworks are not the same: the NVQ organises qualifications into eight levels, whereas the SCQF organises them into 12. However, both frameworks serve an identical purpose, which is to make it easy to compare qualifications and decide whether some are equal to others. The following tables show the qualifications that are discussed in this chapter.

National Qualifications Framework

Level 1	GCSEs graded at D–G
	National Vocational Qualifications at Level 1
	BTEC Introductory Diplomas and Certificates
	OCR Nationals
	Key Skills Level 1
	Skills for Life qualifications
	Foundation Diploma
Level 2 This is the level above which the government will not fund adults but will fund young people	Five GCSEs graded A*–C
	National Vocational Qualifications at Level 2
	Higher Diploma
Level 3	A-levels
	AS-levels
	Advanced Vocational Certificate of Education
	BTEC National Diploma
	National Vocational Qualifications at Level 3
	Advanced Diploma
Level 4	National Vocational Qualifications at Level 4
	Some BTEC diplomas, certificates and awards
	Higher education certificates

Level 5	Higher National Certificates
	Higher National Diplomas
	National Vocational Qualifications at Level 5
	Higher education diplomas
	Foundation degrees
Level 6	Bachelor's degrees (with honours)

Scottish Credit and Qualifications Framework

Level 1	Access 1
Level 2	Access 2
	National Certificates
	National Progression Awards
Level 3	Access 3
	Foundation Standard Grade
	National Certificates
	National Progression Awards
Level 4	Intermediate 1
	General Standard Grade
	National Certificates
	National Progression Awards
	Scottish Vocational Qualifications Level 1

Level 5	Intermediate 2
	Credit Standard Grade
	National Certificates
	National Progression Awards
	Scottish Vocational Qualifications Level 2
Level 6	Highers
	National Certificates
	National Progression Awards
	Professional Development Awards
	Scottish Vocational Qualifications Level 3
Level 7	Advanced Highers
	Professional Development Awards
	Higher National Certificates
	Higher education certificates
	Scottish Vocational Qualifications Level 3
Level 8	Professional Development Awards
	Higher National Diploma
	Higher education diplomas
	Scottish Vocational Qualifications Level 4
Level 9	Professional Development Awards
	Ordinary Degree Graduate Certificate
	Scottish Vocational Qualifications Level 4
Level 10	Professional Development Awards
	Honours degrees
	Graduate diplomas
Level 11	Scottish Vocational Qualifications Level 5

School-based qualifications in England, Wales and Northern Ireland

After you turn 16, the main courses on offer at school are usually:

• GCSE re-takes
• General Certificates of Education (AS- or A-levels)
• Vocational (applied) AS- or A-levels
• 14–19 Diplomas (England)
• Welsh Baccalaureate (Wales), and
• Work-Based Learning Pathways (Wales).

Many people think about re-taking their GSCEs, and they usually only re-sit English and Maths. Students tend to do re-takes in the Autumn term, alongside other courses of study. If you're thinking about doing re-takes, it would be a good idea to speak to your school to make sure this is possible.

General Certificates of Education (A-levels)

What are General Certificates of Education?

General Certificates of Education (GCEs) are subject-based qualifications taken mainly by students aged between 16 and 19. They are Level 3 qualifications and are also known as A levels, which is short for Advanced Level Examinations. GCEs normally take two years to complete, and are broken down into two parts: Advanced Subsidiary (AS) and A2. AS is the first half of a full A-level qualification, but it also counts as a stand-alone qualification. A2 is the second half of an A-level qualification.[2]

Why study for General Certificates of Education?

GCEs require you to study subjects in detail, so if you are really interested in certain subjects and want to learn more, GCEs could be a good choice for you. Plus, they are highly valued by schools, colleges and employers, and they are necessary if you want to move on to higher education, such as a bachelor's degree. Or, if you would rather do something practical and work-related, you can choose GCEs in vocational or 'applied' subjects (see page 114).

How are General
Certificates of Education organised?

Each GCE takes two years to complete and is divided into two parts: AS and A2. AS qualifications count as the first half of a full A-level qualification, and you will usually do AS exams at the end of the first year of study. Once you have done the AS exams, you can choose whether or not to continue to the A2 part of your A-level. If you choose not to continue, your AS qualification will still be recognised in its own right. This means that after your first year of study, you will get an AS certificate to mark what you have achieved so far. You have to go on studying for another year to be awarded the full A-level qualification.

What subjects are available?

GCEs are available in over 50 different subjects. Traditional subjects on offer include English, maths, drama, religious studies, physics, French and history.

Are there any entry requirements?

Normally, you need five GCSEs graded C or above to do a full-time GCE course. Mature students may be accepted without having to meet the normal entry requirements.

How are General Certificates
of Education assessed and graded?

A-level courses are split into units, and each unit is assessed through a mixture of internal evaluation and examinations.

You will study AS units in the first year of your A-level course. Most subjects have two AS units, but some (like sciences and music) have three. If you pass all of the AS units for a subject, you will get an AS qualification in that subject. This qualification is called an AS-level.

A2 units are studied in the second year of your course. Most A-levels have two A2 units, but some subjects (such as sciences and music) have three units. If you pass all of the A2 units for a subject, you will get a full A-level qualification in that subject.

A-levels are awarded on an A to E grading scale or A* to E from September 2009. If you do not meet the minimum standard for an award, your results are recorded as 'unclassified'.

Where do General Certificates of Education lead?

AS- and A-levels are widely recognised by employers and universities. They are the traditional route into university degree courses.

Applied General Certificates of Education

Why study for Applied General Certificates of Education?

Applied General Certificates of Education (AGCEs) are also known as vocational or applied A-levels. By doing AGCEs, you will have the chance to develop broad skills and an understanding of industry and commerce. An AGCE will:

* prepare you for employment, and
* allow you to enter further and higher education and training.

You will spend time completing work-related assignments, and you may work with local employers to learn more about a certain work sector (such as business, leisure and recreation, travel and tourism, or engineering). As you do your assignments, you will be encouraged to develop skills that are valuable in any job, such as communication, numeracy and IT skills.

How are Applied General
Certificates of Education organised?

AGCE subjects have the same structure as GCEs, with courses split into two parts: AS and A2. However, there are four different qualifications available if you do an AGCE:

- Advanced Subsidiary (made up of three AS units, with one unit assessed externally and the rest assessed internally)
- Advanced Subsidiary Double Award (made up of six AS units, with two units assessed externally and the rest assessed internally)
- Advanced (made up of three AS units and three A2 units, with two units assessed externally and the rest assessed internally), and
- Advanced Double Award (made up of six AS units and six A2 units, with four units assessed externally and the rest assessed internally).

What subjects are available?

You can study subjects such as leisure studies, health and social care, travel and tourism, applied ICT and applied business, among others.

How will you be assessed?

AGCEs have internal and external assessment. They are assessed by coursework (a portfolio of work), which is internally assessed, and by a form of external assessment. The type of external assessment you do will depend on what you are studying, so speak to your learning provider for more details. Internal assessment normally makes up two-thirds of your overall grade, and external assessment makes up one-third.[3]

Where do Applied General Certificates of Education lead?

If you want to get a job after school or college, and you have a good idea of the area you want to work in, then you should think about doing an AGCE. Many companies recruit students who have done a vocational course, and employers increasingly value the work skills and vocational knowledge that learners gain on these programmes. However, be aware that some employers may also expect a range of other qualifications, including GCSEs and traditional GCEs.

14–19 Diplomas

What is a Diploma?

The new 14–19 Diplomas are open to students in England who are aged between 14 and 19. They have been created with help from employers and universities, so you can be sure that by doing a Diploma, you're developing valuable skills. You can do a Diploma at school or college, in a number of different subject areas. The new Diploma is different from GCSEs and A-levels because it mixes classroom work with hands-on experience. However, Diplomas are designed to be flexible, so you can study for a Diploma instead of GCSEs or A-levels, or combine a Diploma with GCSEs and A-levels.[4] All Diplomas will require you to:

- achieve a minimum standard in English, maths and ICT
- complete a project, and
- do a minimum of 10 days' work experience.[5]

Why study for a Diploma?

A Diploma gives you more choice about what you learn than other qualifications, and it allows you to keep your options open by giving you the chance to explore an area of work without committing to a career in it. While doing a Diploma, you'll learn in the classroom and you might even spend time at another school or college. You will also do practical projects and work experience. If you enjoy hands-on learning but you're not sure which career path you want to follow, then a Diploma could be a good choice for you.

How are Diplomas organised?

Levels

You can usually study a Diploma at three levels:

- Foundation Diploma (this takes the same time to complete as four or five GCSEs and can be started in Year 10 or above)
- Higher Diploma (this takes the same time to complete as five or six GCSEs and can be started in Year 10 or above)

- Advanced Diploma (this is equal to three and a half A-levels and can be started in Year 12 or above)

There is also a less common Progression Diploma, which is counted as equal to two and a half A-levels.

From 2011, there will be an Extended Diploma. The Extended Diploma will contain extra maths and English, plus more Additional and Specialist Learning. If you do the Extended Diploma at Foundation level, it will be the same as seven GCSEs graded D–G. At Higher level, it will be worth nine GCSEs graded A*–C, and at Advanced level it will be equal to four and a half A-levels.[6]

Programme elements

Each Diploma covers three types of learning:[7]

- Principal Learning (knowledge, understanding and skills relevant to your chosen Diploma subject)
- Generic Learning (functional skills), and
- Additional and Specialist Learning (this offers you the chance to broaden your studies or study a particular topic in more depth).

Principal Learning

Each Diploma aims to give you a set of personal, learning and thinking skills. These skills are assessed through the Principal Learning part of the Diploma. Personal, learning and thinking skills include:

- creative thinking
- reflective learning
- independent inquiry
- team work
- effective participation, and
- self-management.

Generic Learning

The Generic Learning part of the Diploma aims to give you functional skills. Functional skills are the practical English, maths and ICT skills that everybody needs to deal with everyday life. The Diploma will cover all three functional skills. You will need to achieve a pass in functional skills at Foundation level for a Foundation level Diploma, at Higher level for a Higher Diploma, or at Advanced level for an Advanced Diploma.

The Generic Learning element includes a minimum of 10 days' work experience.

Additional and Specialist Learning

This part of the Diploma offers you the chance to broaden your studies, or study a particular topic in more depth. Additional and Specialist Learning includes a wide range of existing and new qualifications, including GCSEs, A-levels and BTECs.

The project for the Advanced Diploma has the same guidelines as the Extended Project done by A-level students.

What subjects are available?

Seventeen broad subject areas will be introduced over the next few years. By 2013, all students will have access to the subjects listed below.[8]

From 2008
- Construction and the Built Environment
- Creative and Media
- Engineering
- Information Technology
- Society, Health and Development

From 2009
- Business, Administration and Finance
- Hair and Beauty

- Land-based and Environmental
- Hospitality and Catering
- Manufacturing and Product Design

From 2010

- Public Services
- Retail
- Sport and Leisure
- Travel and Tourism

From 2011

- Humanities
- Science
- Languages

How will you be assessed?

For each Diploma, Principal Learning is assessed through a mixture of exams and work marked by teachers. Generic Learning is assessed through external examinations, and Additional and Specialist Learning will be assessed according to the arrangements for the specific qualification you have chosen.

Your overall Diploma grade will be worked out by putting together the grades you achieve for Principal Learning and your project. While it is necessary to do functional skills, work experience and Additional and Specialist Learning to achieve the Diploma qualification, the grades for these things do not count towards your overall Diploma grade.[9]

Where do Diplomas lead?

With a Diploma, you will keep your options open. If you do a Foundation or Higher Diploma, you can go on to study for the next level of Diploma, do GCSEs or A-levels, start an apprenticeship, or go on to a job with training. If you do an Advanced Diploma, you can progress to university or start a career.[10]

The Diploma will help you to gain general skills like teamwork, self-management and critical thinking skills, which are essential for success in employment and higher education.[11]

Welsh Baccalaureate

What is the Welsh Baccalaureate?[12]

The Welsh Baccalaureate is a programme that combines personal development with qualifications such as A-levels, National Vocational Qualifications (NVQs) and GCSEs. The programme is split into two parts: the Core Programme and Options. For the Core Programme, you will develop your key skills, do an individual investigation, and complete a number of work-related and community activities. For the Options part of the Welsh Baccalaureate, you will choose and complete a number of established courses, such as GCSEs, A-levels, BTEC qualifications and NVQs. During the programme, you will get help from a personal tutor.

The Welsh Baccalaureate is available at three different levels: Foundation, Intermediate and Advanced. If you complete an Advanced Welsh Baccalaureate, your Core Programme is worth an A-level graded at A. You can study the Baccalaureate in English, Welsh or a combination of both languages.

Why study for the Welsh Baccalaureate?[13]

The Welsh Baccalaureate gives you broader experiences than a traditional learning programme, making you better prepared for work, further and higher education. By getting a Baccalaureate, you will show that you have developed key skills, furthered your personal and social education, gained work experience, done an individual investigation, and been an active member of the community, on top of achieving your A-levels or other traditional qualifications. The programme aims to give you a rounded education, with the flexibility to choose a level and kind of study that suits you. Plus, the Core Programme is designed to help your performance in your Options subjects, and isn't too demanding or time-consuming.

How is the Welsh Baccalaureate organised?[14]

The Welsh Baccalaureate is made up of two parts: a Core Programme and Options. To get the full qualification, you must meet all of the requirements of the Core Programme as well as your Options. You can do the Baccalaureate at one of three levels: Foundation, Intermediate and Advanced. Each level covers a different range of qualifications, which are set out below. There is no fixed timeframe for completing the Welsh Baccalaureate, but students usually complete the Core Programme alongside their Options, and submit their work at the end of the academic year.

Core Programme

The Core Programme aims to give you personal development skills, leaving you better equipped for work and further or higher education, better informed about the wider world, and a more active member of your community. The Core Programme comprises the following areas:

- Wales, Europe and the world, which teaches you more about Wales and its relationship with Europe and the world (this subject includes a language module)
- Work-Related Education, which involves working with an employer and taking part in a team activity to help you understand how businesses work
- Personal and Social Education, which gives you a chance to explore issues in the modern world (this subject includes an activity in the local community)
- Individual Investigation, for which you do an individual research project on a subject that interests you
- Key Skills, which you develop by doing the four subjects listed above

Options

For the Options part of the Welsh Baccalaureate, you will choose approved courses such as GCSEs, Vocational GCSEs, A-levels, Vocational A-levels, BTEC qualifications or NVQs. The number of subjects you do for your Options depends on the level and type of programme you are studying.

Levels and qualifications

If you do a Welsh Baccalaureate at Foundation level, you will work towards:

- the Core Certificate at Foundation level (Level 1), and
- four GCSEs graded at D–G, or a Level 1 NVQ, or a BTEC Introductory Diploma (or equivalent).

If you do a Welsh Baccalaureate at Intermediate level, you will work towards:

- the Core Certificate at Intermediate level (Level 2), and
- four GCSEs graded at A*–C, or a Level 2 NVQ, or a BTEC First Diploma at Pass level.

Your Core Certificate at Intermediate level is roughly worth three GCSEs graded at A*–C.

If you do a Welsh Baccalaureate at Advanced level, you will work towards:

- the Core Certificate at Advanced level (Level 3), and
- two A-levels graded at A–E, or a Level 3 NVQ, or a BTEC National Certificate at pass level (or equivalent).

Your Core Certificate at Advanced level is worth an A-level graded at A, or 120 UCAS (Universities and Colleges Admissions Service) points.

What subjects are available?[15]

Everyone doing the Welsh Baccalaureate takes the same basic subjects for the Core Programme, as described above.

The level of difficulty of the Core Programme depends on whether you are doing the Baccalaureate at Foundation, Intermediate or Advanced level.

For the Options part, there is a wide variety of subjects to choose from. You can do academic subjects (such as GCSEs or A-levels) or vocational subjects (such as vocational GCSEs, A-levels, BTEC qualifications or NVQs). The variety of subjects available to you depends on what your school or learning provider offers, so speak to them for more information.

How will you be assessed?[16]

You will meet the usual national requirements for whichever Options subjects you have chosen to do. This could include sitting exams, depending on the subjects you have picked and the level you are studying at. For information on A-level assessment, see page 113.

There is no exam for the Core Programme. Instead, during the academic year you will gather evidence that you meet the programme requirements. This includes evidence to show you are competent in the relevant key skills. You will submit your evidence to tutors for assessment when you're ready. As part of the Core Programme assessment, you will also present an individual investigation on an aspect of Wales, Europe and the world, personal and social education, or work-related education. The investigation will test your skills in collecting information, analysing it, and presenting it in an appropriate way.

Where does the Welsh Baccalaureate lead?[17]

The options open to you after gaining a Welsh Baccalaureate will depend on the level of your qualification and the subjects you studied. If you are awarded a Welsh Baccalaureate at Advanced level, with at least two A-levels, you will have the option of applying to university. If you do vocational subjects for your Welsh Baccalaureate, you will be well-equipped to enter the world of work once you leave school. You might want to think about starting an apprenticeship, or continuing your work-based education at a further education college or with a training provider. If you choose to do an apprenticeship, the vocational qualifications you have already gained for your Baccalaureate may help you to finish the apprenticeship sooner.

Work-Based Learning Pathways

What are Work-Based Learning Pathways?

Along with the Welsh Baccalaureate, Work-Based Learning Pathways (WBLPs) are a new learning option for students aged 14 to 19 in Wales. The WBLPs programme runs in Years 10 and 11, lasting for two years. If you follow a WBLP, you will still do core National Curriculum subjects (including English, Maths, Welsh, ICT and Science), but you will also work towards getting vocational qualifications. Plus, as part of the programme, you will spend a maximum of 50 days on a work placement, spread over two years. So, by doing a WBLP, you can expect to learn in three different ways: classroom lessons, practical training and work experience.[18]

Why study a Work-Based Learning Pathway?

If you enjoy practical lessons and hands-on learning, and you are eager to gain real-life business and work skills, then WBLPs could be a good choice for you. WBLPs aim to keep your long-term options open by including study for your GCSEs in English, Maths, Welsh, ICT and Science. If you complete these GCSEs during your WBLP with five A*-C grades, this means you can choose to go back to more traditional academic study once your WBLP is finished. Plus, during a WBLP, you will not only work towards your GCSEs, but you will gain nationally recognised vocational qualifications and valuable work experience. You will gain work skills that employers are looking for, and you will learn at firsthand what is expected of you in the workplace. This will give you a clear advantage if you choose to continue with vocational learning, or get a job once your WBLP is over.

How are Work-Based Learning Pathways organised?

The WBLPs programme runs for two years, over Year 10 and Year 11. During this time, you will study for your GCSEs at school, you will spend up to two days each week studying for a vocational qualification, and you will do a maximum of 50 days of work experience.

Your school is responsible for arranging your WBLP, and should give you all of the information you need (including timetables, transport information and employers' contact details). The school will form partnerships with colleges, training providers or employers, so that your teachers and trainers can work together to share responsibility for your learning. If you need extra support during your programme, talk to your school tutor first, but all of the partners in the programme should be willing to help you. When arranging your timetable, your school is responsible for making sure that your work experience and vocational training does not have a negative effect on your GCSE study.[19]

What subjects are available?

Currently, WBLPs are offered in four sectors:

- Construction and the Built Environment
- Technologies
- Sport Management, Leadership and Coaching, and
- the Motor Industry.

If your school has a WBLPs partnership, it will be working with businesses in at least one of these sectors to offer you a WBLPs programme.[20]

How will you be assessed?

Your core GCSEs will be assessed in the same way they are assessed for students who do not take part in a WBLP. Assessment methods for your vocational qualification depend on which qualification you are doing. However, in general, most vocational qualifications will ask you to:

- create a portfolio of work
- develop key skills (such as teamwork, communication, problem solving and the ability to plan and evaluate your work)
- develop people skills
- apply theory to real-life situations
- gain experience, and
- use your initiative.[21]

If you are doing a NVQ, see page 150 for more information on assessment methods.

Your school and college, training provider or employer will work in partnership to check your progress and make sure you are measuring up to learning expectations. Your study programme should have clear milestones set out for you to achieve, and your progress will be measured against these milestones. Your attendance, timekeeping and behaviour will also be regularly checked by the partnership, and information about your progress will be passed on to your parents or carers.[22]

Where do Work Based Learning Pathways lead?

By doing a WBLP, you can work out whether a vocational learning route is suitable for you. If you decide that it is, then you can start a full-time apprenticeship once your WBLP is over. Or, you can continue your vocational studies at college or with a training provider. The experience and qualifications you gained during your WBLP may even help you to finish your apprenticeship or vocational course earlier than usual.

If you decide that a vocational learning route is not the right thing for you, you can return to academic study once your WBLP is over, so long as you have achieved five GCSEs graded at A*-C. If this is the case, you will be able to follow an academic route into college or university.[23]

School-based qualifications in Scotland

After you turn 16, the main courses on offer at school are usually:

• Standard Grade re-takes, and
• National Courses, which cover the following levels of learning:
    – Access 1, 2 and 3
    – Intermediate 1 and 2
    – Highers, and
    – Advanced Highers.

You can choose to do National Courses in traditional academic subjects, or in vocational subjects. If you prefer hands-on learning, you could think about doing Skills for Work subjects, which are available at Access 3, Intermediate and Higher level. If you're interested in academic study in either languages or science, then the Scottish Baccalaureate (available at Advanced Highers level) could be right for you.

Access and Intermediate courses

If your school offers National Courses, you can do Access and Intermediate courses after you turn 16, but most students aged 16 or over will be doing Highers or Advanced Highers. This is because most students will have Standard Grades by time they are 16 years old, and Access 3, Intermediate 1 and Intermediate 2 courses are roughly equal to Standard Grades at Foundation, General and Credit levels respectively. However, Access courses are starter courses, so they could be the right choice if you:[24]

- have been out of learning for a while
- have a learning difficulty, or
- have special educational needs.

Access courses could help to ease your move back into learning and build your confidence to progress to higher levels. You do not have to sit exams at the end of Access courses – instead, your work is assessed by your teacher or lecturer.[25]

Highers

What are Highers?

Highers are subject-based qualifications aimed at students who have already passed their Standard Grades at Credit level or a subject at Intermediate 2 level.[26] Highers are usually taken in S5 and/or S6, and students can do up to six subjects (though most do only five), with each subject taking one year to complete. Generally, Highers are sufficient to gain entry to universities throughout the UK, though some universities may ask for Advanced Highers as well. This is because Highers are roughly equal to AS-level qualifications, whereas Advanced Highers are equal to a full A-level. Highers are Level 6 qualifications on the SCQF (see page 110).

Why study for Highers?

Highers provide a good balance between breadth of study and depth of study. You can take up to six courses, which means you can study a variety of subjects, keeping your options open for the future. Your courses will challenge and stretch your knowledge, so if you want to progress to a university degree, Higher National Certificate or Higher National Diploma, you will usually have to achieve Highers first.

How are Highers organised?

Each Highers subject is made up of three units (called National Units) plus an external examination. To achieve a Higher qualification, you have to pass all of the assessment for your units, and the exam. If you don't pass your unit assessment the first time, you may be able to do extra work and be re-assessed. The type of exam you are set depends on what you're studying, but it could be a written examination, project work or practical tasks.

Each subject unit is a qualification in its own right. So, if you fail the overall subject, but still pass one or two units, you will be awarded a National Unit qualification (rather than a National Course qualification, which you would get for passing the entire subject).

What subjects are available?

There are a wide range of Highers subjects available, covering both academic and vocational study.

Ask your school or college, or check the Scottish Qualifications Authority website (www.sqa.org.uk) to find out what other subjects are available.

How will you be assessed and graded?

The assessment for each subject unit will be set and marked by your teachers or lecturers. The external examination is set by the Scottish Qualifications Authority and marked by an external examiner. If you pass your subject, you will be awarded an overall grade of A, B or C. If you fail your subject, you will be awarded a grade of D or 'No Award'. 'No Award' is given to those students who score 44 per cent or less for their subject as a whole.

Where do Highers lead?

Your options after Highers depend on which subjects you studied. If you chose to study traditional academic subjects (such as maths, science, English, languages, history or politics), you could progress to a university degree. Many universities in the UK will grant entry on the basis of your Highers results, though some universities will ask for Advanced Highers as well. So, depending on where you want to study, you could either enter university straight after finishing your Highers, or you could progress to Advanced Highers instead.

If you studied vocational subjects for your Highers, you could consider going to a further education college or training provider to get further vocational qualifications, such as a Higher National Certificate or Diploma, a BTEC qualification, or a Scottish Vocational Qualification. You could also think about starting an apprenticeship or a job.

Advanced Highers

What are Advanced Highers?

Advanced Highers are advanced subject-based qualifications. They are usually studied in the sixth year of secondary school, or at college. An Advanced Higher can be studied as a qualification in its own right, or it can act as a stepping stone to another qualification, such as a Higher National Diploma. To do Advanced Highers, you normally have to have passed Highers.[27]

Advanced Highers are Level 7 qualifications on the Scottish Credit and Qualification Framework, and they are generally considered equal to A-levels. There is a wide range of subjects available for Advanced Highers, including both academic subjects and subjects with a vocational focus (such as Construction, Accounting and Home Economics).

Why study for Advanced Highers?

You do not need to have an Advanced Highers qualification to go to some universities or colleges in the UK, but because Advanced Highers encourage you to learn through both classroom-based teaching and independent study, they can be a good bridge between the kinds of learning you do in school and in university and college. Sometimes, if you have Advanced Highers, you can skip the first year of a Scottish bachelor's degree. However, if you're applying to a university in England, Wales or Northern Ireland, you may need to have Advanced Highers, since they're considered equal to a full A-level qualification.

Advanced Highers are a good way to prepare for employment and become self-motivated, or you may want to do Advanced Highers simply to broaden your knowledge and skills.[28]

How are Advanced Highers organised?

Advanced Highers are usually made up of three National Units, plus an external assessment.[29] They take two years to complete.

National Units

To pass your National Units, you will have to do independent work, as well as study what is taught in tutorials or the classroom. National Units can include coursework, practical work or tests, and they are qualifications in their own right. This means that if you do not pass your subject overall, but you pass one of the National Units for your subject, your National Unit achievement will be recognised.[30]

External assessment

The external assessment is usually an exam or project which gives you the chance to show that you understand everything you've learned. You will have to show that you can apply what you've learned to a number of new subjects and contexts.[31]

What subjects are available?

Advanced Highers are available in a wide range of subjects, both academic and vocational.

To find out what other subjects are offered, talk to your school or visit the Scottish Qualifications Authority website (www.sqa.org.uk).

How will you be assessed and graded?

To get a National Unit, you need to pass assessment (such as course work, tests or practical work) which is marked by your teacher or lecturer. Your marks will then be checked by the Scottish Qualifications Authority.

The Scottish Qualifications Authority will set your external assessment and appoint professionals to mark it.[32]

If you pass your whole course, you will get an overall grade of A, B or C.[33] If you fail your subject, you will be awarded a grade of D or 'No Award'. 'No Award' is given to those students who score 44 per cent or less for their subject as a whole.

Where do Advanced Highers lead?

Advanced Highers can lead to a number of different things. Universities and colleges can use your Advanced Highers results to offer you a place, or give you direct entry to the second year of a degree programme (this is called 'Advanced Standing'). Advanced Highers can be a useful bridge between the classroom-based learning you do at Highers level and the self-motivated style of learning you will have to do at college or university.

Advanced Highers can also help to prepare you for certain types of employment. Some courses are directly relevant to careers, but no matter what subject you study, your employer will value the self-motivation you develop through Advanced Highers.[34]

Skills for Work courses

What are Skills for Work courses?

Skills for Work courses aim to give you knowledge and skills to prepare you for the world of work. They give you the chance to gain a variety of practical experiences that are linked to a specific vocational area. Courses are usually open to students in their third and fourth year of secondary school, and they are offered at Access 3, Intermediate 1 and 2 and Highers levels. You will usually do a Skills for Work course through a learning centre or college which works in partnership with your school.[35]

Why study Skills for Work courses?

If you want to develop some general employability skills, and you enjoy learning through practical tasks, a Skills for Work course could be the right choice for you. During your course, you will spend some time at a local college or training provider, or with an employer, and this will give you the chance to learn in a different environment and meet new people.

Skills for Work courses will help to improve your self-confidence, and they will give you practical skills that you can use in the workplace. By doing a Skills for Work course, you can develop:

- the skills and attitudes employers look for
- an understanding of the workplace
- skills and knowledge of a broad vocational area, and
- Core Skills.[36]

How are Skills for Work courses organised?

Skills for Work courses at Access Level are usually made up of three 40-hour units. Courses at Intermediate 1, Intermediate 2 and Higher are usually made up of four 40-hour units. You could have the chance to do a work placement during your course, but it is not essential.

The courses have four general learning aims:

- learning through practical experience
- learning by reflecting on your experience
- developing Core Skills, and
- developing employability skills and attitudes.

Learning through practical experience

If you do a Skills for Work course, you will learn through practical experience. Your course will include some of all of the following:[37]

- learning in a real or simulated workplace setting
- learning by role playing vocational activities

- doing case study work, and
- planning and doing practical assignments.

Learning by reflecting on your experience

You will also learn by reflecting on your experiences during the course. Your course will include some or all of the following:[38]

- preparing for and planning your experiences
- reflecting during your experience (such as reviewing your progress and adapting to different circumstances when necessary), and
- looking back over the experience once it is finished, and summarising what you have learnt.

Core Skills

You will develop Core Skills throughout your course. Core Skills are skills in:

- communication
- numeracy
- information technology
- problem solving, and
- working with others.

Employability skills and attitudes

You will gain the general skills and attitudes that employers look for by doing a Skills for Work course. These skills and attitudes include:[39]

- understanding the workplace and your responsibilities in it (such as time-keeping and taking care with your appearance)
- being able to evaluate your own skills
- a positive attitude to learning
- problem-solving in a flexible way
- being able to adapt to change and view it in a positive way, and
- the confidence to set goals and learn from your experience.

You may also obtain some skills and knowledge related to the specific vocational area you have chosen to study.

What subjects are available?

Skills for Work courses are linked to specific vocational areas. These areas include:[40]

- Construction
- Hairdressing
- Hospitality
- Engineering
- Health and social care
- Early education and childcare
- Financial services
- Retail
- Digital media
- Energy
- Sport and recreation
- Rural skills, and
- Uniformed and emergency services.

How will you be assessed?

You will pass your course by successfully completing the individual units which make up the course. Your assessment will be made up of a range of tasks, including practical assignments, short tests and record-keeping. The learning centre that teaches your course will assess your units and decide whether you pass them, and the Scottish Qualifications Authority will then double-check your assessment. If you pass the course, you will not receive a grade. There is no final exam for Skills for Work courses.[41]

Where do Skills for Work courses lead?

Skills for Work courses aim to help you progress to further education, training or employment.

Scottish Baccalaureate

What is the Scottish Baccalaureate?[42]

The Scottish Baccalaureate is a new qualification that will be introduced in August 2009. The qualification is made up of two courses and an interdisciplinary project at Advanced Higher level, and one course at Higher level. There are two different kinds of Baccalaureate:

- Scottish Baccalaureate in Languages, and
- Scottish Baccalaureate in Science.

The qualifications have been designed to encourage young people to study language and science subjects in secondary school, and to help students make a smooth transition from school to higher education, further education, or employment.

Why study for a Scottish Baccalaureate?

By doing a Scottish Baccalaureate, you will not only gain Advanced Highers and Highers qualifications, but you will learn how to apply your knowledge in real-life contexts through the interdisciplinary project. The project will most likely require you to work outside your school – for example, in a college or university, or a community or workplace setting. It will challenge you to think in a different way and develop skills that are valuable to higher education and work, such as initiative, responsibility and the ability to work independently.[43]

How is the Scottish Baccalaureate organised?

The Scottish Baccalaureate is made up of four parts:

- two Advanced Highers courses
- one Highers course, and
- an interdisciplinary project.

You will have to do the usual Highers and Advanced Highers tests, assignments and exams in order to pass those courses. For the interdisciplinary project, you will do an investigation or a practical assignment that is related to your subject knowledge and linked to real-life context. So, for example, you could choose a theme like employability and language use in the Scottish market, or energy options for sustainable solutions. The interdisciplinary project will usually require you to do some work outside your school (for example, in a college, university, community or workplace setting).[44]

What subjects are available?

Scottish Baccalaureate in Languages[45]

If you do the Scottish Baccalaureate in Languages, one of your language courses must be English, ESOL or Gàidhlig, which you can do at Higher or Advanced Higher level. You must also study two other language courses from the following list:

- Cantonese (available at Advanced Higher level from 2010)
- Classical Greek
- Gaelic (Learners)
- German
- French
- Italian
- Latin
- Mandarin (available at Advanced Higher level from 2010)
- Russian (not available at Advanced Higher level)
- Spanish
- Urdu (not available at Advanced Higher level)

If your first language is Gàidhlig, you may study both English and Gàidhlig, along with one of the languages courses from the list above.

You cannot study both Gaelic (Learners) and Gàidhlig for your Baccalaureate.

Scottish Baccalaureate in Science[46]

If you do the Scottish Baccalaureate in Science, one of your courses must be Mathematics or Applied Mathematics, which you can do at

Higher or Advanced Higher level. You must also choose either two science courses or one science course and one technology course from the following list:

Science courses

- Biology
- Biotechnology (not available at Advanced Higher level)
- Chemistry
- Geology (not available at Advanced Higher level)
- Human Biology (not available at Advanced Higher level)
- Physics
- Mechatronics (not available at Advanced Higher level)
- Product Design
- Technological Studies

Technology courses

- Building Construction (not available at Advanced Higher level)
- Computing
- Fabrication and Welding Engineering (not available at Advanced Higher level)
- Graphic Communication
- Information Systems
- Managing Environmental Resources (not available at Advanced Higher level)

How will you be assessed?[47]

Your individual courses and your interdisciplinary project will be given a grade of A, B or C, provided you pass the assessment. You will also receive an overall grade for your Baccalaureate: either a Distinction or a Pass. To achieve a Distinction, you must get:

- Grade A in one Advanced Highers course
- Grade A in one other course or your interdisciplinary project, and
- Grade B in all other parts of your course.

You will be awarded a Pass if you achieve at least a C in all parts of your Baccalaureate and you do not meet the criteria for a Distinction.

Where does a Scottish Baccalaureate lead?

Because you will be achieving three Advanced Highers through your programme, the qualification is excellent preparation for entering university.

Classroom-based vocational qualifications

For those who would like to learn more about a particular area of work, there are many classroom-based vocational qualifications to choose from, including BTECs , City and Guilds qualifications, OCR Nationals, National Certificates and National Progression Awards. Some vocational qualifications help you to develop general skills that can be applied to a variety of jobs, whereas others teach you the skills related to a specific job or sector.[48] These qualifications are usually recognised by certificates and diplomas.

BTECs, City and Guilds qualifications and OCR Nationals 🆄🅺

What are BTECs, City and Guilds qualifications and OCR Nationals?[49]

The Business Training and Education Council (BTEC) has created a number of work-related qualifications that are called BTECs. Their qualifications are offered by the awarding body Edexcel. Similarly, City and Guilds (CG) offers its own range of vocational qualifications, and Oxford Cambridge and RSA Examinations (OCR) supplies work-related qualifications called OCR Nationals. BTECs and CG qualifications are available throughout the whole UK, and OCR Nationals are available in England, Wales and Northern Ireland.

Many BTECs, CG qualifications and OCR Nationals are designed with the help of employers and industry experts, so you can be sure that you're gaining the kind of knowledge and skills employers are looking for. The qualifications can involve a mixture of theory and practice, and sometimes work experience. A BTEC, CG qualification or OCR National can be part of a technical certificate, which is a requirement of some apprenticeships.

Who can do BTECs, City and Guilds qualifications and OCR Nationals?[50]

BTECs and CG qualifications are offered at most levels on the National Qualifications Framework (NQF) and the Scottish Credit and Qualifications Framework (see page 110), and OCR Nationals are offered at Levels 1 to 3 on the NQF. The entry requirements for each qualification will depend on the level you are studying. So, for example, if you want to do a Level 2 BTEC, CG qualification or OCR National, you will usually need to have GCSEs graded at D–G, or a Level 1 qualification in a similar subject. If you want to do a Level 3 BTEC, CG qualification or OCR National, you will usually need to have GCSEs graded at A*–C, or a Level 2 qualification.

BTECs, CG qualifications and OCR Nationals are generally designed for people aged over 16, but some schools offer them to students in the 14–16 age bracket.

How do you study for BTECs, City and Guilds qualifications and OCR Nationals?[51]

BTECs, CG qualifications and OCR Nationals are usually available at colleges, and sometimes at schools. You can study them full-time at colleges and schools, or part-time at colleges. The length of your programme will depend on what you are studying. Most of the qualifications mix theory with practice, and some may also include work experience.

You will be assessed through assignments, case studies, practical activities and a portfolio of your work. Usually, your teacher or trainer will assess your work, but for some qualifications, an external examiner will also look at your work. If you pass, you will be awarded one of three grades: Pass, Merit or Distinction.

Where do BTECs, City and Guilds qualifications and OCR Nationals lead?[52]

These qualifications offer good progression routes to further study, so you might start on an introductory or Foundation programme, and then move up to higher awards. The higher-level qualifications are often recognised by universities and could allow you to progress to a degree course. Or your BTEC, CG qualification or OCR National could lead to a job, since these qualifications are well regarded by employers and industry experts.

National Certificates and National Progression Awards (S)

What are National Certificates and National Progression Awards?[53]

National Certificates (NCs) and National Progression Awards (NPAs) prepare you for employment, career development or progression to further study by improving your knowledge and skills. You can do NCs and NPAs in a range of subjects, but the qualifications are only available in Scotland. Most NCs and NPAs are short, full-time programmes of study centred on a particular job area or industry. You can do NCs and NPAs at Levels 2–6 on the Scottish Credit and Qualifications Framework (see page 110), and the awards are linked to National Occupational Standards. They are run by colleges (sometimes in partnership with schools and employers), and they are aimed at adults or young people aged 16–18. Check the Scottish Qualifications Authority website for more information (www.sqa.org.uk).

Higher education qualifications

Higher education is the university-level phase of education that you can do after you leave school or college at age 18. Universities arrange many of the learning programmes at this level, but some learning programmes may be run by colleges instead.

Higher education offers a range of advanced courses and qualifications. You will usually study just one or two subjects: either traditional subjects like art, history, or English literature, or modern topics like sports science, music production, or multimedia programming. The higher education qualifications on offer are:

- bachelor's degrees (sometimes called a Master of Arts in Scotland)
- Foundation Degrees (England, Wales and Northern Ireland)
- Higher National Certificates and Higher National Diplomas (UK-wide), and
- Diplomas of higher education and Certificates of higher education.

Bachelor's degrees

What kinds of undergraduate degrees are available?

The most common university degree is a bachelor's degree. Almost all universities will expect you to do a bachelor's degree with Honours, and this will take three or four years to complete. Some universities may offer a bachelor's degree without Honours.

If you go to one of the older universities in Scotland, you may do a Master of Arts degree instead of a bachelor's degree. Master of Arts degrees are basically the same as bachelor's degrees, except they take four years to complete and can be awarded with or without Honours. Older universities offer a Master of Arts degree for certain subjects only, usually fine art, humanities, social sciences and theology. A Master of Arts degree is not the same as a postgraduate Masters degree.

Some universities offer undergraduate masters degrees, mostly in engineering and science subjects. These degrees usually include honours, take four years to finish, and are not as common as bachelor's degrees.

Your degree programme could include a sandwich course. This involves taking one year out of your studies (a 'sandwich' year) to work in industry or abroad.

How will you learn at university?

At university, you will learn through lectures, seminars and tutorials, and possibly practical sessions, depending on which subject area you choose to study. Seminars, tutorials and lectures are not lessons as such, but they provide support and guidance for your own reading. While you're at university, you will need to manage your time responsibly and effectively, particularly if you are going to meet deadlines. You will also need to develop new academic skills for tasks such as writing research essays. You will develop these techniques over time, but lots of help is available. For tips on how to get the most out of lectures, visit the Student UK website (www.studentuk.com).

What kinds of social activities are available at university?

Each university is different, but most will have clubs and societies for all popular sports, hobbies and interests. 'Raising and Giving' (RAG) societies are often busy on campus all year, organising stunts and fundraising for good causes. The major political parties usually have student branches, and most universities will have cultural, religious and faith group societies as well. To get an idea of the types of clubs at universities, visit the Student Zone Clubs and Societies Directory at www.studentzone.org.uk.

University living arrangements

If you decide to move away from home to go to university, you don't just have to think about your course and finances, you also have to think about where you're going to live. Most universities have accommodation on campus or nearby (usually this accommodation is either halls of residence or privately run housing). In August and September each year, lots of students arc going to be looking for accommodation, so as soon as your place on at university is confirmed, you need to sort out your accommodation. Most first-year students choose to live in halls on campus or in university-managed accommodation, because it's easy to meet people, it can be safer, and there are no bills to worry about.

After the first year you may decide to rent a house with your friends. This can be lots of fun, but you'll need to be ready to live with other people and to budget as a group.

Foundation Degrees

What is a Foundation Degree?

A Foundation Degree is an alternative to a traditional undergraduate degree (such as a bachelor's degree), and it gives you more hands-on work experience and practical skills than a standard university degree. Foundation Degrees are work-based degrees run by colleges, universities and other training providers, and employers have an important say in the design of the degrees, so you can be sure that a Foundation Degree meets current employment needs.[54]

Who can do a Foundation Degree?

Foundation Degrees are open to:

• people who are already in work

• people who want to kick-start a career change, and

• students who have finished their Level 3 qualifications (for example, A-levels, an Advanced Apprenticeship or a Level 3 National Vocational Qualification).

Sometimes formal qualifications will not be necessary to start a Foundation Degree. There are no set entry requirements, so you should check whether you are eligible to do a Foundation Degree with your university or college.

Foundation Degrees are not available in Scotland.

You can apply for a full-time Foundation Degree through the Universities and Colleges Admissions Service website, www.ucas.com. To apply for a part-time Foundation Degree, speak to the education provider in charge of the course you want to do. [55]

How long does it take to do a Foundation Degree?

It usually takes two years to finish a Foundation Degree, if you are a full-time student, or three or four years if you study part-time.[56]

What subjects can you study?

There are over 2,500 Foundation Degree courses available,[57] covering a wide range of subjects, including veterinary nursing, e-commerce, health and social care, and forensic science.[58]

How are you assessed?

Most degree courses mix exams, coursework and workplacelearning assessments. You may even have to submit a written dissertation at the end of your course, depending on what you are studying. Foundation Degree coursework and assessments are usually awarded either a Pass or a Fail, though some courses might also offer Distinctions.

Where do Foundation Degrees lead?

Foundation Degrees are stand-alone qualifications, roughly equal to the first two years of a bachelor's degree. A Foundation Degree will significantly improve your career prospects, especially if you want to become a higher-level technician, marketing consultant, associate professional or personnel officer. [59] The degree will often lead you straight into a job, since it is designed in partnership with businesses.

Once you have finished your Foundation Degree, you have the option of converting it to a bachelor's degree by doing another year of full-time study.[60]

Higher National Certificates and Higher National Diplomas (UK)

What are Higher National Certificates and Higher National Diplomas?

Higher National Certificates (HNCs) and Higher National Diplomas (HNDs) are vocational higher education qualifications. They aim to give you both theoretical knowledge and practical skills, and they are run by further education colleges and some universities and training centres.[61] HNCs and HNDs are available in all parts of the UK.

Who can do a Higher National Certificate or Higher National Diploma?

To do a HNC or HND, you will need to already have some qualifications. For most HND courses, you will need to have one A-level (or equivalent).[62] If you are doing a HNC or HND in Scotland, you will usually be expected to have a Level 3 General Scottish Vocational Qualification, two passes at Higher or above, or an equivalent qualification.[63]

How long does it take to do a Higher National Certificate or Diploma?

HNCs take one year to complete if you study full-time, and two years to finish if you are a part-time student. HNDs take two years to complete if you study full-time, or longer if you do the programme part-time.[64]

What subjects can you study?

HNCs and HNDs cover a wide range of subjects, with more than 1,000 courses on offer, including:

- Agriculture
- Computing and IT
- Construction and Civil Engineering
- Engineering
- Health and Social Care
- Business and Management
- Sport and Exercise Sciences
- Performing Arts
- Retail and Distribution
- Hospitality and Management[65]
- Travel and Tourism
- Broadcasting
- Information and Office Management
- Accounting, and
- Video Production.[66]

How are you assessed?

Generally speaking, you will be assessed through assignments, projects and practical tasks. You will be awarded a Pass, Merit or Distinction for each subject unit. You may be able to re-take certain projects or tasks if you are unhappy with your results.[67]

Where do Higher National Certificates and Diplomas lead?

You can convert your HNC or HND into a bachelor's degree if you are willing to do extra study. If you have a HNC, you can enter the second year of some degree courses, and if you have a HND, you can enter the second or third year of some degree courses.

If you aren't interested in going on to a university degree, you can use your HNC or HND to launch a career, or to progress within your current career: you could use the qualification as a stepping-stone to gaining professional status.[68] Your HNC or HND can give you the knowledge and skills required for some Scottish Vocational Qualifications, and having a HNC or HND can also permit you to join some professional bodies.[69]

Diplomas of higher education and Certificates of higher education[70]

Diplomas of higher education are similar to HNDs. They are professional qualifications which take two years to finish, and you can often convert your diploma to a degree, if you are prepared to do an extra year of study. Diplomas are available in a variety of subjects, including accounting, construction, engineering, nursing, science, technology and textile design.

Certificates of higher education are broadly equal to HNCs, but they are academic (not vocational) qualifications. Certificates require one year of full-time study.

Work-based learning

If you want to stay in learning so you can increase your knowledge of a specific area of work or trade, you could choose to take part in work-based learning.

Work-based learning brings together a number of essential learning experiences to create a single learning programme. So, instead of studying a range of subjects, you will follow one programme which has been designed to meet the requirements of a particular work sector or industry. Here are a few key facts you should know about work-based learning:

- Work-based learning lets you earn while you learn.
- Courses are designed to fit around your needs and the needs of your employer.
- You can learn skills that are essential to your future career, such as computer literacy, communication skills, teamwork and how to meet deadlines.
- There are lots of qualifications available to you while you're working, including apprenticeships, pre-employment programme qualifications, National Vocational Qualifications and Scottish Vocational Qualifications.

To find out more about work-based learning, try searching the web, calling your local university or college, or looking in newspapers and trade magazines. More information can be obtained from the Direct Government website (www.direct.gov.uk), the Skills Development Scotland website (www.scottish-enterprise.com), and the Careers Scotland website (www.careers-scotland.org.uk).

There are currently three work-based learning programmes:

- National Vocational Qualifications and Scottish Vocational Qualifications
- pre-employment programmes, including:
  - New Deal for Young People and Flexible New Deal (UK)

- Entry to Employment (England)
- Skill Build (Wales)
- Get Ready for Work (Scotland)
- Skillseekers (Scotland)
- Training for Work (Scotland)
- Training for Success (Northern Ireland)
- Bridge to Employment (Northern Ireland)
- Steps to Work (Northern Ireland), and
- apprenticeships.

National Vocational Qualifications and Scottish Vocational Qualifications

National Vocational Qualifications

What are National Vocational Qualifications?

National Vocational Qualifications (NVQs) are qualifications linked to a particular industry or job sector, and they can be studied at college, work, or as part of an apprenticeship.

NVQs assess your occupational competence – that is, your ability to apply knowledge and skills in the workplace to get jobs done correctly and on time. So, for a NVQ you will do practical, work-related tasks designed to help you develop the skills and knowledge to do a particular job. NVQs make sure that you can cope with the unexpected and respond to the demands, pressures and problems that come up at work every day. Once you have shown that you can meet the occupational standards for your NVQ, you will be awarded the appropriate NVQ certificate.

Why study for National Vocational Qualifications?

If you want to get a recognised qualification linked to a particular industry or work sector, a NVQ could be the right option for you. You will learn how to actually do a job in a certain area of work, so pursuing a NVQ may be a good choice for you if you have a sound idea about which area you would like to work in. Also, because NVQs can be studied alongside a job you are already doing, or as part of an apprenticeship, they can be a great way to get qualifications in the sector where you already work.

Who is eligible for National Vocational Qualifications?

NVQs are open to young people and adults. You can start a NVQ if:

- you are employed, or
- you are studying at college and have a part-time job or access to a work placement.

You can also take a NVQ at Level 2 or 3 as part of an apprenticeship, and in some cases if you are at school.

How are National Vocational Qualifications organised?

NVQs are organised into five levels, based on competency. NVQs at Levels 1, 2 and 3 are usually done by learners aged 14 to 19. NVQs at Level 4 and above are usually done by mature students.

A Level 1 NVQ assesses your competency in performing a range of varied but routine and predictable work activities. As you move up through the levels, you will be expected to use your knowledge to do more varied activities, and you will have more personal responsibility and freedom in your work.

Because NVQs are designed to be done at a pace that suits your needs, there is no formal time limit on completing the qualification. Most learners need about one year to complete a NVQ at Level 1 and 2, and around two years for a NVQ at Level 3.[71]

What subjects are available?

NVQs are available in most job sectors. There are over 1,300 NVQs to choose from, including:

- Sales, Marketing and Distribution
- Healthcare
- Construction and Property
- Business and Management
- Manufacturing, Production and Engineering, and
- Food, Catering and Leisure Services.[72]

How will you be assessed?

Because NVQs are work-related qualifications, you are assessed through practical assignments and a portfolio of evidence. An assessor will observe you completing real work activities in the workplace, and he or she will test your knowledge and understanding as well as your actual performance.

NVQs are made up of individual units, which an assessor will 'sign off' when you reach the standard required. You are assessed as being either 'competent' or 'not yet competent'.[73]

Where do National Vocational Qualifications lead?

If you complete a NVQ, you can go on to further training at the next NVQ level, up to Level 5, or you could do a professional qualification, usually in a similar area to your NVQ.

If you've studied a NVQ at Level 3, you could also go on to a higher education course in a related vocational area, such as a:

- Higher National Certificate
- Higher National Diploma
- Foundation Degree, or
- another vocational qualification.

You could also think about going on to a Modern Skills Diploma, if you live or work in Wales. The Modern Skills Diploma is an work-based programme for people who are employed, and it provides opportunities for learners to improve their skills and knowledge at NVQ Level 4. To enter this programme, you would normally be expected to hold a technician and/or people management position.[74]

Scottish Vocational Qualifications

What are Scottish Vocational Qualifications?

Scottish Vocational Qualifications (SVQs) are very similar to NVQs, since they are qualifications linked to a particular industry or job sector. The main difference is that SVQs take into account Scotland's different legal, education, and enterprise systems. SVQs prove that you are competent – that you really can do the work the SVQ covers. If you do a SVQ, you will collect and submit evidence to show that you are competent.

SVQs are not training programmes, but a way to recognise that you are capable of doing something. So you may have to get training or do other learning in order to achieve the level (or standard) of competency set out by a SVQ. You can do SVQs through training providers and colleges, as well as through your workplace.[75] The standard of competency for each SVQ covers the skills, knowledge and understanding you need to achieve the qualification. The standards for SVQs are the same as the standards for NVQs.[76]

Why do a Scottish Vocational Qualification?

If you want to get a recognised qualification linked to a particular industry or work sector, a SVQ could be valuable for you. The award shows that you know how to actually do a job in a certain work sector, so a SVQ is a good choice if you have a sound idea about which area you would like to work in the long term.

Who is eligible for a Scottish Vocational Qualification?

SVQs can be done by people at all ages, and at all different points in their career. There are no entry requirements for SVQs.[77]

How are Scottish Vocational Qualifications organised?

SVQs are organised into five levels, based on competency. A Level 1 SVQ will assess your competency in doing a range of varied but routine and predictable work activities. As you move up through the levels, you will be expected to use your knowledge to do more difficult activities, and you will have more personal responsibility and freedom in your work. The levels cover the following :[78]

- Level 1: basic, routine and repetitive work skills
- Level 2: broad range of skills including non-routine activities and individual responsibility

- Level 3: supervisory skills
- Level 4: management skills
- Level 5: senior management skills

For each SVQ, competency is broken down into units. Each unit covers one part of the work you have to prove you can do to get the SVQ. You will have to pass all of the units to get your SVQ.

Units are further broken down into elements. Each element describes a task you have to perform to pass the unit. So, for example, one of your units may be 'Maintain business relationships.' In order to pass that unit, you will have to show you can do all of the individual elements, which are:

- Create and maintain external working relationships
- Enhance productive working relationships with colleagues, and
- Enhance productive working relationship with immediate manager.[79]

What subjects are available?

SVQs are available in most job sectors. There are over 650 SVQs to choose from. You can get an information sheet for each SVQ from the Scottish Qualifications Authority website (www.sqa.org.uk).[80]

How will you be assessed?

Because SVQs are work-related qualifications, you will be assessed by producing evidence to show you are competent. There are no rules about how long it should take to complete an assessment.[81] Your assessor will usually be a supervisor or manager, and their assessment will be double-checked internally by the company.[82] Their assessment may also be double-checked externally by the Scottish Qualifications Authority. Your assessor will make one of three possible judgements when they assess you:[83]

- you are competent
- you are not yet competent, or
- there is not enough evidence to make a judgement.

There are three main types of evidence you can collect for your assessment:

- Performance evidence
- Knowledge evidence, and
- Evidence of prior learning.

SVQs at Levels 1 and 2 will usually be assessed by your performance at work. However, sometimes an assessor might want to observe you doing something which is not part of your normal work. You may have to spend some time in another department, or do special tasks which have been set.

SVQs at Levels 3, 4 and 5 will usually be assessed using a number of methods. This could include observing you in the workplace, doing simulations, role-play and special tasks, and spending some time in another department.[84]

Performance evidence

Performance evidence shows that you can do the activities set out in each element. It can include:[85]

- observations recorded by your assessor or another competent person
- work products, and
- your answers to questions about activities and products (answers should show that you know why you have done what you have done).

Knowledge evidence

Knowledge evidence usually comes from answers to written or oral questions, case studies, your own record of your activities, and witnesses. It shows that:[86]

- you know why things are done in a particular way
- you can transfer your skills to different situations, and
- you can deal with things that may be difficult for your assessor to fully observe or simulate.

Evidence of prior learning

This proof that you are competent is based on things you have already done. It can include evidence of work experience, training and hobbies.[87]

Where do Scottish Vocational Qualifications lead?

SVQs encourage you to go on to further qualifications. Once you have a SVQ, you can do another SVQ at the next level, or you could do a different professional qualification. If you've studied a SVQ at Level 3, you could go on to a higher education course in a related vocational area, such as a Higher National Certificate or Higher National Diploma.

Pre-employment programmes

New Deal for Young People and Flexible New Deal

New Deal for Young People (NDYP) and Flexible New Deal (FND) are run by Jobcentre Plus throughout the UK for people aged over 18. The programmes aim to help people who are claiming welfare benefits to move into sustainable work.[88] Through the programmes, Jobcentre Plus provides a wide variety of support, which can include training, advice, help with jobsearch, and work experience.

NDYP has been running for some time, but it will be gradually replaced by FND, which is a new programme. Jobcentre Plus is introducing FND in phases, so programme availability will depend on where you live. If you live in a Phase One area, and you have done six months of supported jobsearch, you will move onto FND in October 2009. Those who live in a Phase One area and are taking part in NDYP in October 2009 will also move onto FND. If you live in a Phase Two area, FND will be introduced from October 2010 for those who have done six months of supported jobsearch, and for those who are taking part in NDYP at the time. This means that NDYP will run in Phase Two areas up until October 2010.

If you would like to know more about which programme runs in your area, the programme structure and criteria, contact your local Jobcentre Plus or refer to *Inclusion's Welfare to Work Handbook*.

Entry to Employment

What is Entry to Employment?

Entry to Employment (e2e) is a learning programme that can help you if you:

- are aged 16 to 18
- live in England, and
- are not ready or able to enter apprenticeship programmes, further education or employment.

E2e can give you the skills you will need to prepare for employment, employment with training, an apprenticeship programme or further education.

The programme is:

- not limited to a fixed amount of time
- has no fixed number of guided learning hours or attendance, but you do have to meet the minimum requirements
- not driven by qualifications, but you may want to get qualifications to help you progress and develop
- flexible, and learning providers have developed a range of options to suit the needs of the individual learner.

Who is eligible for Entry to Employment?

You are eligible to join e2e if you:

- are aged 16 to 18
- live in England
- are not taking part in any other kind of post-16 learning, and
- need help to progress to further learning and/or a job.

Young people who fall under the Extended Guarantee can also take part in e2e. This means that the local Learning and Skills Council (LSC) can use its discretion to allow older young people into the programme, provided that they are not eligible for New Deal, and that they will finish their learning programme by their 25th birthday.

Is Entry to Employment right for you?

E2e may be right for you if you are not ready to enter training, employment or further education. Young people who take up e2e will have different levels of ability. In general, you are likely to benefit from e2e programmes if you:

- have significant learning difficulties and/or disabilities
- are currently not doing any form of learning and may have had a negative experience of school
- have one or more barriers to work and learning, such as alcohol abuse, drug abuse, depression or homelessness.

How do you get involved in Entry to Employment?

Staff from your local Connexions Service will advise you about e2e opportunities in your local area. Connexions staff will refer you to e2e if they think the programme is appropriate for you. Other agencies, such as Social Services, youth offending teams, and work-based learning providers can also identify young people who may benefit from e2e learning programmes. However, your Connexions adviser is the key to getting you onto an e2e programme, even if you refer yourself to an e2e programme or are advised to apply by a local learning provider.

Your Connexions adviser will confirm that e2e is appropriate by doing assessment, planning, implementation and review (APIR) with you (see page 16). APIR is used to assess your needs and work out your goals, so that your adviser can draw up a personal action plan for you. Your personal action plan will set out your learning and support needs and should be recorded on a Personal Adviser Referral Form. Your learning needs are the skills, knowledge and abilities that you need to gain in order to help you reach your goals. Your support needs are the extra help you need in order to address and overcome any barriers that you may have to learning or work.

The personal action plan is then used to set out what you will do on e2e. You will have an e2e passport which details what you have agreed to do on e2e (see page 158).

How long does Entry to Employment last?

The e2e programme is not limited to a fixed amount of time because it is based on the needs of each individual. The programme recognises that there can be no 'quick fix' for many of the young people who enter e2e. Some young people prepare to enter an apprenticeship, employment or further vocational learning opportunities in a very short time. Others will require much longer before they are ready to enter and stay in training and employment, if they have more complex personal and social needs.

How many hours per week will you spend on Entry to Employment?

The amount of time you spend on e2e each week depends on your individual needs, but it is likely to be between 16 and 40 hours per week. In exceptional circumstances, your local LSC may agree that you can attend for 8 to 16 hours per week.

What will you learn on Entry to Employment?

E2e aims to help you:

- improve your motivation and confidence
- develop your basic and/or key skills (see page 109), and gain knowledge, skills and understanding by sampling different work and learning contexts.

By the end of an e2e programme you should have gained:

- vocational knowledge and understanding
- up-to-date work skills
- some related knowledge and understanding that goes beyond vocational areas

- career awareness and career management skills
- skills in:
  - communication
  - numeracy
  - ICT
  - effective thinking, enterprise and problem solving
  - personal relations and teamwork, and
  - citizenship.

Entry to Employment Passport

You will have a period of initial assessment as part of e2e, in order to clearly work out your learning and support needs. This might last from two to eight weeks, depending on your needs. The aim is to use this period of initial assessment to help you develop your personal and social skills.

The arrangements for meeting your learning and support needs will be set out in a document called the e2e Passport. This passport is your overall plan, and it records your initial assessment, learning plan and progress reviews.

The passport is made up of the:

- Personal Adviser Referral Form
- Initial Assessment Summary
- e2e Programme
- e2e Activity Plan and Review

How is the learning programme structured?

You will do learning in three core areas:

- Basic and key skills
- Vocational development, and
- Personal and social development.

Your level of learning for each core area will be decided according to your needs. Learning will be introduced at the right time for you. For example, if you have complex emotional and social needs, you may not be ready to undertake vocational learning until these needs are addressed.

Each core area has a range of learning options at different levels of work, and you will be able to select appropriate options.

Where and how will learning take place?

Learning takes place in a range of indoor and outdoor settings, using different methods. These methods include classroom-type activities, one-to-one coaching, group activities, discussions, projects, presentations from speakers, online learning, open learning, work placements and experience, external visits, outward bound activities and volunteering.

Will you work towards qualifications?

Wherever possible, you will work towards some kind of qualification, because getting a qualification can motivate you to continue learning. There is a range of qualifications that you can gain. You may take national qualifications, or others such as first aid courses, computer literacy and information technology, European Computer Driving Licence, or the City and Guilds Profile of Achievement.

Working with support agencies

Local support agencies have a valuable role in e2e. These agencies may work with you if you need extra support. Learning providers may refer you to local support agencies to get help with issues such as drug or alcohol dependency, sexual health or child abuse.

Financial support

See page 220.

Skill Build

What is Skill Build?

Skill Build (SB) helps young people who have left school and are still unsure about what they want to do. It is aimed at people who are:

- unemployed and need vocational skills training
- are unsure what they want to do, and require work taster placements to figure it out
- lack confidence or motivation, or
- have poor basic skills.[89]

SB can help you to improve skills such as writing, reading and working with numbers, or you could try out a job through the programme and see if it's the right thing for you. By taking part in SB, you can also get skills and training relevant to a certain job, or work towards NVQs.[90] The programme will:

- identify any learning barriers that might stop you from taking part in vocational learning at Level 1, 2 or 3
- identify and address any of your basic skills needs
- give you learning opportunities, so that you have the skills to better participate in work and in society, and
- give you the chance to do vocational learning at Level 1, 2 or 3.[91]

Who can take part in Skill Build?

You can take part in SB if you:

- are aged 16 or over, and
- have left full-time compulsory education, and
- are ordinarily resident in Wales, or your employment or work placement is in Wales.[92]

You will not be able to join SB if you:

- have not reached the school leaving age
- are in full-time school, further or higher education

- are taking part in a vocational training programme funded by the UK government, Welsh Ministers or the European Union
- are getting an Assembly Learning Grant (see page 234), or
- are an ineligible overseas national.[93]

Programme elements

Initial assessment

Before you enter SB, or as soon as you enter SB, you will have an initial assessment with your programme provider to work out your previous learning, your current learning and skills needs, and any support needs you might have. Once these are known, your provider will work with you to draw up an Individual Learning Plan, which will set out a learning programme to meet your needs. Your Individual Learning Plan should be drawn up within four weeks of starting the programme, and must be agreed by both you and your SB provider. It will set out the length of your SB programme, your attendance requirements, how often you will have progress reviews, and the qualifications you aim to achieve. If your learning and support needs change during the programme, your Individual Learning Plan will be updated, and you must agree any changes to your programme.[94]

Ongoing assessment

During SB, you will have ongoing assessment to check your progress against your Individual Learning Plan. Assessments make sure that you are on track to achieve your aims, and give you a chance to talk about any problems or needs that have come up since your initial assessment. Your provider will review your progress as often as necessary, and at least once every 31 days. Both you and your provider will have to sign your review.[95]

Exit interview

Your provider should interview you before you leave SB, to talk about your options and learning needs for the future.[96]

What range of careers does Skill Build cater for?

SB caters for a wide range of different careers. The areas in which you can do training will depend on your SB provider, so you should speak to them to find out what they offer. Some examples of the areas covered by the training on offer are:[97]

- business administration
- motor mechanics
- agriculture, and
- carpentry.

You could also improve your chances of employment by doing general training in areas such as First Aid and basic food hygiene.[98]

How do you join Skill Build?

The Welsh government has a Youth Guarantee and Extended Guarantee which means that certain young people (mainly those aged under 18) are entitled to a place on SB. If you fall into this group, you must enter the SB programme via Careers Wales. Speak to an adviser at Careers Wales, and they will refer you to SB with a written 'endorsement'.

If you are aged 18 or over, Jobcentre Plus must confirm that you are eligible to enter SB.[99]

How long does Skill Build last?

SB training lasts for at least 13 weeks. If you are working towards NVQs, your SB programme could last for up to one year.[100]

How many hours per week does the programme take?

If you are taking part in SB and you are not employed, you will usually attend the programme for at least 30 hours per week. The maximum amount of time you can spend on the programme is 40 hours per week (not counting meal breaks).

If you entered SB under the Youth Guarantee and Extended Guarantee (that is, you entered via Careers Wales), you are not employed, and you are attending the programme for less than 30 hours per week, your learning allowance will be reduced accordingly.[101]

Financial support

See page 220.

Absences and holiday leave

Generally, if you are absent from the programme for 10 working days in a row without prior authorisation, you will be suspended from the learning programme for a maximum of 13 weeks. This rule does not apply to learners aged 18 or over who are receiving an allowance from the Department for Work and Pensions. During your suspension, your SB provider will decide whether you can return to learning in some form. You will not receive a learning allowance while you are suspended.[102]

If you are aged 18 or over and you are receiving an allowance from the Department for Work and Pensions, and you are absent from the programme for 10 working days in a row without prior authorisation, your SB provider will assume that you have left the programme.[103]

Those who are not employed and are receiving a learning allowance are entitled to at least one and a half days of holiday per month, along with time off for bank holidays. You can take up to 15 days of holiday at a time, so long as you speak to your SB provider ahead of time and they authorise your absence.[104]

Re-joining Skill Build

You can only re-join SB if you still meet the eligibility criteria. You will have a progress review if you re-join SB after a suspension.[105]

Get Ready for Work

What is Get Ready for Work?

Get Ready for Work (GRFW) is a programme which helps young people to move into a job, further training or a college. It helps you to focus on working out what you want to do. Through the programme, you will figure out your individual needs and get the skills and confidence to move into work, either directly or via training and further education.[106]

Who can take part in Get Ready for Work?

You can take part in GRFW if you:[107]

- are aged 16 to 19 (first priority is given to people aged 16 to 17)
- have reached the school leaving age
- have left full-time education
- are in need of essential skills to stay in work and make progress (for example, personal and learning skills, literacy and numeracy, employability and core skills), and
- are capable of, and available to progress to, work, full-time training, or further learning within a reasonable amount of time.

You cannot take part in the programme if you are already doing employment, training or a similar programme which is funded by the government or Skills Development Scotland.

Programme elements

GRFW sets out to do the following:[108]

- Assess your needs and skills
- Identify your positive achievements
- Identify any barriers that might stop you from making progress
- Create an Individual Learning Plan (ILP) for you
- Offer you a programme of support based on your ILP
- Support you while you plan and move through the transition into work or further education

Initial assessment

Your local Careers Service will do an initial assessment before you start GRFW. The initial assessment will work out your goals, which will be recorded in your ILP. When you meet with your GRFW provider, they will use the results from your initial assessment to plan your training course, in discussion with you. Your personal adviser will work with the GRFW provider to make sure that your course meets your needs.[109]

Individual Learning Plan

Using the results of your initial assessment, your personal adviser will draw up an ILP with you. The ILP will be drawn up no more than four weeks before you start your GRFW programme, and you and your personal adviser will both sign it. Your ILP will set out the details and time-frame of your GRFW programme. Your GRFW provider should check that the goals on your ILP are reasonable and you have a good chance of completing the plan successfully.[110]

If you are claiming Incapacity Benefit and you wish to continue receiving the benefit during your GRFW programme, this must be stated on your ILP. You will not be able to get a Training Allowance if you are getting Incapacity Benefit.[111]

Trainee Agreement

As well as drawing up and signing an ILP with your adviser, you will also have to agree and sign a Trainee Agreement with your GRFW provider. The agreement will set out the details and time-frame of your programme. It should be kept up-to-date.[112]

Training and support

The programme will be geared towards meeting your individual needs. Depending on your needs, you could get help with the following:[113]

- interview techniques
- completing application forms
- drawing up a CV
- building self-confidence
- developing your computer skills
- applying for jobs
- developing your communication skills
- improving you literacy and numeracy skills
- managing your money.

GRFW will also give you the chance to do work 'tasters' and placements, to help you decide the best kind of job or career for you.

Ongoing assessment and reviews

As part of GRFW, you will have ongoing assessment to check your goals and your progress. You will have a formal review at least once every four weeks, and the results of your review will be recorded on your ILP. The goals on your ILP can be changed to take account of what's been happening.[114]

In-work support

If you move into work as a result of GRFW, your programme provider should make sure that you get in-work support for up to 26 weeks after you start your job.[115]

How long does the programme last?

Because GRFW focuses on the individual, the length of the programme will depend on your needs. However, the maximum amount of time you can spend on GRFW is usually 26 weeks.

The time-frame for your programme will be set out in your ILP. The time-frame can only be changed if your personal adviser agrees to it.[116]

How do you join Get Ready for Work?

If you're thinking about joining GRFW, contact your local Careers Service. Your personal adviser will be able to give you more information about the programme and let you know if you're eligible to join.

Financial support
See page 220.

Absences and holiday leave

If you do not attend the programme, and you do not give a reason for your absence or fill out the required forms, you will have an 'unauthorised absence'. This could affect the amount of your Training

Allowance. If you have five days of unauthorised absence in a row, your GRFW provider will assume that you have left the programme.[117]

While you are on GRFW, you are entitled to some paid holidays. You should be entitled to at least one and a half days of paid holiday per month. You must get approval from your provider for your holiday time in advance.[118]

There are guidelines for taking time off because of sickness and other reasons. You should talk to your GRFW provider to find out what they are before you have time off from the programme, otherwise your Training Allowance could be affected.

Training for Work

What is Training for Work?[119]

Training for Work (TfW) is a voluntary programme which gives training support to people who are unemployed and actively looking for work. Through the TfW programme, you can go on work placements and get access to formal training. In many cases, you will have a good chance of moving into a full-time job. TfW also helps people to start up their own businesses.

Who can take part in Training for Work?[120]

You can take part in TfW if you:

- are aged 18 or over, and
- need training to help you get a job, and
- are not taking part in any other government-funded programmes, including:
    - a business start-up scheme
    - Positive Moves
    - Work Trials
    - Jobcentre Plus Rehabilitation Programme
    - Skillseekers
    - New Deal for Young People, and
    - New Deal for 25 Plus.

How does the programme work?

If you join TfW, you will get help from a network of training providers. The programme covers a wide variety of skills and jobs, and local employers will give you on-the-job training as part of the programme. [121]

TfW offers two programmes to help people get ready for work:[122]

- Occupational training, which is for specific jobs and aims to improve and update your skills for re-entering employment, and
- Customised training, which is flexible training for people who are capable of moving into work quickly (this training is often carried out in response to things like large-scale redundancies).

Your TfW provider will assess your needs and draw up an Individual Training Plan. This plan sets out the kind of training you will do, activities to improve your core skills (see page 109), and your employment goals.

You will do training at provider sites, at an employer's premises, or at a combination of these two places. You can do a mixture of skills training, work experience and test trading, depending on your needs. You may even work for an employer but continue to follow the steps set out in your Individual Training Plan.

How long is the programme?

There is no set length of a TfW programme. Your time on the programme will depend on your needs.[123]

How many hours per week does the programme take?

The amount of time you spend on the programme each week depends on whether you are doing TfW full-time or part-time. If you are taking part in the programme full-time, you will attend TfW for 30 hours per week, spread over five days. If you cannot do TfW full-time because of personal or domestic reasons, your TfW provider will decide if you can do the programme part-time instead. If you do TfW part-time, you will attend for 15 to 29 hours per week, spread over five to seven days.[124]

How do you join Training for Work?

Referral[125]

If you think you could be eligible to take part in TfW, contact your local Jobcentre Plus. They will do a 'better off' calculation before referring you to TfW. The calculation tests your motivation, job readiness, and commitment to doing a training course.

If Jobcentre Plus decides that you are eligible for TfW, they will phone a TfW provider to arrange an appointment for you. They will give you written confirmation of the appointment and details of how to get to the TfW site.

A referral does not guarantee you a place on a TfW course. You may have to compete with other people for places on the course.

Interviews

At your appointment, the TfW provider will interview you. They will discuss the options that are open to you and assess whether you are eligible to join the programme. If you are eligible to join, and you decide to go ahead, you will have a Pre-entry Interview at your local Jobcentre Plus. You will be interviewed by a TfW officer.[126]

At the Pre-entry Interview, the TfW officer will make sure that:

• you are eligible for TfW

• you are fully aware of your responsibilities while taking part in TfW

• you have correct information about the benefits and/or allowances you will get while on TfW, and

• you have form AT40, which you must use to tell Jobcentre Plus about any change in your circumstances.[127]

Re-joining Training for Work[128]

Once you have finished a TfW course, you will have to wait another 26 weeks to re-qualify for another TfW course.

If you stopped training because of sickness, maternity or jury service, you may be allowed to re-enter TfW. It is up to your TfW provider to decide whether you can re-enter the programme. If you were getting Jobseeker's Allowance after you stopped your training, this should not disqualify you from re-joining the programme. You will have to have another Pre-entry Interview at Jobcentre Plus before you can re-join TfW.

Financial support

See page 220.

Skillseekers

What is Skillseekers?

Skillseekers is a training programme which helps young people to develop their skills and equip themselves for work. As a Skillseeker, you will work towards Scottish Vocational Qualifications, starting at a level that suits you. Young people who take part in Skillseekers are usually employed, but the programme is also open to people who are having trouble finding work.[129]

Who can take part in Skillseekers?

You can join Skillseekers if you:[130]

- are aged 16 to 19
- have reached the legal school leaving age
- have left full-time education, and
- are not taking part in higher education.

If you are aged over 20 and doing training in engineering or construction, you might be able to get funding to do skills qualifications at a higher level.[131]

Guarantee group

You will be guaranteed a place on Skillseekers if you:

- are aged 16 or 17
- have left full-time education
- are unemployed, and
- are currently looking for entry to training.

You will also be guaranteed a place on Skillseekers if you are:

- aged 18 or 19
- unemployed
- currently looking for entry to training, and
- your entry to training has been delayed, or you have been unable to finish training in the past, because of disability, ill health, pregnancy, language problems, a custodial sentence, remand in custody or a care order.[132]

How many hours per week does Skillseekers take?

The time you spend on Skillseekers per week will depend on whether you are an employed Skillseeker (that is, you are doing Skillseekers alongside a paid job) or a non-employed Skillseeker (that is, you have no paid employment).

Employed Skillseekers

If you are an employed Skillseeker, the time you spend on the programme will be worked out with your employer.

Non-employed Skillseekers

If you are a non-employed Skillseeker, you will attend training for 30 to 40 hours per week (not counting meal breaks), usually spread over five days.

You may be able to arrange to do part-time training with your programme provider. If you do part-time training, you will spend around 15 hours per week on the programme (not counting meal breaks).[133]

How long does Skillseekers last?

The length of your programme will depend on what level of qualification you are doing. Most people doing a Level 2 qualification will spend about two years on Skillseekers.[134]

Programme elements (S)

Initial assessment

Usually before the end of your first week on Skillseekers, you will have an initial assessment to work out your qualifications and experience, and previous employment and learning. Your programme provider may refer to your National Record of Achievement during the assessment.

The results of your initial assessment will be used to draw up an Individual Training Plan and a Training Agreement which you will sign with your programme provider. Your provider should give you guidance and support during the assessment, and make sure that you are making appropriate decisions about your learning and work.[135]

Training Agreement

After your initial assessment, you will complete and agree a Training Agreement with your Skillseekers provider. The agreement will record your training activities and make sure that the training is relevant to your job and needs. The aim of every Training Agreement is to achieve a qualification. Your agreement should be kept up-to-date and changed if your training or needs vary. [136]

Individual Training Plan

Once you have a Training Agreement, and within two weeks of starting Skillseekers, you will draw up and agree an Individual Training Plan (ITP) with your programme provider. The ITP will set out:

- your past learning
- your assessed needs
- the timescale of your Skillseekers programme
- the support you will get through Skillseekers, and
- the type and level of any qualification you are aiming to get.

Your provider should make sure that the aims of your ITP are achievable for you.[137]

Training

The type of training you do on Skillseekers will depend on your area of work and the qualification level you are aiming for. If you are an employed Skillseeker, your employer will organise your training, probably with the help of a training provider or college. If you are a non-employed Skillseeker, your training must still involve a named employer.[138] You will do a work placement with this employer, though you will not technically be employed by them. Your training will give you the chance to work towards a vocational qualification and also:[139]

* improve your jobsearch skills
* get help with interviews, letter writing, literacy, numeracy and confidence
* get work experience
* develop work-related skills, and
* get references.

Regardless of whether you are an employed or non-employed Skillseeker, you can do training in a workplace, at a college or training centre, or at a mixture of these places. Your ITP should set out how much time you will be spending in the workplace and/or at a college or training centre.

Reviews

You will have a formal review to check your progress at least once every 13 weeks. During the review, your programme provider will also check and record your core skills progress. You will have to sign the review and you will be given a copy.[140]

Financial support

See page 220.

Absences and holiday leave

If you are a non-employed trainee, you must get approval from your

Skillseekers provider for any absences. If you are absent without approval (or without a good reason) for five days in a row, your provider can assume that you have left the programme.[141] There are guidelines about sick leave, time off for interviews and exams, and compassionate leave, and you should talk to your provider before taking leave for these reasons.[142]

If you are an employed trainee, you will have to follow your employer's usual guidelines about notification of absences and taking leave.[143]

If you are a non-employed Skillseeker, you are entitled to 20 days of paid holiday leave per year, or one and a half days per month. You must get approval from your programme provider and the company where you are doing your work placement before taking any leave.[144]

How do you join Skillseekers?

If you are interested in joining Skillseekers, you should talk to an adviser at your local Careers Scotland centre, or talk to your school careers adviser (if you are still in school).

Where does Skillseekers lead?

When you have finished the Skillseekers programme, you could have the chance to go on to a Modern Apprenticeship. A Modern Apprenticeship will let you increase your training to Level 3 and above.

Training for Success

What is Training for Success?

Training for Success (TfS) gives you the extra learning you may need to find work. It will help you to build confidence and gain recognised skills and qualifications. TfS aims to help you go on to employment, further education or an apprenticeship. The programme has three parts:

- Personal Development (this will be re-named 'Skills for Your Life' in September 2009. It helps you to address your personal and development needs)
- Skills for Work (this helps you to gain skills and a vocational qualification at Level 1), and

- Pre-Apprenticeship (this gets you ready for starting employment as an apprentice).[145]

Who can take part in Training for Success?

You can join TfS if you have reached the school leaving age, and you:[146]

- are aged under 18 and unemployed, or
- have a disability, are aged under 22 and unemployed, or
- are aged under 24, unemployed, and qualify under the Children (Leaving Care) Act (NI) (2002).

Guarantee group

If you are aged 16 or 17, are unemployed and want to join or re-join TfS, you will be guaranteed a place on the programme.

If you turn 18 on or after 1 July, but before the second Monday in September, you will be guaranteed a place on TfS – so long as you start the programme during the week which includes the first Monday in September.[147]

Programme elements

Assessment period

When you start the TfS programme, you will have a 12-week assessment period to work out your strengths and weaknesses. The assessment may be carried out with the help of your Careers Adviser, parents, school, Social Services, or other organisations. The point of the assessment period is to check your personal, training, or basic skills needs, and to see which parts of the TfS programme would best suit your needs. The assessment will also check your motivation to make sure that you have chosen the right job area.

Assessment methods can include:

- watching while you do certain tasks
- asking you questions
- self-assessment

- looking at your past achievements and experience
- getting reports from other people, and
- testing.[148]

If you are taking part in Skills for Work or Pre-Apprenticeship, your assessment period could include some employability skills training.[149] If your assessment is finished before 12 weeks have passed, the time left over on your assessment period will be used for employability skills training.

Personal Training Plan

As part of your assessment, you will draw up a Personal Training Plan (PTP). Your PTP will set out your personal and training aims, including essential skills training (if you need it). It will record:

- your qualifications and achievements
- your previous work experience or employment (if you have any)
- your career aims
- the results of your assessment
- any barriers to employment (such as time-management and interpersonal skills)
- your essential skills needs (this covers literacy, numeracy and ICT), and
- your training aims and arrangements.[150]

Your PTP will be agreed four to 12 weeks after you start the TfS programme.[151] You cannot do any work placements until your PTP has been agreed.

Personal Development, Skills for Work and Pre-Apprenticeship

TfS is split up into three parts:

- Personal Development (or Skills for Your Life)
- Skills for Work, and
- Pre-Apprenticeship.

You will participate in one of these parts, depending on your individual needs and aims.

Personal Development (or Skills for Your Life)

This part of TfS can include the following:[152]

- Essential skills (these are numeracy, literacy and ICT)
- Personal and social development (including homelessness, independent living, healthy lifestyle, and coping with authority)
- Preparation for working life
- Mentoring and pastoral care
- Social and cultural awareness
- Recreation and creativity

Your time will usually be split between in-house training and work placements.

Skills for Work

Through this part of TfS, you will have the chance to gain the following:[153]

- a vocational qualification at Level 1
- an Essential Skills qualification, if you have a basic skills need
- the ability to work independently and as part of a team
- problem-solving, creative, and information skills
- the ability to apply for jobs and interviews
- the ability to find opportunities for training, employment and progression.

If you are taking part in Skills for Work, you should also have the chance to do work experience. This could include spending some time in a workplace, or getting advice from employers and other people in specific job areas about work opportunities.[154] Your time will usually be split between in-house training and work placements.

PRE-APPRENTICESHIP

The skills and qualifications you get through this part of TfS will depend on what kind of job sector you want to work in. In the first 12 weeks of the Pre-Apprenticeship programme (the assessment period), you will develop your employability skills. After this, your time will be split between in-house training and work placement.

If you haven't found a work placement as an apprentice after 12 weeks, you can stay on the Pre-Apprenticeship programme and do in-house training to work towards vocational qualifications.[155] The training you do should include skills that you would expect to gain from a work placement. You will also do directed jobsearch during this time.[156]

Reviews and ongoing assessment

Your TfS provider will do regular reviews to check your progress and talk about what you aim to achieve before your next review. The results of your review must be recorded in your PTP.

Your provider will also do ongoing assessment to check that you have achieved a certain level of learning. They will mainly check your progress towards getting a recognised qualification, but they will also check your progress towards your essential skills, personal and social aims.[157]

How many hours per week does the programme take?

The time you spend on the programme depends on what part of the programme you are doing, and whether or not you are in your assessment period.[158]

Personal Development (or Skills for Your Life)

For the first two weeks of your assessment period, you will do in-house training and assessment for 10 to 35 hours per week. For the remaining 10 weeks of your assessment period, you will attend the programme for 21 to 35 hours per week. There is no set number of days per week over which your hours will be spread.

Between weeks 13 and 25 of TfS, you will do at least 21 hours per week of in-house training. Outside your training, you will do work placements and job sampling. Your training and work placements or job sampling should add up to 35 hours per week by the time you reach week 26 of TfS.

Between weeks 26 and 52 of TfS, you will be expected to spend 35 hours per week on the programme. At least 14 hours per week will be spent on in-house training. The rest of the time will be spent on work placements and job sampling.

Skills for Work

During your assessment period, you will do at least 21 hours per week of assessment and employability skills training. There is no set number of days per week over which your hours will be spread.

Between weeks 13 and 25 of TfS, you will spend at least 21 hours per week on the programme. At least 14 hours will be used for in-house training, and the rest of the time (a maximum of 21 hours per week) will be used for work placement. If you are not capable of doing a work placement, you will spend 21 hours per week on in-house training.

Between weeks 26 and 52 of TfS, you will spend 35 hours per week on the programme. Each week, you will spend 14 hours on in-house training, and the rest of the time on work placements.

Pre-Apprenticeship

During your assessment period, you will spend at least 21 hours per week on in-house training, and a maximum of 14 hours per week on work placements. However, you can't start doing work placements until your PTP has been agreed (this will happen at least four weeks after you start TfS).

After your assessment period, you will spend 35 hours per week on the programme. Each week, you will spend at least 14 hours on in-house training and no more than 21 hours on work placement. If you can't get a work placement, you will do in-house training for at least 21 hours per week.

Financial support

See page 220.

Absences and holiday leave

You are allowed to take a reasonable amount of time off from the programme in the following situations:[159]

- To attend interviews for jobs or further education
- To attend interviews with the:
    - Department for Employment and Learning
    - Social Security Agency
    - Jobs and Benefits Office, and
    - Careers Office
- To do exams and assessments for your qualifications
- To attend court or a Community Service Order
- For domestic emergencies (including when someone in your family has died)
- To attend annual training courses or camps (for example, if you are a member of the Auxiliary or Reserve Forces)
- To attend hospital, doctor or dentist appointments (but only in emergencies or if you cannot arrange your appointments outside your programme hours)
- To attend regular hospital visits or health checks (if you have a disability)
- To attend events directly related to TfS

You should ask permission for your absence before you spend time away from the programme. If you are absent without permission, or without a good reason, you will not get your Educational Maintenance Allowance for the time you are away. If you are absent without permission for five days in a row, your provider will assume that you have left TfS.[160]

There are also guidelines for taking time off because of sickness. You should talk to your TfS provider to find out what they are before you have time off from the programme, otherwise your Educational Maintenance Allowance could be affected.

You will be entitled to 25 days of paid holiday leave per year while you are on TfS (this works out to two days per month). You will need to agree your holiday leave in advance with your programme provider.[161]

Re-joining Training for Success

If your programme is interrupted because of pregnancy, a custodial sentence or a care order, you can re-join TfS once you are able to, and finish whatever is left of your programme. If you turn 18 during your time away from the programme, you can still re-join and finish whatever is left.[162]

Bridge to Employment

What is Bridge to Employment?

Bridge to Employment (BTE) is a training programme that helps you to find a job, no matter how little (or how much) work experience you already have. Employers use BTE to find and train unemployed people to fill current job vacancies.[163] If you successfully finish the programme, you will have a job interview with the employer.

Who can take part in Bridge to Employment?

You can take part in BTE if you are:[164]

- aged 18 or over, and
- unemployed.

What happens on the programme?

BTE is a training programme and it is run in response to employers with job vacancies. So each BTE training course is tailored to meet the skills required for a particular kind of job, and no two training courses are the same.[165] Depending on what's on offer, you could do a BTE training course for just one employer, or you could do a course that is being run for a group of employers who have similar needs.[166]

Your training will take place at a training provider's site, at the employer's company, or at a mixture of both.[167] Your course could involve working for the employer to get hands-on experience.

Once you have successfully finished your BTE programme, you will have a job interview with the employer. If you do well at the interview, you have a good chance of getting the job.[168]

What kind of job can you get through Bridge to Employment?

A range of employers offer opportunities through Bridge to Employment. You could train for a job in one of the following areas:[169]

- Manufacturing
- Information and Communication Technology
- Hospitality and Tourism
- Construction
- Engineering
- Transport
- Banking

How do you join Bridge to Employment?

BTE is a voluntary programme and you need to apply for it. Programme vacancies are advertised in your local Jobcentre, Jobs and Benefits Office, newspapers and community groups. You can also check vacancies on the Jobcentre website: www.jobcentreonline.com.

If you want to apply for BTE, you should pick up an application form from your local Jobcentre, along with an information leaflet which explains the company and the training. Fill out the form and return it to the Jobcentre before the closing date.[170] You should then get a letter seven days after the closing date for applications, and this letter will invite you to do an aptitude test and/or interview. You will find out the results of your test and/or interview within five working days. If you are successful, you will be offered a place on the programme.[171]

Financial Support[172]

See page 220.

Steps to Work

What is Steps to Work?

Steps to Work (StW) helps you to find work by giving you a 'menu' of work-related activities to choose from, so that you can create a programme to suit your needs. If you take part in StW, you will have a personal adviser to help you decide which options will best help you towards getting ready for employment. Through the progamme, you will have a chance to:

- improve your existing skills
- gain recognised qualifications
- do work experience
- get help with finding and staying in work, and
- get personalised advice and guidance.[173]

Who can take part in Steps to Work?

You can participate in StW if you are:[174]

- aged 18 or over, and
- unemployed, or working for less than 16 hours per week.

You can also join StW if you are a lone parent aged 16 or under, and unemployed or working for less than 16 hours per week.

You can take part in the programme whether or not you are claiming benefits.

How does the programme work?

StW is made up of three different 'steps'. You will get help through one of the steps, depending on your needs. At first, you will speak to an adviser, who will work out which parts of the programme are best suited to you. Your adviser will help you to draw up an Action Plan which sets out your aims and the courses, assessment, and other parts of the programme you will do.[175]

Step One[176]

If you are almost ready to apply for jobs, but need some extra help brushing up your skills, you will join Step One. On this step, your adviser will help you to work on the things employers are looking for, such as presentation and communication skills. You can take part in a number of short courses, sessions and assessments. You will have access to:

- essential skills assessment (a one-day assessment for those who have problems with reading, numeracy and writing)
- a personal assessment (this lasts for up to three days, assesses your training needs and helps you to overcome any barriers to work)
- a Core Gateway course (you can choose to do all or some of the topics offered on this ten-day course, which include jobsearch, interview skills, CV building, completing application forms, employability skills (such as teamwork and time-keeping), and introduction to IT and the internet)[177]
- a self-employment awareness session (this half-day session gives you information on self-employment and the chance to discuss a business idea)
- Start a Business programme (this lasts for five days and gives you support, mentoring and help to develop a Business Plan),[178] and
- an assessment to check if you would benefit from special support from a music industry adviser (if you have work experience or an employment history in the music industry).

Step Two[179]

If you have particular trouble with finding or keeping a job, and you could benefit from intensive one-to-one help, you will join Step Two. On this step, you will have access to:

- the Back to Work programme (this lasts for up to 13 weeks and is made up of work experience and a short course)
- essential skills training (this lasts for up to 26 weeks, improves your skills in reading, numeracy and writing and helps you to get a qualification while you gain experience in a workplace)

- a range of qualifications (you can spend 52 weeks working towards a Level 2 NVQ, finish a NVQ if you already have some units, get a qualification to improve your job-related language skills (if English is not your first language), and do a work placement for up to 26 weeks)
- self-employment test trading (if you are receiving benefits and you are interested in starting your own business, you can do 'test trading' for up to 26 weeks to try out your idea), and
- an employer subsidy (if you are offered a job while you are on StW, your employer may be able to get a subsidy for the first 26 weeks of your job).

Step Three[180]

If you have not found a job after taking part in Step Two, you will join Step Three. On this step, you will get extra support from your adviser for up to six weeks. You will be encouraged to use your new skills to improve your chances of finding a job.

How long does Steps to Work last?

The time you spend on StW depends on your needs and the step you are on. You could spend just a few weeks on the programme, or you could spend up to one year.[181]

How do you join Steps to Work?

If you want to join StW, contact your local Jobcentre or Jobs and Benefits office and speak to an adviser.

Financial Support

See page 220.

Apprenticeships

What is an apprenticeship?

An apprenticeship is a qualification which builds your knowledge, skills and expertise, and tests your competence in a specific industry or work sector. Apprenticeships are, in most cases, a job with training. Apprenticeships give you on-the-job and off-the-job training, so that you can apply your knowledge and skills in a practical way, and they allow you to earn money while you learn.

By doing an apprenticeship, you will:

- develop your personal and social skills
- gain the technical knowledge and skills you need to do the job
- develop other skills that will help you to be successful in the workplace (such as skills in communication, numeracy, information technology, working with others, and problem solving), and
- practise applying what you have learnt.

There are apprenticeships for a wide range of industries, including engineering, retail, information technology, floristry, accounting and financial services. This provides a great variety of occupations in which to work and train.[182]

Apprenticeship programmes are run throughout the UK, but they are slightly different depending on where you live. The programmes on offer are:

- Foundation Apprenticeships and Advanced Apprenticeships (England)
- Pre-Apprenticeship Learning, Foundation Modern Apprenticeships and Modern Apprenticeships (Wales)
- Modern Apprenticeships (Scotland), and
- ApprenticeshipsNI (Northern Ireland).

Apprenticeships in England

There are two kinds of apprenticeships available in England:

- Foundation Apprenticeships, and
- Advanced Apprenticeships.

What is the difference between a Foundation Apprenticeship and an Advanced Apprenticeship? **E**

Foundation Apprenticeships are qualifications at Level 2 (which is counted as equal to five GCSEs graded at A*–C). On a Foundation Apprenticeship, you'll usually have a job and a wage. However, if employment is not possible, you can still do a Foundation Apprenticeship with a training provider, in which you will go on a work placement and receive an Education Maintenance Allowance. A Foundation Apprenticeship takes at least 18 months to finish and gives you the chance to gain a Level 2 NVQ, Technical Certificates and Key Skills qualifications. The work you do will be mainly practical: you'll develop technical skills and gain valuable work experience. At the end of a Foundation Apprenticeship, you could have the opportunity to progress to an Advanced Apprenticeship.

Advanced Apprenticeships are a Level 3 qualification (which is counted as equal to two A-levels graded at A–C, or A* from September 2009). On an Advanced Apprenticeship, you'll be in full-time employment with an appropriate wage. You should be aiming for a technical, supervisory or junior management role. The training, which usually lasts for at least two years, gives you the chance to gain a Level 3 NVQ, Technical Certificates and Key Skills qualifications. An Advanced Apprenticeship may be used as a stepping-stone to university, where you can start a Foundation Degree.[183]

Who is eligible to do an apprenticeship? **E**

You could be eligible to do an apprenticeship if you are:

- living in England, and
- aged 16 to 24, and
- not taking part in full-time education.

However, it is unusual for people aged 19 or over to be accepted on an apprenticeship programme. Your local Learning and Skills Council (LSC) can make an exception if they feel that you stand to benefit a great deal from the programme.

The kind of skills and attributes employers look for in an apprentice are:

- motivation to succeed in the sector of your choice
- an interest in learning and applying your learning in the workplace
- the potential to complete the qualifications which are part of the programme
- willingness to communicate with a range of people, and
- willingness to have a police check (you need to do this for employment in sectors such as childcare).

Even though there are no rules about having certain qualifications before you can enter an apprenticeship, the Sector Skills Councils (which set out the framework for apprenticeships) may ask for certain GCSE passes before you can start an Advanced Apprenticeship. This is because the councils want you to be successful, and they know that an Advanced Apprenticeship can be very demanding. To start an Advanced Apprenticeship, you should ideally have five GCSEs graded at C or above, or have completed a Foundation Apprenticeship.

For many apprenticeships, you will have to show well-developed study skills. However, if you can't show that you have study skills, but you can demonstrate enthusiasm for the sector and a willingness to learn, some employers and learning providers will allow you onto the apprenticeship programme. If you are allowed onto the programme without qualifications, your employer or learning provider will often ask you to do extra work to give you the skills you need to be successful. For example, you may have to do extra work on your basic skills, if necessary. Ultimately, it is up to an employer to select the person they feel is right for their business.

What qualifications can you get through an apprenticeship?

The level of your qualifications will depend on which kind of apprenticeship you are doing, but as you progress through either apprenticeship programme, you will have the chance to collect a number of certificates. As you develop your technical knowledge and skills, you will collect Technical Certificates. When you develop general workplace skills, you will collect Key Skills qualifications. Once you have shown that you can apply the knowledge and skills needed to do a job, you will be awarded the appropriate NVQ (see page 148 for more information about NVQs). For a Foundation Apprenticeship, you will earn a Level 2 NVQ, and for an Advanced Apprenticeship, you will earn a Level 3 NVQ.

After you have been awarded all of these certificates, you can claim your Apprenticeship Certificate. This is like a final diploma that confirms you have completed all the requirements of the learning framework. In addition, you may also get a reference from your employer.[184]

Key Skills qualifications

Key Skills are a range of general skills that you will need in your work and personal life. There are currently six Key Skills in England:

- communication
- application of number
- information and communication technology (ICT)
- working with others
- improving own learning and performance, and
- problem solving.

During your apprenticeship, you will have the chance to earn certificates that recognise your key skills and show you can communicate effectively, understand numbers and use ICT.

For Advanced Apprenticeships, it is compulsory to do Level 2 key skills qualifications in communication and application of number. However, it is a good idea to go beyond this minimum requirement and do key skills qualifications in communication and application of number at Level 3. You may even want to get other key skills qualifications at different levels, in areas such as ICT, improving own learning and performance, problem solving, and working with others. It is up to you to make the most of the key skills qualifications on offer.

Technical Certificates

As part of your apprenticeship, you will have to earn Technical Certificates, which show that you have the knowledge needed to do a specific job. You will gain this knowledge through off-the-job training, being taught in a classroom or following a distance-learning course over the internet. To be awarded a Technical Certificate, you will have to do an external assessment which could include:

- completing a case study, project or assignment that is externally marked
- taking a multiple-choice test
- doing a written exam, or
- attending a 'viva', where you do a presentation and answer interview questions.

For some apprenticeships, Technical Certificates have been newly developed to meet the needs of a particular sector. For other apprenticeships, existing qualifications such as BTEC National Diplomas or City and Guilds vocational certificates have been included in the learning framework to meet the Technical Certificate requirement.

Where and how will you learn?

Learning takes place through a mixture of off-the-job and on-the-job training.

The amount of off-the-job training you will do on an apprenticeship depends on what Technical Certificates are included in your framework. You will spend time with a learning provider to study for your Technical Certificates and Key Skills.

When you are in the workplace, you will be able to practise what you have learnt, so that you develop the knowledge and skills you need for the job.

How long does an apprenticeship last?

An apprenticeship does not have a fixed length of time – it will end when you have finished all of the necessary elements and satisfied the employer's requirements. However, as a general guide, apprenticeships tend to last from 18 months to three years.

How much will you be paid?

All employed apprentices must get a wage of at least £80 per week. This amount will rise to £95 per week from August 2009. You could get more than this, depending on your employer.[185]

Do you get holidays?

Like most other employees, you will have at least 20 days of paid holiday leave per year, as well as bank holidays.

How do you get started on an apprenticeship?

There are several ways to become an apprentice. You can apply for an apprenticeship online (at www.apprenticeships.org.uk), or you can apply through the Connexions Service (Connexions should be able to tell you which local employers offer apprenticeships). Or, you may simply respond to an advertisement, since employers can advertise apprenticeships in the same way that they advertise other jobs. You should contact the Connexions Service anyway, if you are not already in touch, because it can give you the guidance you need.

Can you become an apprentice if you're already in work?

It is possible to become an apprentice when you are already in a job. Your employer might decide to invest in your future and ask you if you want to be an apprentice, or you could approach your employer and ask if they're interested in making you an apprentice. Either way, you can always get advice from the Connexions Service.

Leaving an apprenticeship before completion

If you want to leave your apprenticeship, if you get made redundant, or if your relationship with your employer breaks down, the normal rules stated in your work contract will apply. However, your learning provider has a duty to find you an alternative apprenticeship programme.

Where do apprenticeships lead?

An apprenticeship will open up a range of options to you. The qualifications you gain on an Advanced Apprenticeship can help you to go on to higher education, or you could stay with your employer and develop your career. If you have completed a Foundation Apprenticeship, you can go on to an Advanced Apprenticeship, or you could work for a different employer. You could even become self-employed or go to a further education college and do some higher qualifications.

Apprenticeships in Wales

In Wales, you can do a Pre-Apprenticeship Learning programme in addition to the two apprenticeship programmes on offer:

- Foundation Modern Apprenticeships, and
- Modern Apprenticeships.

Pre-Apprenticeship Learning

What is Pre-Apprenticeship Learning?

Pre-Apprenticeship Learning (PAL) is for people who need to brush up their literacy and numeracy skills before they can progress onto a full apprenticeship. The programme is for people who are already in employment.[186]

Who can take part in Pre-Apprenticeship Learning?

You can take part in PAL if you are employed and you:

- are aged 16 or over
- have left full-time compulsory education, and
- are ordinarily resident in Wales, or your employment or work placement is in Wales.[187]

You will not be able to join PAL if you:

- have not reached the school leaving age
- are in full-time school, further or higher education

- are taking part in a vocational training programme funded by the UK government, Welsh Ministers or the European Union
- are getting an Assembly Learning Grant (see page 234), or
- are an ineligible overseas national.[188]

The Welsh government has a Youth Guarantee and Extended Guarantee which means that certain young people (mainly those aged under 18) are entitled to a place on PAL.[189]

What qualifications can you get through Pre-Apprenticeship Learning?

PAL allows you to study for the following qualifications:

- Certificate in Adult Literacy and Certificate in Adult Numeracy at Entry Level 1, 2 and 3
- Level 1 Key Skills qualifications in Communication and Application of Number
- An approved qualification at Level 1, which is relevant to your current job role (as specified in the Learning and Skills Act 2000)[190]

Programme Elements

INITIAL ASSESSMENT

Before you enter PAL, or as soon as you enter PAL, you will have an initial assessment with your programme provider to work out your previous learning, your current learning and skills needs, and any support needs you might have. Once these are known, your provider will work with you to draw up an Individual Learning Plan, which will set out a learning programme to meet your needs. Your Individual Learning Plan should be drawn up within four weeks of starting the programme, and must be agreed by both you and your PAL provider. It will set out the length of your PAL programme, your attendance requirements, how often you will have progress reviews, and the qualifications you aim to achieve. If your learning and support needs change during the programme, your Individual Learning Plan will be updated, and you must agree any changes to your programme.[191]

ONGOING ASSESSMENT

During PAL, you will have ongoing assessment to check your progress against your Individual Learning Plan. Assessments make sure that you are on track to achieve your aims, and give you a chance to talk about any problems or needs that have come up since your initial assessment. Your provider will review your progress as often as necessary, and at least once every 31 days. Both you and your provider will have to sign your review.[192]

EXIT INTERVIEW

Your provider should interview you before you leave PAL, to talk about your options and learning needs for the future.[193]

How do you join Pre-Apprenticeship Learning?

Contact Careers Wales if you're interested in joining the PAL programme. They will be able to give you more information about the application procedure and programme providers.

Financial Support

You cannot get a learning allowance or help with expenses because you are already receiving wages from your employer.

Absences and holiday leave

If you are absent from the programme for 10 working days in a row without prior authorisation, you will be suspended from the PAL learning programme for a maximum of 13 weeks. During your suspension, your provider will decide whether you can return to learning in some form. You will not receive a learning allowance while you are suspended.[194]

You can take up to 15 days of holiday at a time, so long as you speak to your PAL provider ahead of time and they authorise your absence.[195]

What is the difference between a Foundation Modern Apprenticeship and a Modern Apprenticeship?

Foundation Modern Apprenticeships (FMAs) are a Level 2 qualification (which is equal to five good GCSE passes). On a FMA, you'll be employed with a wage, or you'll do training through a provider and get a training allowance. The training, which usually lasts for up to two years, gives you a chance to gain a Level 2 vocational qualification (and a qualification at Level 3, if you choose), along with Key Skills qualifications and Technical Certificates (where appropriate to your work sector). After finishing a FMA, you can go on to a Modern Apprenticeship or a job.

Modern Apprenticeships are a Level 3 qualification (which is equal to two A-level passes). On a Modern Apprenticeship, you'll be in full-time employment with an appropriate wage. The training usually lasts for up to three or four years, and leads to a Level 3 vocational qualification, Technical Certificates and Key Skills qualifications. If you didn't do a FMA before starting a Modern Apprenticeship, you can get the Level 2 qualification you would have earned through a FMA while you are studying for your Level 3 Modern Apprenticeship qualifications. A Modern Apprenticeship can act as a stepping-stone to a Higher National Diploma, Higher National Certificate, or university degree.[196]

Who is eligible to do an apprenticeship?

You can do an apprenticeship if you:

- are aged 16 or over
- have left full-time compulsory education, and
- are ordinarily resident in Wales, or your employment or work placement is in Wales.[197]

You will not be able to do an apprenticeship if you:

- have not reached the school leaving age
- are in full-time school, further or higher education
- are taking part in a vocational training programme funded by the UK government, Welsh Ministers or the European Union

- are getting an Assembly Learning Grant (see page 234), or
- are an ineligible overseas national.[198]

You do not need to be employed to do a FMA, but you do need to have a job to do a Modern Apprenticeship.

To enter a FMA, you may need to have certain GCSE grades (or an equivalent qualification), depending on the area of work you want to do. To enter a Modern Apprenticeship, you will usually need four or five GCSEs graded at C or above (or an equivalent qualification).[199]

What qualifications can you get through an apprenticeship?

The apprenticeship learning framework is drawn up by the Sector Skills Council responsible for your area of work, and approved by the Approvals and Advisory Group, which specifies the qualifications for each apprenticeship. Generally speaking, the level of your qualifications will depend on which kind of apprenticeship you are doing, but as you progress through either apprenticeship programme, you will have the chance to collect a number of certificates. For both types of apprenticeship, when you develop general workplace skills, you will collect Key Skills qualifications. Depending on your apprenticeship sector and your learning framework, you may also collect Technical Certificates as you develop your knowledge and skills. Regardless of the apprenticeship you do, you will be awarded with an appropriate vocational qualification once you have shown that you can apply the knowledge and skills needed for a job. For FMAs, you will earn a Level 2 or 3 vocational qualification, and for Modern Apprenticeships, you will earn a Level 3 vocational qualification.

Key Skills

There are currently six Key Skills in Wales:

- communication
- application of number
- information and communication technology (ICT)
- working with others

- improving own learning and performance, and
- problem solving.

On a FMA, you will work towards Key Skills qualifications at Level 2 or above, and on a Modern Apprenticeship, you will work towards qualifications at Level 3 or above. The specific Key Skills you are required to study depends on your learning framework and the Learning Agreement you draw up with your training provider.

The key skills of communication, application of number and ICT will be replaced by essential skills in September 2010.[200] Essential skills will be a suite made up of communication, application of number and ICT, and these skills will be available from Entry Level 1 through to Level 4. In the future, the remaining key skills (working with others, Improving own learning and performance, and problem solving) may be added to the essential skills suite.

Technical Certificates

As part of your apprenticeship, you may have to earn Technical Certificates, which show that you have the knowledge needed to do a specific job. You gain this knowledge through off-the-job training, in a classroom or via a distance-learning course over the internet. To be awarded a Technical Certificate, you will usually have to do an external assessment which could include:

- completing a case study, project or assignment that is externally marked
- taking a multiple-choice test
- doing a written exam, or
- attending a 'viva', where you do a presentation and answer interview questions.

For some apprenticeships, Technical Certificates have been newly developed to meet the needs of a particular sector. For other apprenticeships, existing qualifications such as BTEC National Diplomas or City and Guilds vocational certificates have been included in the learning framework to meet the Technical Certificate requirement.

Where and how will you learn?

Apprenticeship learning takes place through a mixture of off-the-job and on-the-job training.

The amount of off-the-job training you will do on an apprenticeship depends on what Technical Certificates are included in your framework. You will spend time with a learning provider to study for your Technical Certificates and Key Skills.

When you are in the workplace, you will be able to practise what you have learnt, so that you develop the knowledge and skills you need for the job.

How long does an apprenticeship last?

The length of your apprenticeship will depend on what kind you are doing and the learning framework for your job sector. Generally speaking, if you are doing a FMA, you can expect your training to last for up to two years. If you are doing a Modern Apprenticeship, you can expect your training to last for up to three or four years.

How much will you be paid?

On a FMA, you will be paid a wage or training allowance of at least £50 per week, depending on whether you are employed or doing an apprenticeship through a training provider. If you are getting a training allowance, you may also get help with travel costs and childcare: you can expect the same financial assistance that a learner on Skill Build receives (see page 161).[201] On a Modern Apprenticeship, you will be paid a wage which usually amounts to the going rate for your job.[202]

How do you get started on an apprenticeship?

If you are interested in becoming an apprentice, you should contact Careers Wales for advice and guidance. They will be able to tell you about the opportunities and vacancies available in your area.

For both kinds of apprenticeship, you may have to sit an entrance test and be interviewed by the employer.[203]

Where do apprenticeships lead?

Apprenticeships can offer you a range of options for the future. After you have finished a FMA, you could go on to a Modern Apprenticeship, or you could look for a job with a different employer. If you have done a Modern Apprenticeship, you could use this as a stepping-stone to a Higher National Diploma, Higher National Certificate or university degree.[204]

You could also think about going on to a Modern Skills Diploma, if you live or work in Wales. The Modern Skills Diploma is an work-based programme for people who are employed, and it provides opportunities for learners to improve their skills and knowledge at NVQ Level 4. To enter this programme, you would normally be expected to hold a technician and/or people management position.[205]

Apprenticeships in Scotland

There is only one kind of apprenticeship available in Scotland: a Modern Apprenticeship. You can do this apprenticeship at one of three levels:

- craft
- technician, or
- management.[206]

Who is eligible to do an apprenticeship?

To do a Modern Apprenticeship, you have to be aged at least 16, but there is no upper age limit. However, under a UK-wide government training guarantee, funding is prioritised for people aged 16 or 17.[207]

What qualifications can you get through an apprenticeship?

You will have the chance to collect a number of certificates and qualifications during your apprenticeship. The number and type of qualifications you get will depend on the learning framework for your chosen occupation or job sector, but you will usually have the chance to collect core skills and sector-specific qualifications. You might also have the chance to get a qualification in a foreign language. Once you have shown that you can apply the knowledge and skills needed to do a job, you will be awarded the appropriate SVQ (see page 148 for more information on SVQs). Modern Apprentices will study for SVQs at Level 6 or above on the Scottish Credit and Qualifications Framework.[208]

After you have worked your way through all of the above qualifications, you will get a final certificate from the Sector Skills Council (or its equivalent) for your occupation to recognise that you have finished the Modern Apprenticeship framework.[209]

Core skills qualifications

Scotland has five core skills: numeracy, communication, information technology, problem solving and working with others. As an apprentice, you will be expected to achieve all of the core skills at a minimum of Level 4 on the Scottish Credit and Qualifications Framework (see page 110). Usually, your core skills will be assessed and certified separately, unless they are already included in one of the Level 3 SVQ (or NVQ) units you are doing. If this is the case, you will not have to get a separate core skills qualification.[210]

Sector-specific qualifications

Along with general core skills qualifications, you will work towards qualifications that recognise the special knowledge and skills you need to do a job in the sector you have chosen. These qualifications will make sure that your training meets the standards required by the sector, so the type and number of qualifications you have to do will depend on which sector you are working and training in.

Modern Apprenticeships in Scotland do not include Technical Certificates. This is because your knowledge should be recognised through sector-specific qualifications and other certificates in the learning framework. However, for some apprenticeships, you may have to do a Scottish equivalent to a Technical Certificate, such as a Scottish Progression Award.[211]

Foreign language qualifications

If you are doing an apprenticeship in a sector where using a foreign language is important to business, you may be encouraged to get a foreign language qualification. It is up to the Sector Skills Council for your occupation to decide whether or not to include foreign language learning in your apprenticeship framework.[212]

How will you know which qualifications and training to do?

There are two main agreements which set out the details of your qualifications and training: the Modern Apprenticeship Agreement (MAA) and the Individual Training Plan (ITP).

You and your employer will sign the MAA, and in some cases, your parents or carers may also be required to sign. The MAA will set out your commitments during the apprenticeship.

You will agree an ITP with your employer or training provider. The ITP sets out the on-the-job training you will do with your employer, as well as the off-the-job learning you will do. The ITP should be drawn up before you start your training.[213]

Where and how will you learn?

Learning takes place through a mixture of off-the-job and on-the-job training.[214]

The amount of off-the-job training you do on an apprenticeship depends on the learning framework for your chosen sector. You will spend time with a learning provider to study for your sector-specific qualifications and core skills.

When you are in the workplace, you will be able to practise what you have learnt, so that you develop the knowledge and skills you need for the job.

How long does an apprenticeship last?

There is no fixed time-span for a Modern Apprenticeship. The time you spend on an apprenticeship will depend on your abilities and experience, as well as the difficulty of your training and the requirements for your sector. The Sector Skills Council (or its equivalent) for your occupation may set out the minimum expected time-frame for doing an apprenticeship.[215]

How much will you be paid?

As a Modern Apprentice, you will get a wage from your employer, which usually amounts to the going rate for your job.[216]

Do you get holidays?

You will have the same rights to holiday leave as the other employees at your workplace. You should be entitled to at least 20 days of holiday leave per year, plus bank holidays.

How do you get started on an apprenticeship?

If you think a Modern Apprenticeship could be the right choice for you, speak to your school careers adviser or get in touch with your local Careers Scotland centre. It is a good idea to contact Careers Scotland because they can tell you about the opportunities and training providers in your local area. A Careers Scotland adviser can also help you to apply for an apprenticeship, build your CV and prepare for an interview.

Modern Apprenticeship vacancies are also advertised in your local press, or you can visit www.mappit.org.uk to find a position.

If you are already employed, you can ask your employer if they are interested in running Modern Apprenticeships.[217]

Can you become an apprentice if you're already in work?

It is possible to become an apprentice when you are already in a job. Your employer might decide to invest in your future and ask you if you want to be an apprentice, or you could approach your employer and ask if they're interested in making you an apprentice. Either way, you can always get advice from your local Careers Scotland centre.

Apprenticeships in Northern Ireland

There are two kinds of apprenticeship available in Northern Ireland:

- Level 2 ApprenticeshipsNI, and
- Level 3 ApprenticeshipsNI.

What is the difference between a Level 2 Apprenticeship and a Level 3 Apprenticeship?

As the titles suggest, on a Level 2 Apprenticeship you will work towards Level 2 qualifications, and on a Level 3 Apprenticeship, you will work towards Level 3 qualifications. You will usually have to complete a Level 2 Apprenticeship before you can start a Level 3 Apprenticeship. However, you could go straight onto a Level 3 Apprenticeship if you already have a lot of work experience and your current job allows you to work to a Level 3 standard.[218]

Who is eligible to do an apprenticeship?

ApprenticeshipsNI are open to people of all ages. However, you must be employed during your apprenticeship. You can take part in an apprenticeship if:[219]

- you have reached the school leaving age
- you are about to start a permanent paid job in Northern Ireland
- you are contracted to work for at least 21 hours per week (the 21 hours can include the time you spend doing off-the-job training for your apprenticeship)
- you have the potential to successfully complete the apprenticeship requirements
- you meet any health requirements specific to the occupation you have chosen, and
- you meet the entry requirements set out for your job sector (such as GCSE and entry-test passes).

If you are aged 16 and you are entitled to leave school after 30 June, you will have to wait until the first Monday in September to start your apprenticeship.

If you are aged 17 and you leave school or further education during June, you will also have to wait until the first Monday in September to start your apprenticeship. However, if you are aged 17 and you leave school or college before June, you can start an apprenticeship at any time after you have left.

What qualifications can you get through an apprenticeship?

As you progress through either apprenticeship programme, you will have the chance to collect a number of qualifications. The level of your qualifications will usually depend on whether you are doing a Level 2 or a Level 3 Apprenticeship. However, for both types of apprenticeship, when you develop general workplace skills, you will collect Essential Skills qualifications, and as you gain knowledge and skills specific to your occupation, you will be awarded Technical Certificates.[220] Plus, you will have the chance to gain either Level 2 or Level 3 NVQs through your apprenticeship.[221] When you have shown that you can apply the knowledge and skills needed to do a job, you will be awarded the appropriate NVQ (see page 148 for more information about NVQs). For Level 2 Apprenticeships, you will earn Level 2 NVQs, and for Level 3 Apprenticeships, you will earn Level 3 NVQs.

Once you have met all of the requirements for your learning framework, the Department for Employment and Learning will give you an ApprenticeshipsNI Certificate, to show that you have completed your apprenticeship.[222]

Essential Skills qualifications

During your apprenticeship, you will work towards Essential Skills qualifications in communication and application of number. From September 2009, it may also be compulsory to get an Essential Skills qualification in ICT (currently, you will either get a Key Skills qualification in ICT, or you will be part of the Essential Skills ICT pilot). You may not have to get an Essential Skills qualification in communication and application of number if you already have an equivalent qualification (such as an A-level or GCSE in English or maths), or if the essential skill is covered by your NVQ.[223]

Technical Certificates

By studying for Technical Certificates, you will gain knowledge of your job area, which is vital for career progression.[224] You will gain this knowledge through off-the-job training, and you could be taught in a classroom or follow a distance-learning course over the internet. To be awarded a Technical Certificate, you will have to do an external assessment which could include:

- completing a case study, project or assignment that is externally marked
- taking a multiple-choice test
- doing a written exam, or
- attending a 'viva', where you do a presentation and answer interview questions.

For some apprenticeships, Technical Certificates have been newly developed to meet the needs of a particular sector. For other apprenticeships, existing qualifications such as BTEC National Diplomas or City and Guilds vocational certificates have been included in the learning framework to meet the Technical Certificate requirement.

How will you know which qualifications and training to do?

You will agree and sign a Personal Training Plan (PTP) with your employer and training provider (if you are aged under 18, your parents may also have to sign your PTP). The PTP will set out your training and Essential Skills aims, as well as the assessment methods which will be used during your apprenticeship. It should tell you the time-frame for achieving these aims and your hours of work and training. Your employer and training provider should review your PTP every six to eight weeks to make sure that it still reflects your needs.[225]

Where and how will you learn?

Apprenticeships include on-the-job training and off-the-job training.[226] The amount of off-the-job training you do on an apprenticeship depends on the learning framework for your chosen sector. You will spend time with a learning provider to study for your Technical Certificates and Essential Skills.

When you are in the workplace, you will be able to practise what you have learnt, so that you develop the knowledge and skills you need for the job.

How long does an apprenticeship last?

There are no rules about how long your apprenticeship will last. The length of your apprenticeship will depend on the level of qualifications you are working towards and your experience and skills. Different job sectors have different requirements for an apprenticeship, so your area of work could also affect the time you spend doing an apprenticeship. As a rough guideline, most apprenticeships take two to four years to complete.[227]

How much will you be paid?

During your apprenticeship, you will be paid a wage that is equal to the industry rate for your job.[228]

How do you get started on an apprenticeship?

If you're interested in becoming an apprentice, you should contact the Careers Service run by the Department for Employment and Learning for more information. You can call the helpline number for advice on apprenticeships (0800 0854 573) or contact the service by e-mail (ApprenticeshipsNI@delni.gov.uk). The Careers Service may ask you to attend a careers guidance interview before you register for ApprenticeshipsNI.[229] Plus, if you need extra information or support during your apprenticeship, you can go back to the Careers Service for help.

Your school careers adviser may also be able to give you information on apprenticeships, or put you in touch with someone who can help.

Can you become an apprentice if you're already in work?

It is possible to become an apprentice if you already have a job. To do this, you must:

- be in permanent paid employment with a company based in Northern Ireland from day one of your apprenticeship
- be contracted to work for at least 21 hours per week (the 21 hours can include the time you spend doing off-the-job training for your apprenticeship)
- have reached the school leaving age
- have the potential to successfully complete the apprenticeship requirements
- meet any health requirements specific to the occupation you have chosen, and
- meet the entry requirements set out for your job sector (such as GCSE and entry-test passes).[230]

Endnotes

1 www.unionlearn.org.uk/policy/learn-1849-f0.pdf Accessed on 9 March 2009

2 www.aqa.org.uk/over/qual/gceas.php Accessed on 9 March /2009

3 www.qca.org.uk/qca_13406.aspx Accessed on 16 June 2009

4 www.direct.gov.uk/en/EducationAndLearning/QualificationsExplained/ DG_070676 Accessed on 9 February 2009

5 www.dcsf.gov.uk/14-19/index.cfm?go=site.home&sid=3&pid=224&ctype Accessed on 9 March 2009

6 yp.direct.gov.uk/diplomas/what_is_a_diploma/Accessed on 9 March 2009

7 www.dcsf.gov.uk/14-19/index.cfm?go=site.home&sid=3&pid=224&lid=454&ctype=Text&ptype=Single Accessed on 9 March 2009

8 www.ucas.ac.uk/students/beforeyouapply/diplomas/14-19diplomas/ Accessed on 9 March 2009

9 www.dcsf.gov.uk/14-19/index.cfm?go=site.home&sid=3&pid=224&lid=455&ctype=Text&ptype=Single Accessed on 9 March 2009

10 yp.direct.gov.uk/diplomas/ Accessed on 9 March 2009

11 www.dcsf.gov.uk/14-19/index.cfm?go=site.home&sid=3&pid=224&ctype Accessed on 9 March 2009

12 Welsh Assembly Government and WJEC (2007) Be Informed...The Welsh Baccalaureate Qualification Explained

13 Welsh Assembly Government and WJEC (2007) Be Informed...The Welsh Baccalaureate Qualification Explained

14 Welsh Assembly Government and WJEC (2007) Be Informed...The Welsh Baccalaureate Qualification Explained

15 Welsh Assembly Government and WJEC (2007) Be Informed...The Welsh Baccalaureate Qualification Explained

16 Welsh Assembly Government and WJEC (2007) Be Informed...The Welsh Baccalaureate Qualification Explained

17 Welsh Assembly Government and WJEC (2007) Be Informed...The Welsh Baccalaureate Qualification Explained

18 Welsh Assembly Government, Work Based Learning Pathways: Young People, Parents & Guardians – Your questions answered, p.2, 4

19 Welsh Assembly Government, Work Based Learning Pathways: Young People, Parents & Guardians – Your questions answered, p.2, 4

20 Welsh Assembly Government, Work Based Learning Pathways: Guide for parents & guardians, p.3

21 Welsh Assembly Government, *Work Based Learning Pathways: Guide for young People*, p.11

22 Welsh Assembly Government, *Work Based Learning Pathways: Young People, Parents & Guardians – Your questions answered*, p.5

23 Welsh Assembly Government, *Work Based Learning Pathways: Young People, Parents & Guardians – Your questions answered*, p.3

24 www.ceg.org.uk/nq/accessframe.htm Accessed on 31 March 2009

25 www.ceg.org.uk/nq/ Accessed on 31 March 2009

26 Scottish Qualifications Authority (2004) *Scotland's National Qualifications: A Quick Guide*, p.2

27 Scottish Qualifications Authority (2006) *Introducing Advanced Higher*

28 Scottish Qualifications Authority (2006) *Introducing Advanced Higher*

29 Scottish Qualifications Authority (2006) *Introducing Advanced Higher*

30 www.sqa.org.uk/sqa/333.html Accessed on 30 March 2009

31 Scottish Qualifications Authority (2006) *Introducing Advanced Higher*

32 Scottish Qualifications Authority (2006) *Introducing Advanced Higher*

33 www.sqa.org.uk/sqa/334.html Accessed on 30 March 2009

34 Scottish Qualifications Authority (2006) *Introducing Advanced Higher*

35 www.sqa.org.uk/sqa/25259.998.html#overview Accessed on 31 March 2009

36 www.sqa.org.uk/sqa/25259.998.html#overview Accessed on 31 March 2009

37 www.sqa.org.uk/sqa/25259.998.html#overview Accessed on 31 March 2009

38 www.sqa.org.uk/sqa/25259.998.html#overview Accessed on 31 March 2009

39 www.sqa.org.uk/sqa/25259.998.html#overview Accessed on 31 March 2009

40 www.sqa.org.uk/sqa/5951.html Accessed on 31 March 2009

41 www.sqa.org.uk/sqa/25259.998.html#overview Accessed on 31 March 2009

42 SQA (2009) *Scottish Baccalaureates*

43 SQA (2009) *Scottish Baccalaureates*

44 SQA (2009) *Scottish Baccalaureates*

45 www.sqa.org.uk/sqa/35858.1826.html Accessed on 9 June 2009

46 www.sqa.org.uk/sqa/35858.1826.html Accessed on 9 June 2009

47 www.sqa.org.uk/sqa/35858.1826.html Accessed on 9 June 2009

48 www.direct.gov.uk/en/EducationAndLearning/QualificationsExplained/ DG_10039020 Accessed on 9 February 2009

49 www.direct.gov.uk Accessed on 8 June 2009

50 www.direct.gov.uk Accessed on 8 June 2009

51 www.direct.gov.uk Accessed on 8 June 2009

52 www.direct.gov.uk Accessed on 8 June 2009

53 www.sqa.org.uk/sqa/24067.html Accessed on 8 June 2009

54 Foundation Degree Forward, *What is a Foundation degree?*

55 Foundation Degree Forward, *What is a Foundation degree?*

56 www.direct.gov.uk Accessed on 8 June 2009

57 Foundation Degree Forward, *What is a Foundation degree?*

58 www.direct.gov.uk Accessed on 8 June 2009

59 Foundation Degree Forward, *What is a Foundation degree?*

60 www.direct.gov.uk Accessed on 8 June 2009

61 www.direct.gov.uk Accessed on 8 June 2009

62 www.direct.gov.uk Accessed on 8 June 2009

63 www.sqa.org.uk/sqa/168.html Accessed on 8 June 2009

64 www.direct.gov.uk Accessed on 8 June 2009

65 www.direct.gov.uk Accessed on 8 June 2009

66 www.sqa.org.uk/sqa/168.html Accessed on 8 June 2009

67 www.direct.gov.uk Accessed on 8 June 2009

68 www.direct.gov.uk Accessed on 8 June 2009

69 www.sqa.org.uk/sqa/168.html Accessed on 8 June 2009

70 www.direct.gov.uk Accessed on 8 June 2009

71 www.qca.org.uk/14-19/qualifications/index_nvqs.htm Accessed on
19 March 2009

72 www.direct.gov.uk/en/EducationAndLearning/QualificationsExplained/
DG_10039029 Accessed on 16 March 2009

73 www.qca.org.uk/qca_6640.aspx Accessed on 16 March 2009

74 www.torfaen.gov.uk/EducationAndLearning/TrainingAndDevelopment/
TorfaenTraining/ProgrammesAvailable/ModernSkillsDiploma.aspx Accessed on
16 June 2009

75 www.sqa.org.uk/sqa/4409.html Accessed on 1 April 2009

76 Scottish Qualifications Authority (2002) *SVQs – a user's guide*, pp.2–3

77 Scottish Qualifications Authority (2002) *SVQs – a user's guide*, p.10

[78] www.sqa.org.uk/sqa/4409.html Accessed on 1 April 2009

[79] Scottish Qualifications Authority (2002) *SVQs – a user's guide*, pp.3–4

[80] www.sqa.org.uk/sqa/4409.html Accessed on 1 April 2009

[81] Scottish Qualifications Authority (2002) *SVQs – a user's guide*, p.25

[82] Scottish Qualifications Authority (2002) *SVQs – a user's guide*, p.13

[83] Scottish Qualifications Authority (2002) *SVQs – a user's guide*, p.14

[84] Scottish Qualifications Authority (2002) *SVQs – a user's guide*, p.21

[85] Scottish Qualifications Authority (2002) *SVQs – a user's guide,* p.18

[86] Scottish Qualifications Authority (2002) *SVQs – a user's guide,* p.18

[87] Scottish Qualifications Authority (2002) *SVQs – a user's guide,* p.18

[88] DWP Provider Guidance ch 11, and Jobcentre Plus Decision Makers' Guide, Vol. 3, Ch. 14

[89] Welsh Assembly Government, *Programme Specification for Welsh Assembly Government Work Based Learning Programmes 1 August 2007 – 31 July 2010*, para. A6.2

[90] www2.ceredigion.gov.uk/ Accessed on 1 April 2009

[91] Welsh Assembly Government, *Programme Specification for Welsh Assembly Government Work Based Learning Programmes 1 August 2007 – 31 July 2010*, para. A6.6

[92] Welsh Assembly Government, *Programme Specification for Welsh Assembly Government Work Based Learning Programmes 1 August 2007 – 31 July 2010*, para. A1.1

[93] Welsh Assembly Government, *Programme Specification for Welsh Assembly Government Work Based Learning Programmes 1 August 2007 – 31 July 2010*, para. A3.1

[94] Welsh Assembly Government, *Programme Specification for Welsh Assembly Government Work Based Learning Programmes 1 August 2007 – 31 July 2010*, para. E3.1–2, E5.2

[95] Welsh Assembly Government, *Programme Specification for Welsh Assembly Government Work Based Learning Programmes 1 August 2007 – 31 July 2010*, para. E6.1–4

[96] Welsh Assembly Government, *Programme Specification for Welsh Assembly Government Work Based Learning Programmes 1 August 2007 – 31 July 2010*, para. E8.1

[97] www2.ceredigion.gov.uk/ Accessed on 1 April 2009

[98] www.rathboneuk.org/ Accessed on 3 April 2009

99 Welsh Assembly Government, *Programme Specification for Welsh Assembly Government Work Based Learning Programmes 1 August 2007 – 31 July 2010*, paras A6.3, A6.4, B1.1

100 www.skillsmartretail.com Accessed on 1 April 2009

101 Welsh Assembly Government, *Programme Specification for Welsh Assembly Government Work Based Learning Programmes 1 August 2007 – 31 July 2010*, para. C2.1–2

102 Welsh Assembly Government, *Programme Specification for Welsh Assembly Government Work Based Learning Programmes 1 August 2007 – 31 July 2010*, para. C3.1

103 Welsh Assembly Government, *Programme Specification for Welsh Assembly Government Work Based Learning Programmes 1 August 2007 – 31 July 2010*, para. C4.1

104 Welsh Assembly Government, *Programme Specification for Welsh Assembly Government Work Based Learning Programmes 1 August 2007 – 31 July 2010*, para. C1.4, C5.1

105 Welsh Assembly Government, *Programme Specification for Welsh Assembly Government Work Based Learning Programmes 1 August 2007 – 31 July 2010*, para. B2.1, C5.3

106 www.hie.co.uk/getready.htm Accessed on 1 April 2009

107 Skills Development Scotland, *Programme Rules for Get Ready for Work 2009–10*, para. 2.1–2.2

108 Skills Development Scotland, *Programme Rules for Get Ready for Work 2009–10*, para. 1.2

109 Skills Development Scotland, *Programme Rules for Get Ready for Work 2009–10*, para. 3.1

110 Skills Development Scotland, *Programme Rules for Get Ready for Work 2009–10*, paras 5, 7.4

111 Skills Development Scotland, *Programme Rules for Get Ready for Work 2009–10*, para. 5.3

112 Skills Development Scotland, *Programme Rules for Get Ready for Work 2009–10*, para. 6.1

113 www.hie.co.uk/getready.htm and www.scottish-enterprise.com Accessed on 1 April 2009

114 www.hie.co.uk/getready.htm

115 Skills Development Scotland, *Programme Rules for Get Ready for Work 2009–10*, para. 4.3

[116] Skills Development Scotland, *Programme Rules for Get Ready for Work 2009–10*, para. 4.3, 7.4

[117] Skills Development Scotland, *Programme Rules for Get Ready for Work 2009–10*, para. 11

[118] Skills Development Scotland, *Programme Rules for Get Ready for Work 2009–10*, para. 14.1

[119] www.hie.co.uk/trainingforwork.htm Accessed on 20 March 2009

[120] DWP, *Provider Led Pathways to Work Guidance*, Section 13, Part 2, para. 30

[121] www.hie.co.uk/trainingforwork.htm Accessed on 20 March 2009

[122] DWP, *Provider Led Pathways to Work Guidance*, Section 13, Part 2, paras 6–8

[123] DWP, *Provider Led Pathways to Work Guidance*, Section 13, Part 2, para. 7

[124] DWP, *Provider Led Pathways to Work Guidance*, Section 13, Part 2, para. 15

[125] DWP, *Provider Led Pathways to Work Guidance*, Section 13, Part 2, paras 29, 32–37

[126] DWP, *Provider Led Pathways to Work Guidance,* Section 13, Part 2, paras 49–50

[127] DWP, Provider Led Pathways to Work Guidance, Section 13, Part 2, para. 55

[128] DWP, *Provider Led Pathways to Work Guidance*, Section 13, Part 2, paras 61–64

[129] www.careers-scotland.org.uk/Education/Training/Skillseekers.asp Accessed on 7 April 2009

[130] Scottish Enterprise (2007) *Programme Rules for Skillseekers and Modern Apprenticeships 2007/08*, para. 2.1

[131] www.hie.co.uk/skillseekers.htm Accessed on 7 April 2009

[132] Scottish Enterprise (2007) *Programme Rules for Skillseekers and Modern Apprenticeships 2007/08,* para. 2.1

[133] Scottish Enterprise (2007) *Programme Rules for Skillseekers and Modern Apprenticeships 2007/08*, para. 14.1

[134] www.hie.co.uk/ss_employers.htm Accessed on 7 April 2009

[135] Scottish Enterprise (2007) *Programme Rules for Skillseekers and Modern Apprenticeships 2007/08*, paras 3.1–3.2 and 3.4

[136] Scottish Enterprise (2007) *Programme Rules for Skillseekers and Modern Apprenticeships 2007/08*, paras 5.1–5.2

[137] Scottish Enterprise (2007) *Programme Rules for Skillseekers and Modern Apprenticeships 2007/08*, para. 6

[138] www.careers-scotland.org.uk/Education/Training/Skillseekers.asp Acessed on 7 April 2009

[139] www.careers-scotland.org.uk/Education/Training/Skillseekers.asp Acessed on 7 April 2009

[140] Scottish Enterprise (2007) *Programme Rules for Skillseekers and Modern Apprenticeships 2007/08*, para. 11.1–11.3

[141] Scottish Enterprise (2007) *Programme Rules for Skillseekers and Modern Apprenticeships 2007/08*, para.12.3

[142] Scottish Enterprise (2007) *Programme Rules for Skillseekers and Modern Apprenticeships 2007/08*, para. 14

[143] Scottish Enterprise (2007) *Programme Rules for Skillseekers and Modern Apprenticeships 2007/08*, para. 15

[144] Scottish Enterprise (2007) *Programme Rules for Skillseekers and Modern Apprenticeships 2007/08*, para. 14.2.2

[145] www.delni.gov.uk Accessed on 3 April 2009

[146] Department for Employment and Learning (2008) *Training for Success 2008 Operational Guidelines*, para. 5.2

[147] Department for Employment and Learning (2008) *Training for Success 2008 Operational Guidelines*, para. 5.1

[148] Department for Employment and Learning (2008) *Training for Success 2008 Operational Guidelines*, para. 1.4.2

[149] Department for Employment and Learning (2008) *Training for Success 2008 Operational Guidelines*, para. 4.5

[150] Department for Employment and Learning (2008) *Training for Success 2008 Operational Guidelines*, para. 1.4.3

[151] Department for Employment and Learning (2008) *Training for Success 2008 Operational Guidelines*, para. 4.5

[152] Department for Employment and Learning (2008) *Training for Success 2008 Operational Guidelines*, para. 1.5

[153] Department for Employment and Learning (2008) *Training for Success 2008 Operational Guidelines*, para. 1.5

[154] Department for Employment and Learning (2008) *Training for Success 2008 Operational Guidelines*, para. 1.6

[155] Department for Employment and Learning (2008) *Training for Success 2008 Operational Guidelines*, para. 1.5

[156] Department for Employment and Learning (2008) *Training for Success 2008 Operational Guidelines*, para. 4.5

[157] Department for Employment and Learning (2008) *Training for Success 2008 Operational Guidelines*, para.1.7–1.8

[158] Department for Employment and Learning (2008) *Training for Success 2008 Operational Guidelines*, para. 4.5

[159] Department for Employment and Learning (2008) *Training for Success 2008 Operational Guidelines*, para. 4.2

[160] Department for Employment and Learning (2008) *Training for Success 2008 Operational Guidelines*, para. 4.3

[161] Department for Employment and Learning (2008) *Training for Success 2008 Operational Guidelines*, para. 4.9

[162] Department for Employment and Learning (2008) *Training for Success 2008 Operational Guidelines*, para. 4.4

[163] www.delni.gov.uk Accessed on 3 April 2009

[164] www.delni.gov.uk Accessed on 3 April 2009

[165] www.delni.gov.uk Accessed on 3 April 2009

[166] www.jobcentreonline.com/jcolfront/Template.aspx?articlename=OurProducts_B2E.htm Accessed on 6 April 2009

[167] www.jobcentreonline.com/jcolfront/Template.aspx?articlename=OurProducts_B2E.htm Accessed on 6 April 2009

[168] Department for Employment and Learning, *Catch 22: Training Opportunities for Jobs*, p.2

[169] www.jobcentreonline.com/jcolfront/Template.aspx?articlename=OurProducts_B2E.htm Accessed on 6 April 2009

[170] Department for Employment and Learning, *Catch 22: Training Opportunities for Jobs,* p.2

[171] www.delni.gov.uk Accessed on 3 April 2009

[172] www.delni.gov.uk Accessed on 3 April 2009

[173] www.delni.gov.uk/index/finding-employment-finding-staff/fe-fs-help-to-find-employment/stepstowork.htm Accessed on 6 April 2009

[174] www.delni.gov.uk/index/finding-employment-finding-staff/fe-fs-help-to-find-employment/stepstowork.htm Accessed on 6 April 2009

[175] Department for Employment and Learning, *A Guide to Steps to Work*, p.2

[176] www.delni.gov.uk/index/finding-employment-finding-staff/fe-fs-help-to-find-employment/stepstowork/stw-stepone.htm Accessed on 6 April 2009

[177] Department for Employment and Learning, *Core Gateway – Improve your chances of getting work*, p.2

[178] Department for Employment and Learning, *Starting your own business*, p.2

[179] www.delni.gov.uk/index/finding-employment-finding-staff/fe-fs-help-to-find-employment/stepstowork/stw-steptwo.htm Accessed on 7 April 2009

[180] www.delni.gov.uk/index/finding-employment-finding-staff/fe-fs-help-to-find-employment/stepstowork/stw-stepthree.htm Accessed on 7 April 2009

[181] Department for Employment and Learning, *A Guide to Steps to Work*, p.2

[182] www.apprenticeships.org.uk/Be-An-Apprentice/Other-Questions/FAQDetails3.aspx Accessed on 9 February 2009a

[183] www.apprenticeships.org.uk/Parents/Whats-it-all-about/Levels.aspx Accessed on 9 February 2009

[184] www.apprenticeships.org.uk/Be-An-Apprentice/What-do-I-get-out-of-it.aspx Accessed on 9 February 2009

[185] www.apprenticeships.org.uk/Be-An-Apprentice/Other-Questions/FAQDetails6.aspx Accessed on 9 February 2009

[186] Welsh Assembly Government, *Programme Specification for Welsh Assembly Government Work Based Learning Programmes 1 August 2007 – 31 July 2010*, para. A7.1

[187] Welsh Assembly Government, *Programme Specification for Welsh Assembly Government Work Based Learning Programmes 1 August 2007 – 31 July 2010*, para. A1.1

[188] Welsh Assembly Government, *Programme Specification for Welsh Assembly Government Work Based Learning Programmes 1 August 2007 – 31 July 2010*, para. A3.1

[189] Welsh Assembly Government, *Programme Specification for Welsh Assembly Government Work Based Learning Programmes 1 August 2007 – 31 July 2010*, paras A6.3, A6.4, B1.1

[190] Welsh Assembly Government, *Programme Specification for Welsh Assembly Government Work Based Learning Programmes 1 August 2007 – 31 July 2010*, para. A7.1

[191] Welsh Assembly Government, *Programme Specification for Welsh Assembly Government Work Based Learning Programmes 1 August 2007 – 31 July 2010*, paras E3.1–2, E5.2

[192] Welsh Assembly Government, *Programme Specification for Welsh Assembly Government Work Based Learning Programmes 1 August 2007 – 31 July 2010*, para. E6.1–4

[193] Welsh Assembly Government, *Programme Specification for Welsh Assembly Government Work Based Learning Programmes 1 August 2007 – 31 July 2010*, para. E8.1

[194] Welsh Assembly Government, *Programme Specification for Welsh Assembly Government Work Based Learning Programmes 1 August 2007 – 31 July 2010*, para. C3.1

[195] Welsh Assembly Government, *Programme Specification for Welsh Assembly Government Work Based Learning Programmes 1 August 2007 – 31 July 2010*, paras C1.4, C5.1

[196] www.careerswales.com/youngpeople/choices16/apprenticeships_training. asp Accessed on 8 April 2009 and Welsh Assembly Government, Programme Specification for Welsh Assembly Government Work Based Learning Programmes 1 August 2007 – 31 July 2010, paras A9.1–2, A10.1–2

[197] Welsh Assembly Government, *Programme Specification for Welsh Assembly Government Work Based Learning Programmes 1 August 2007 – 31 July 2010*, para. A1.1

[198] Welsh Assembly Government, *Programme Specification for Welsh Assembly Government Work Based Learning Programmes 1 August 2007 – 31 July 2010*, para. A3.1

[199] www.careerswales.com/youngpeople/choices16/apprenticeships_training.asp Accessed on 8 April 2009

[200] accac.org.uk/eng/content.php?mID=752 Accessed on 8 April 2009

[201] Welsh Assembly Government, *Programme Specification for Welsh Assembly Government Work Based Learning Programmes 1 August 2007 – 31 July 2010*, para. D5.5

[202] www.careerswales.com/youngpeople/choices16/apprenticeships_training.asp Accessed on 8 April 2009

[203] www.careerswales.com/youngpeople/choices16/apprenticeships_training.asp Accessed on 8 April 2009

[204] www.careerswales.com/youngpeople/choices16/apprenticeships_training.asp Accessed on 8 April 2009

[205] www.torfaen.gov.uk/EducationAndLearning/TrainingAndDevelopment/ TorfaenTraining/ProgrammesAvailable/ModernSkillsDiploma.aspx Accessed on 16 June 2009

[206] www.hie.co.uk/modern_apprenticeships.htm Accessed on 8 April 2009

[207] Scottish Executive, *Scottish Qualifications Authority, Highlands & Islands Enterprise and Scottish Enterprise, Modern Apprenticeships in Scotland: Overview of Policy and Practice*, p.9

[208] Scottish Executive, *Scottish Qualifications Authority, Highlands & Islands Enterprise and Scottish Enterprise, Modern Apprenticeships in Scotland: Overview of Policy and Practice*, pp.7–8

[209] Scottish Executive, *Scottish Qualifications Authority, Highlands & Islands Enterprise and Scottish Enterprise, Modern Apprenticeships in Scotland: Overview of Policy and Practice*, pp.5 and 10

[210] Scottish Executive, *Scottish Qualifications Authority, Highlands & Islands Enterprise and Scottish Enterprise, Modern Apprenticeships in Scotland: Overview of Policy and Practice*, p.7

[211] Scottish Executive, *Scottish Qualifications Authority, Highlands & Islands Enterprise and Scottish Enterprise, Modern Apprenticeships in Scotland: Overview of Policy and Practice*, pp.8 and 10

[212] Scottish Executive, *Scottish Qualifications Authority, Highlands & Islands Enterprise and Scottish Enterprise, Modern Apprenticeships in Scotland: Overview of Policy and Practice*, p.8

[213] Scottish Executive, *Scottish Qualifications Authority, Highlands & Islands Enterprise and Scottish Enterprise, Modern Apprenticeships in Scotland: Overview of Policy and Practice*, pp.8–9

[214] Scottish Executive, *Scottish Qualifications Authority, Highlands & Islands Enterprise and Scottish Enterprise, Modern Apprenticeships in Scotland: Overview of Policy and Practice*, p.9

[215] Scottish Executive, *Scottish Qualifications Authority, Highlands & Islands Enterprise and Scottish Enterprise, Modern Apprenticeships in Scotland: Overview of Policy and Practice*, p.9

[216] www.scottish-enterprise.com/sds-modernapprenticeships Accessed on 8 April 2009

[217] www.hie.co.uk/future_apprentices.htm Accessed on 8 April 2009

[218] Department for Employment and Learning (2009) *ApprenticeshipsNI 2008 Level 2/Level 3 Operational Guidelines*, para. 2.11

[219] Department for Employment and Learning (2009) *ApprenticeshipsNI 2008 Level 2/Level 3 Operational Guidelines*, para. 2.1.1

[220] Department for Employment and Learning (2009) *ApprenticeshipsNI 2008 Level 2/Level 3 Operational Guidelines*, para. 1.3

[221] Department for Employment and Learning (2009) *ApprenticeshipsNI 2008 Level 2/Level 3 Operational Guidelines*, para. 1.1

[222] Department for Employment and Learning (2009) *ApprenticeshipsNI 2008 Level 2/Level 3 Operational Guidelines*, para. 4.4

[223] Department for Employment and Learning (2009) *ApprenticeshipsNI 2008 Level 2/Level 3 Operational Guidelines*, para. 3.12

[224] Department for Employment and Learning (2009) *ApprenticeshipsNI 2008 Level 2/Level 3 Operational Guidelines*, para. 1.4

225 Department for Employment and Learning (2009) *ApprenticeshipsNI 2008 Level 2/Level 3 Operational Guidelines*, para. 3.9

226 Department for Employment and Learning (2009) *ApprenticeshipsNI 2008 Level 2/Level 3 Operational Guidelines,* para. 1.1

227 Department for Employment and Learning (2009) *ApprenticeshipsNI 2008 Level 2/Level 3 Operational Guidelines*, para. 1.1

228 Department for Employment and Learning (2009) *ApprenticeshipsNI 2008 Level 2/Level 3 Operational Guidelines*, para. 1.2

229 Department for Employment and Learning (2009) *ApprenticeshipsNI 2008 Level 2/Level 3 Operational Guidelines*, para. 4.2

230 Department for Employment and Learning (2009) *ApprenticeshipsNI 2008 Level 2/Level 3 Operational Guidelines*, para. 2.1.2

5 Financial Support for Learning

You may be able to get some financial help to make it easier for you to stay in learning. Generally speaking, if you are aged 16 to 18, and you have left school but would like to do another learning course, you will not have to pay for the course. This is because you are entitled to free education: the government will pay for all of the costs of your learning programme, so long as you provide appropriate proof of enrolment. This applies to all learners aged 16 to 18 across the whole UK, including learners on part-time programmes.

However, there are also specific types of funding you could apply for, depending on which type of learning you are doing and where you live. This section sets out the financial help you could get according to your learning programme.

Financial support for student learning

If you decide to stay in learning as a student, there are a lot of funding opportunities for you to look into. Funding is available for a wide range of purposes: certain types of funding will pay your course fees, but there are also other types of funding that will pay for smaller expenses, such as textbooks and transport. Whether you are staying in school, attending a further education college, doing a classroom-based vocational qualification, or moving on to higher education, there is a good chance that you will be able to get some kind of financial help, if you need it. Some of the funding described below is available to a wide range of learning programmes, whereas other funding applies to just one kind of programme. In the same way, some funding is available across the whole UK, and other funding is only available in specific areas, so make sure you read over this section carefully.

Education Maintenance Allowance (UK)[1]

What is Education Maintenance Allowance?

Education Maintenance Allowance (EMA) helps you stay in education after the age of 16, and is available across all areas in the UK. Under the EMA scheme, students aged 16 to 19 can get a maximum of £30 per week.[2] EMAs cover a large number of qualifications, including NVQs, SVQs, BTECs, and basic skills. Depending on your family's income, EMA usually comes in weekly payments of £10, £20 or £30, which go directly into your bank account. You can use the extra money for anything you want (for example, driving lessons, transport or food). If you claim EMA in Wales or Northern Ireland, you will be paid fortnightly instead of weekly. Normally, you can get EMA for up to three years (or four years in some circumstances).

Even though EMA is available in all areas of the UK, it is not awarded by the central government. Instead, the separate English, Welsh, Scottish and Northern Irish governments are responsible for EMA in their countries. This means that you need to apply to the EMA scheme in the country where you study (and not the country where your family lives, if this is different from the country you are studying in).

England E

Who can get Education Maintenance Allowance?

To claim EMA in England, you must:

- be aged 16, 17 or 18
- have left (or be about to leave) compulsory education
- belong to a household which has an annual income below £30,810 (for the tax year 2009–10), and
- be enrolled on a course in England which is:
    - a full-time further education course at a college or school, or
    - an Entry to Employment course funded by the Learning and

Skills Council (if your Entry to Employment course started on or after 30 June 2008, you'll get the maximum weekly EMA payment, regardless of your household income), or
- – a Diploma funded by the Learning and Skills Council (where available), or
- – a course that leads to an apprenticeship.

To receive EMA, you have to attend lessons regularly and work hard at your course. You also have to sign a contract with your school or college to agree what's expected of you, and show that you are progressing over the course of the year.

How much will you be paid?

For the 2009–10 academic year, you can get:

- £30 per week if your household income is £20,817 per year or less, or
- £20 per week if your household income is between £20,818 and £25,521 per year, or
- £10 per week if your household income is between £25,522 and £30,810 per year.

Along with your weekly amount, you can also receive bonuses, but only if you do well on your course and meet the targets set by your teacher, tutor or learning provider.

How do you apply for Education Maintenance Allowance?

You can apply for EMA at any time of the year (but there is a deadline if you want to backdate your payments to the date your course started).

You can apply by calling the Learner Support Helpline on 0800 121 8989, and the staff will go through your application with you. Or you can get an EMA application form from your school, college or learning provider, or by contacting your personal adviser at Connexions. If you were getting EMA last year, and are returning to learning again this year, you will automatically be sent an application form.

As well as filling out the EMA application form, you will need to get your parents or carers to send proof of your household income. This proof might be their P60 or Tax Credit Award Notice (TC602).

Wales

Who can get Education Maintenance Allowance?

To claim EMA in Wales, you must:

- have been aged between 16 and 18 in the previous year (so, if you are studying in the 2009–10 academic year, your date of birth must be on or between 1 September 1990 and 31 August 1993), and
- be doing an 'eligible' course in Wales that is:
    - a full-time, school-based academic or vocational course up to and including Level 3, or
    - at least 12 hours per week of guided learning at college.[3]

'Eligible' courses include GCSEs, A-levels, BTECs, NVQs, and Basic Skills courses which last for at least 10 weeks.

You will sign a Learning Agreement with your school or college, and this covers all of the attendance and performance rules set by your school or college. You must meet the rules in order to get your weekly allowance.

How much will you be paid?

For the 2009–10 academic year, you can get:[4]

- £30 per week if your household income is £21,885 per year or less, or
- £20 per week if your household income is between £21,886 and £26,840 per year, or
- £10 per week if your household income is between £26,841 and £32,400 per year.

As well as a weekly allowance, you may also receive bonus payments of £100 in January and July if you achieve your learning aims. You could get a further bonus if you were receiving EMA last year and return to school or college this year (provided you are still eligible for EMA).

How do you apply for Education Maintenance Allowance?

You can get an EMA application form from your school or college, or online at www.cyllidmyfyrwyrcymru.co.uk. Application forms are available in spring, and you should apply as soon as possible before the academic year starts. If you apply late, your payments can be backdated to the start of the academic year, so long as you submit your form by 31 October. If you submit your form after 31 October, your EMA will be paid from the first full week after your form is received. Application forms should be completed and returned to the EMA Wales customer services team.

If you got EMA last year, and you are going into your second year of EMA, an application form will automatically be posted to your home. If you are going into your third or fourth year of EMA, a letter will be sent to your home. Contact the EMA Wales customer services team if you do not receive an application form or letter in Spring. You can phone them on 0845 602 8845, or send an e-mail to emawales@slc.co.uk.

Scotland (S)

Who can get Education Maintenance Allowance?

To claim EMA in Scotland, you must:[5]

- be aged 16 to 19
- have reached the legal school-leaving age
- belong to a household which has an annual income of £32,316 or less, and
- have signed a Learning Agreement with your school or college (your parents or carers may also have to sign this agreement).[6]

You can only get EMA if you have full attendance at your school or college. The payments will be stopped if you fail to follow your Learning Agreement.

How much will you be paid?

For the 2008–09 academic year, you can get:

- £30 per week if your household income is £21,835 per year or less, or
- £20 per week if your household income is between £21,836 and £26,769 per year, or
- £10 per week if your household income is between £26,770 and £32,316 per year.

You may also be able to get two bonuses per year of £150, if you stay on your course and make good progress with your learning. Bonuses are paid in January or February and June or July.[7]

How do you apply for Education Maintenance Allowance?

You should ask your school, college or Local Education Authority for an application form. You can get EMA even if you apply after the start of the school term. For example, if you are eligible for EMA when the school year starts in the autumn and you apply by 30 September, your payments will be backdated to the start of the term. Or, if you are eligible for EMA from the winter term, and you apply before the last day in February, your payments will be backdated to the start of the January term. However, no applications will be processed for the current academic year after 31 March.[8]

Northern Ireland

Who can get Education Maintenance Allowance?

To claim EMA in Northern Ireland, you must:

- be aged 16 to 19
- belong to a household with an annual income of £32,400 or less
- be doing at least 15 hours per week of guided learning at a further education college, or be studying full-time at school in Northern Ireland.[9]

How much will you be paid?

For the 2008–09 academic year, you can get:

- £30 per week if your household income is £21,885 per year or less

- £20 per week if your household income is between £21,886 and £26,840 per year, or
- £10 per week if your household income is between £26,841 and £32,400 per year.

You could also get bonus payments of £100 in January and June if you stay on your course and make enough progress with your learning.[10]

How do you apply for Education Maintenance Allowance?

EMA application forms for the next academic year are available in April, and you should apply as soon as possible before the start of the academic year. You can get a form from your school, college or local Jobs and Benefits Office or Jobcentre, or you can download it from www.delni.gov.uk.

If you are an existing EMA student, a renewal application form will be sent to your home address. If you do not receive your renewal application form, you should contact the EMA customer services team on 0845 601 7646 for advice.[11]

Individual Learning Accounts

What are Individual Learning Accounts?

Individual Learning Accounts (ILAs) help people who are on benefits, have a low income, or have a low level of qualifications, to cover their course costs. ILAs can be used for a wide range of courses in Wales and Scotland, so you can get help to learn at a level and in a way that suits you. Depending on where you live and what kind of course you're doing, you could get a payment of £100 or £200 in Wales, or £200 or £500 in Scotland. In Scotland, the higher amount is for people who are studying part-time higher education courses.

Wales

Who can open an Individual Learning Account?

To be eligible for an Individual Learning Account (ILA) in Wales, you must be aged 18 or over and living in Wales, and:

- you or your partner must be claiming an income-related benefit, such as:
  - Income Support
  - Jobseeker's Allowance
  - Pension Credit
  - Housing Benefit
  - Working Tax Credit
  - Council Tax Benefit, or
- you must have qualifications at Level 2 or below on the National Qualifications Framework.[83]

How much will you be paid?

The amount of your ILA will depend on how you qualify and your course costs. If you qualify for an ILA because you are on benefits, you could get the full amount for an ILA, which is £200. If you are eligible because you have low qualifications, you will get the lower amount for an ILA, which is £100. However, if you qualify through benefits, but your course costs are less than £200, you may not get the full ILA payment – your payment will only cover your costs.[84]

How do you apply for an Individual Learning Account?

To apply for an ILA in Wales, contact Learndirect on 0800 100 900 and ask for an application form. Learndirect will be able to give you information and advice on finding a learning course to suit you, if you need it.[85]

Scotland S

Who can open an Individual Learning Account?

To be eligible for an ILA in Scotland, you must:

- be aged 16 or over
- be living in Scotland, and
- have a personal income of £22,000 per year or less.[86]

How much will you be paid?

The amount of your ILA will depend on what kind of course you are doing. You can open an account for £200 if you are interested in learning something new or brushing up your skills. Visit www.ilascotland. org.uk to find out what courses are available. You can open an account for £500 if you are studying a part-time higher education course such as a Higher National Certificate, Higher National Diploma or a degree course at ILA-approved colleges or universities. You must be studying at least 40 SCQF credits to get funding. It's important that you choose your type of account carefully, because you can only have one ILA.[87]

How do you apply for an Individual Learning Account?

You can request an application pack for a £200 or £500 ILA online at www.ilascotland.org.uk. Or, you can call the ILA Scotland Helpline on 0808 100 1090, or send an e-mail to enquiries@ilascotland.org.uk.

Adult Learning Grant

What is an Adult Learning Grant?

If you're aged 19 or over and going back to full-time education, Adult Learning Grants (ALGs) can help to pay for some of the costs you will face. The grants can be used for a wide range of qualifications, including BTECs, NVQs, GSCEs and A-levels. They are meant to help you cover the cost of things such as travel and study materials. The amount you get for an ALG will depend on the income you received over the past tax year.[88]

You can get ALG payments weekly during term-time, and the money is paid directly into your bank account. An ALG is usually paid for up to two years, but you could get the grant for three years if you're studying for a first full Level 2 qualification, then going straight on to a first full Level 3 qualification, and you expect to complete your learning within three years.[89]

Who can get an Adult Learning Grant?

To get an ALG, you need to be:

* aged 19 or over

- studying in England
- doing a course that will lead to your first full Level 2 or 3 qualification
- doing a course with a learning provider who is funded by the Learning and Skills Council
- be studying full-time (at least 12 hours per week), and
- attending college regularly.[90]

You also need to meet some rules about income and benefits. You can't get an ALG if you are getting 'out of work' benefits such as Jobseeker's Allowance or Income Support. Plus, you need to have earned less than the income threshold during the previous financial year. For courses starting between autumn 2008 and summer 2009, the income threshold is:

- under £19,513 per year if you're single, or
- a combined income under £30,810 per year if you're living with a partner.[91]

How much will you be paid?

If you're single, the amount of your ALG will depend on your total income for the last tax year. You can get:

- £30 per week if you earned up to £11,810 in the past tax year, or
- £20 per week if you earned between £11,811 and £15,405 in the past tax year, or
- £10 per week if you earned between £15,406 and £19,513 in the past tax year.

If you live with a partner, the amount of your ALG will depend on your total combined income for the last tax year. You can get:

- £30 per week if your combined income was up to £20,817 in the past tax year
- £20 per week if your combined income was between £20,818 and £25,521 in the past tax year, or
- £10 per week if your combined income was between £25,522 and £30,810 in the past tax year.[92]

You'll only get ALG payments if your attendance rate at college is satisfactory. It's up to your college to decide if your attendance rate is satisfactory.

How do you apply for an Adult Learning Grant?

To apply for an ALG, contact your college's student services team, who will help you find out if you qualify, and take you through the application process. Or, you can call the Learner Support Helpline on 0800 121 8989.

You should apply for an ALG well in advance of your course, so that you don't miss out on any payments. However, you can apply after your course has started, and in some cases, your payments can be backdated.

You'll need to give proof of the taxable income and taxable benefits you got during the last tax year, along with your application. If you live with a partner, you'll need to give evidence of their taxable income and taxable benefits as well.[93]

Care to Learn

What is Care to Learn?

If you are a parent, you may struggle to continue with your education because of the cost and responsibility of childcare. If you are in this situation, you could benefit from Care to Learn (CtL). CtL can give you financial support if you are a teenage parent and you want to continue in (or return to) learning by helping to pay for your childcare and travel costs.

You can get help from CtL no matter what subject or skill you're learning, and your learning does not have to lead to a qualification. Plus, there are no firm rules about how long you can learn for – you can choose a course or learning programme that lasts for just a couple of days, or one that lasts for several years. There are no set hours, so you can study either part-time or full-time.[94]

Who can get help through Care to Learn?

You can normally get help through CtL if you are a young parent living in England and you are:

- aged under 20 on the day your course or learning programme began
- the main carer of your child, and[95]
- doing:
    - a course that receives some public funding at a college, school or sixth form
    - a course in your community (such as a course at a Children's Centre or another form of community learning), or
    - an Entry to Employment or apprenticeship programme (with non-employed status).

To receive CtL funding, you must be caring for your own child, and the other parent of your child must be unable to provide childcare. The other parent must not be claiming the childcare element of Working Tax Credit or Child Tax Credit.[96]

How much will you be paid?

On CtL, you can get up to £160 (£175 in London) per child per week to cover the cost of:

- childcare while you learn, are on a placement, doing private study or travelling for your study
- registration fees (up to £80) and deposit (up to £250)
- a childcare taster and/or settling your child into care before your learning starts
- childcare fees you may need to pay during holidays
- extra travel costs you may have to pay to take your child to childcare.

CtL will pay your childcare provider directly. Travel costs will be paid to your learning or training provider, who will then reimburse you.

CtL allows you to choose the type of childcare that you feel is best for you and your child. The only condition is that the childcare provider must be registered in the compulsory part of the Ofsted Childcare Register or Early Years Register.

How do you apply for Care to Learn?

To apply for CtL, complete an application form, which you can get from the Learner Support Helpline on 0800 121 8989, or download from www.direct.gov.uk. You must complete and sign the form, and get your learning provider and your childcare provider to sign the form as well.

You will need to take your child's birth certificate or Child Benefit notification to the learning provider so that they can photocopy it and declare on the application form that they have verified the existence of your child. The childcare provider will also need to submit a copy of their Ofsted registration certificate with your application.[97]

If you need help with you application, you can contact:

* your college, school or training provider, or
* Sure Start.

If you need any more information about CtL, you can phone the Learner Support Helpline on 0800 121 8989.

Dance and Drama Awards

What are Dance and Drama Awards?

If you're interested in a career as a dancer, actor or stage manager, you may be able to get help with the cost of learning through a Dance and Drama Award. The government introduced Dance and Drama Awards to increase access to vocational dance, drama and stage management training for young people who are talented and ambitious.

Dance and Drama Awards are for students aged 16 or over who want to work in the performing arts, and they are available at some of England's leading private dance and drama schools. They can help you pay for a place on a course, no matter what your financial circumstances are. The award will pay for most of your tuition fees, and can also help with your living costs, but you will also be expected to make a contribution.[98]

Who can apply for a Dance and Drama Award?

To apply for a Dance and Drama Award, you must:

- be aged 16 or over (to apply for a dance course), or aged 18 or over (for an acting or stage management course), and
- be a national of a European Union (EU) or European Economic Area (EEA) country, and
- have been resident in an EU or EEA country for three years before the first academic year of your course, and
- apply for the Trinity College London qualification at one of the 22 accredited providers.

You will not be able to get an EMA as well as a Dance and Drama Award, even if you are studying for A-levels alongside your performing arts course.

Dance and Drama Awards are given to the students who show the most talent at the audition stage. The awards do not depend on your financial circumstances.

What courses can you do with a Dance and Drama Award?

In order to get a Dance and Drama Award, you must take the Trinity College London qualification, which is available from 22 private dance and drama schools in England.

These qualifications cover:

- professional acting
- professional dance
- professional music theatre
- professional production skills, and
- professional classical ballet.[99]

How do you apply for a Dance and Drama Award?

To apply for a Dance and Drama Award, you need to contact the school you want to go to, and let them know that you want to apply for an award. The school will then send you information about their courses and how to apply, and they may send you an application form to fill out and return to them. They should also send you an application form for help with living costs.

Demand for these courses is high, so you need to contact the school you wish to go to as early as possible.[100]

If you need more information about Dance and Drama Awards, contact the Learner Support Helpline on 0800 121 8989.

Assembly Learning Grant

What is the Assembly Learning Grant?

The Assembly Learning Grant (ALG) is for students in further education in Wales, to encourage them to continue learning. An ALG pays up to £1,500 if you are studying full-time, and up to £750 if you are studying part-time. Your eligibility for an ALG depends on your household income. Payment is made directly to your bank or building society account, and the grant can be used in any way you like.

Who can get an Assembly Learning Grant?

To get an ALG:[101]

- you must be aged 19 or over (so, if you are studying in the 2009–10 academic year, your date of birth must be on or before 1 September 1990), and
- your course must:
  - be at least 275 hours
  - be at a participating college
  - lead to a nationally recognised qualification, and
  - be eligible (eligible courses include GCSEs, A- or AS-levels, BTECs, NVQs and Basic Skills courses).

How much will you be paid?

The amount of your ALG will depend on your household income and whether you are studying full-time or part-time. Full-time study lasts for 500 or more hours per year, and part-time study lasts for between 275 and 499 hours per year.

In the 2009–10 academic year, if you are studying full-time, you can get:

- £1,500 if your household income is £5,895 per year or less, or
- £750 if your household income is between £5,896 and £11,790 per year, or
- £450 if your household income is between £11,791 and £17,700 per year.

If you are studying part-time, you can get:

- £750 if your household income is £5,895 per year or less, or
- £450 if your household income is between £5,896 and £11,790 per year, or
- £300 if your household income is between £11,791 and £17,700 per year.[102]

How do you apply for an Assembly Learning Grant?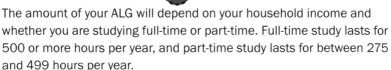

You can get an ALG application form from your school or college, or online at www.studentfinancewales.co.uk. Fill out the form and return it to the ALG (FE) Wales customer services team. You should apply as soon as possible before your course starts (application forms are usually available in spring). If you apply late, you may still be able to get an ALG. However, you must apply within nine months of starting your course, which usually means that you must apply by 31 May.

If you got an ALG last year and are going into your second year of study, an application form will be sent straight to your home address. If you haven't received this form by spring, you should contact the ALG (FE) Wales customer services team. You can do this by phoning 0845 602 8845, or you can send an e-mail to algfe@slc.co.uk.

Discretionary funds[12]

Across all parts of the UK, there are discretionary funds to help students who are having trouble meeting the cost of learning. Individual schools, colleges and universities usually have their own discretionary funds, and they take applications from students, and then choose who to give the funding to. Availability of discretionary funds is different across the UK. For example, students in the sixth form in England can access discretionary funds, but in Scotland, only those who are doing higher or further education programmes can get help from the funds. Discretionary funds also have different names across the UK. They are:

- Discretionary Support Funds in England
- Financial Contingency Funds in Wales
- Discretionary Funds in Scotland, and
- Support Funds in Northern Ireland.

Since discretionary funds are managed and handed out by individual learning providers, the eligibility criteria and the amount of funding on offer will differ from institution to institution.

Discretionary Support Funds E

What are Discretionary Support Funds?

In England, Discretionary Support Funds are available to help with learning costs in colleges and school sixth forms. Students facing financial hardship have priority for funding. The amount you receive from a Discretionary Support Fund will vary according to where you learn, because individual schools and colleges have their own criteria and procedures for the funding.

Discretionary Support Funds can be used for:

- financial hardship and emergencies
- childcare costs (for Ofsted-regulated childcare)
- accommodation costs
- equipment and materials essential to your course, and
- travel costs (if you are over 18).

Who can get help from a Discretionary Support Fund?

To apply for a Discretionary Support Fund you must:

- be aged 16 or over, and
- have been accepted onto, and be studying, a learning programme funded by the Learning and Skills Council.

You will have high priority if you:

- are on a low income or receiving benefits, or
- are aged 19 or over and do not have a Level 2 qualification, or
- have been in care, are on probation, or are a parent.

You can't claim help from a Discretionary Support Fund if you are:

- aged under 16
- an asylum seeker aged over 19
- receiving full public funding for higher education
- on a Learndirect course
- on a New Deal programme (except New Deal for Lone Parents)
- on an apprenticeship training scheme, or
- on a work-based learning course.

You can get help from a Discretionary Support Fund in addition to other forms of financial help, including:

- an Education Maintenance Allowance (see page 221)
- Care to Learn (see page 230)
- New Deal for Lone Parents
- Disability Living Allowance (see page 299)
- a Career Development Loan (see page 283), and
- an Adult Learning Grant (see page 228).

Financial Contingency Funds

In Wales, Financial Contingency Funds are available through your university or college. The funds are used to provide discretionary help to students who are facing financial difficulties, or who might not otherwise be able to afford to enter or stay in higher or further education.[13] Each university or college has its own eligibility rules and procedures for providing support, so you should ask your university or college if you need more information on Financial Contingency Funds.

Discretionary Funds

What are Discretionary Funds?

The Scottish government gives Discretionary Funds to publicly funded higher and further education institutions, so that students with financial difficulties, or students who may not be able to enter higher or further education for financial reasons, can get help. Each institution is responsible for deciding which students should get a payment and how much the payment will be. Support can come in the form of scholarships or bursaries, and students who have trouble meeting the cost of living will usually have priority for funding.[14]

Who can get help from a Discretionary Fund?

The eligibility rules usually depend on your higher or further education provider. However, as a general guide, you can apply for help from a Discretionary Fund if:

- you are a full-time, part-time or sandwich-course student in further or higher education
- your learning institution is publicly funded and eligible to apply for a payment from these funds, and
- you meet the residence conditions for a student loan.

There is no age limit for higher education students who wish to apply for payments from Discretionary Funds.[15] You will usually have to apply for a full student loan before you can get help from a Discretionary Fund.

If you need more information about Discretionary Funds, talk to the student support or student services office at your institution.

Support Funds in Northern Ireland

What are Support Funds?[16]

Support Funds help students who have low income and need extra support to stay in higher education. They are available through your university or college and are used to meet particular course and living costs which are not already covered by other grants you might have. Support Funds can also help you if you are suffering financial hardship. Payments are usually given as grants and do not have to be repaid, but sometimes you will receive help from a Support Fund in the form of a short-term loan. Your university or college will choose whether to pay you in a lump sum or in instalments.

Who can get help from a Support Fund?[17]

Your university or college will take into account your individual situation and needs when deciding whether or not you can get help from a Support Fund. In general terms, the following groups of students will be prioritised to receive help:

- students with children, especially lone parents
- mature students, especially those with existing financial commitments
- students from lower income families
- disabled students who are not getting Disabled Student's Allowance
- students who have been in care
- students who are homeless
- students in their final year.

Bursaries UK

What are bursaries?

A bursary is a financial award that does not have to be paid back. Many colleges and universities across the UK offer support to students in the form of bursaries. Bursaries are usually administered by individual institutions, and the eligibility rules and payment amounts will differ from place to place. You should talk to your learning provider if you are interested in applying for help from a bursary fund.

Bursaries in England[18]

What are bursaries?

Bursaries are an extra source of financial help which you can get if you're studying at college or university. Bursaries are paid on top of student loans and other grants. Usually, your bursary award will be made as a direct payment from your college or university, but sometimes you will receive your award in the form of discounts on things such as accommodation, books or transport.

Who can get help from a bursary?

Bursaries are handed out by either individual colleges and universities, or Student Finance England. The arrangements will depend on your college or university, and the eligibility criteria can differ from institution to institution. If you're interested in applying for a bursary, speak to your university or college.

Completing the main student finance application for Student Finance England is a good way to find out whether you're eligible for support from a bursary. The application will ask whether you consent to Student Finance England sharing your details with your university or college. If your university or college handles their own bursary scheme, your consent allows them to use your information to work out what support you're entitled to.

How much will you be paid?

It's up to your university or college to decide how much you'll be paid, but they have to meet the minimum bursary amount for students who get a full Maintenance Grant or Special Support Grant.

The minimum payment amount depends on your tuition fees, but for 2009–10, universities and colleges that charge the maximum amount for tuition fees (£3,225) have to offer you at least £319 as a bursary award. Many universities and colleges will pay you a lot more than the minimum bursary amount – you could get around £800.

Bursaries in Wales

What is the Welsh Bursary Scheme?

The Welsh Bursary Scheme has been running since September 2007, and under the scheme, universities and colleges that charge flexible fees are committed to providing extra financial support in the form of bursaries. Not all universities and colleges in Wales take part in the scheme, so you may want to get in touch with your institution to ask if they are offering these bursaries, or any other kind of bursary. If your institution is participating in the scheme, and you are starting a higher education course in Wales, your institution will automatically consider you for a means-tested Welsh National Bursary.[19]

Who can get help from the Welsh Bursary Scheme?

You could qualify for help from the Welsh Bursary Scheme if you are a full-time student and you are:

- from Wales, and have a household income of up to £18,370 per year, or
- from England, and have a household income of up to £18,360 per year, or
- from Northern Ireland, and have a household income of up to £18,360 per year, or
- from Scotland, and have a household income of up to £18,820 per year.

When you fill out the application for financial support from the government, it is important to make sure that you and your sponsors consent to share your information. This way, if your college or university is participating in the Welsh Bursary Scheme, you will automatically be assessed for a Welsh National Bursary. Your institution may also assess you for other bursaries or scholarships.[20]

How much will you be paid?

For the academic year 2008–09, the bursary amount is £310. Your university or college may be offering an increased amount, so you should ask for more details.[21]

Bursary funds in Scotland

What are bursary funds?

The Scottish Funding Council supplies bursary funds to colleges every April, along with guidelines for giving the funding to students. Bursary funds are generally available to people who are studying at a further education college, and doing a course below Higher National level.[22] Funding is limited, and will usually go to the students with the greatest need. Bursary awards can help you with:

- living costs
- some of your care responsibilities
- the cost of travelling to and from college
- the cost of your study equipment, and
- extra travel or study costs you may face because of a disability.

Who can get help from a bursary fund?

Because bursary funds are handed out by individual colleges, eligibility differs from institution to institution. However, the Scottish Funding Council gives general guidelines about which students the colleges may fund, and how to work out the amount of an award. Broadly speaking, to apply for help from a bursary fund, you must:

- have no other source of support
- be past your school leaving date
- be attending (or applying to) a Scottish further education college
- be attending (or applying for) a course below Higher National level, and
- be ordinarily resident in Scotland.[23]

How much will you be paid?

A bursary will usually pay you a certain amount for maintenance support, and depending on your personal circumstances, you may also get other payments for things such as childcare, study and travel expenses. The maintenance rate depends on your age, your household income, and whether or not you are living in your parental home, as follows:

- If you are aged 18 to 24, studying full-time and your household income is less than £23,085 per year, you could get a weekly maintenance allowance of £67.01 if you are living at a parental home, or £84.69 if you are living away from your parental home. If your household income is £23,085 or more per year, you may get a reduced maintenance bursary. Your household will be expected to contribute to your support.

- If you are aged 16 or 17, studying full-time and your household income is less than £19,350 per year, you could get a weekly maintenance allowance of £33.66 if you are living away from a parental home. If your household income is £19,350 or more per year, you may get a reduced maintenance bursary. Your household will be expected to contribute to your support.[24]

Bursaries in Northern Ireland

What are bursaries?

Universities and colleges provide bursaries as a form of extra financial support for students on a low income. If you are charged the full tuition fee of £3,225, and you receive the full amount of Maintenance Grant or Special Support Grant, your college or university has a duty to give you extra financial help.[25]

Who can get help from a bursary?

You can get support from a bursary if you are eligible for the full Maintenance Grant or Special Support Grant. However, some colleges may offer you a bursary if you receive less than the full Maintenance Grant or Special Support Grant.[26]

How much will you be paid?

Your bursary payment will be at least £310, and could be more than that, depending on your college. [27]

Student loans and sponsorship

If you are entering a course of higher education, you can get help with your living costs and course fees through a student loan. There are government-owned student loans companies in all areas of the UK. Although you will have to pay back the loan, you will not have to make any payments until you have graduated and are earning a certain amount of money. Visit www.slc.co.uk for details of the loan scheme that runs in your area. The main bodies that administer loans are:

- Student Finance England
- Student Finance Wales
- Student Awards Agency for Scotland, and
- Student Finance NI.

Another option for higher education funding is to find a company that will sponsor your studies. As well as having your tuition fees (and sometimes your living costs) paid for, you are usually guaranteed a job once you get your degree. If you have a particular career in mind, you should research companies in that field and find out if they offer any sponsorship programmes. However, you should bear in mind that the competition for sponsored funding is steep. To search for scholarships, visit www. studentmoney.org.

Disabled Student's Allowance

If you are a student and you face extra course costs as a direct result of your disability or specific learning difficulty, you could get a Disabled Student's Allowance (DSA). The amount you receive does not depend on your income, and you will not have to repay anything. If you are studying part-time, you may also be able to get a DSA.

England[28] E

Who can apply for a Disabled Student's Allowance?

You can apply for a DSA if you are doing:

- a full-time course that lasts at least one year, or

- a part-time course that lasts at least one year (your part-time course must not run for more than twice the time of an equivalent full-time course).

When you apply for a DSA, you will have a needs assessment to work out the level of support that is suitable for you. The assessment will take place at an independent assessment centre, or at a centre within your college or university.

How much will you be paid?

If you're a full-time student, the maximum amount of support you can get is:

- up to £20,520 per year if you need a non-medical helper
- a one-off payment of up to £5,161 for specialist equipment, and
- up to £1,724 per year as a general allowance.

If you're a part-time student, the maximum amount of support you can get is:

- up to £15,390 per year if you need a non-medical helper (the amount of support will depend on the intensity of your course)
- a one-off payment of up to £5,161 for specialist equipment, and
- up to £1,293 per year as a general allowance.

Full-time and part-time students getting DSA can also claim 'reasonable spending' on extra travel costs for the academic year.

Your DSA will be paid into your bank account, or straight to the person or business supplying you with services (for example, your university, college, or equipment supplier).

Wales[29] **W**

Who can apply for a Disabled Student's Allowance?

Full-time and part-time students can apply for support from a DSA. Apply for a DSA when you do your main application for Student Finance Wales (either online at www.studentfinancewales.co.uk, or by printing out forms from the website). If you do your application on paper, you will have to return the forms to your local authority, along with certain pieces of evidence. If you apply online, you will also have to send evidence to your local authority.[30]

For help with your application, contact your local authority or phone Student Finance Wales on 0845 602 8845.

How much will you be paid?

If you're a full-time student, the maximum amount of support you can get is:

- up to £20,520 per year if you need a non-medical helper
- a one-off payment of up to £5,166 for specialist equipment, and
- up to £1,729 per year as a general allowance.

If you're a part-time student, the maximum amount of support you can get is:

- up to £15,390 per year if you need a non-medical helper
- a one-off payment of up to £5,166 for specialist equipment, and
- up to £1,293 per year as a general allowance.

Scotland[31]

Who can apply for a Disabled Student's Allowance?

Full-time and part-time students can apply for a DSA. You should apply for a DSA when you do your main application to the Student Awards Agency for Scotland. To get a DSA, you must be eligible for support from the agency, even if you do not plan to take out a student loan or allow the agency to pay for your tuition.[32]

How much will you be paid?

In Scotland, DSA is made up of three allowances:

- Basic Allowance, which pays up to £1,680 per year, and can help with general costs such as audio tapes, Braille paper, radio aids, medically certified special dietary needs and small items of equipment.

- Special Equipment Allowance, which pays up to £5,030 for your whole course, to help you buy major items of equipment (for example, a word processor or a portable loop).
- Non-medical Personal Help, which pays up to £20,000 per year for non-medical personal help (for example, for a reader if you are blind, or for someone to take notes for you).

You may also get help with your travel costs if you have to pay extra because of your disability.

Northern Ireland[33]

Who can apply for a Disabled Student's Allowance?

Full-time and part-time students can apply for help from a DSA. However, if you are studying part-time, your study load must be at least 50 per cent of a full-time course.

You apply for a DSA when you do your main application for student support from Student Finance NI. You can apply for DSA at any time before or during your course, but it's usually best to apply for financial help as soon as you have applied for a place on a course, before your place is confirmed. You can apply online at www.studentfinanceni. co.uk, or you can get an application form from your Education and Library Board. If your course choice changes after you apply for financial support, tell your Education and Library Board straight away.

For help with your application, contact your local Education and Library Board, or phone Student Finance NI on 0845 600 0662.[34]

How much will you be paid?
You can expect to receive:

- up to £20,000 per year if you need a non-medical helper
- a one-off payment of up to £5,030 for specialist equipment
- up to £1,680 per year as a general allowance, and

- help with extra travel costs you have to pay to attend your university or college course because of your disability.

If you're a part-time student, you will be eligible to get the full specialist equipment allowance (if you need it), but you will only receive a percentage of the non-medical helper's allowance and general allowance, depending on the intensity of your course.

Adult Dependant's Grant

If you're a full-time student in higher education and you have an adult dependant, you could get help with the cost of your education through an Adult Dependant's Grant (ADG). An 'adult dependant' is an adult partner (including a same-sex partner if you started your course in 2005 or after), or another adult (usually a member of your family, but not one of your children) who depends on you financially. The amount of your grant depends on your income and the income of your adult dependant. The grant is usually paid at the beginning of each term and does not have to be repaid.

England

Apply for an ADG by filling out the relevant sections on the main application form for Student Finance England. You can do your application online or on paper. The amount you receive will depend on your income and the income of your dependant, but you could get up to £2,575 per year.[35]

For help with your application, phone Student Finance England on 0845 300 5090.

Wales[36]

Apply for an ADG when you do your main application for Student Finance Wales. You can apply online at www.studentfinancewales.co.uk, or you can print out forms from the website. If you do your application on paper, you will have to return the forms to your local authority, along with certain pieces of evidence. If you apply online, you will also have to send evidence to your local authority.[37]

The maximum amount you can get for an ADG is £2,647. If you are studying part-time, the amount of your grant will be scaled to match the intensity of your study.

For help with your application, you can contact your local authority or phone Student Finance Wales on 0845 602 8845.

Scotland[38]

These grants are called Dependant's Grants (DG) in Scotland. Apply for a DG by filling out the relevant sections on your main application form for the Student Awards Agency for Scotland. The amount of the grant is based on your dependant's income, and the most you can get is £2,640.[39] The agency will pay the grant provisionally at the start of the academic year, and assess the actual income of your husband, wife, partner or civil partner at the end of the academic year. If your spouse or partner earned more than expected during the academic year, you may have to pay back part of the grant.

If you get married, form a civil partnership or start living with a partner after your course starts, you can claim the an ADG for your husband, wife, civil partner or partner from the date that you got married, formed the civil partnership or started living with your partner. You cannot claim an ADG if your dependant receives student support.

For help with your application, you can call the Student Awards Agency for Scotland. The number you need to call depends on what course you are doing. Visit www.student-support-saas.gov.uk to find the number you need, or fill out an e-mail enquiry form on the website.

Northern Ireland[40]

You apply for an ADG when you do your main application for student support from Student Finance NI. To guarantee a payment at the start of the first term of your course, you should apply for financial help as soon as you have applied for a place on a course, before your place is confirmed. You can apply online at www.studentfinanceni.co.uk, or you can get an application form from your Education and Library Board. If your course choice changes after you apply for financial support, tell your Education and Library Board straight away.

The amount that you get depends on your income and the income of your dependant, but the maximum you can receive is £2,575 per year.

For help with your application, contact your local Education and Library Board, or phone Student Finance NI on 0845 600 0662.[41]

Special Support Grant E W NI

What is a Special Support Grant?

Special Support Grants (SSGs) help with costs such as accommodation, books, equipment, travel and childcare while you're doing a full-time higher education course. You do not have to repay the grants. Usually, you will qualify for a SSG if you receive Income Support or another means-tested benefit, such as Housing Benefit. If you qualify for SSG, you will not be able to get a Maintenance Grant (see page 263).[42] However, a SSG will not reduce the amount of your Student Loan for maintenance, if you have one.

England E

Who can get a Special Support Grant?

You will qualify for a SSG if you are a 'prescribed person' under the rules for Income Support or Housing Benefit during the academic year. You are likely to qualify if you are a:

- single parent
- parent, and your partner is also a student, or
- student with a certain disability.

However, other students may also be eligible for a SSG. To get a SSG, in some cases you don't have to receive or even apply for Income Support or Housing Benefit.[43]

How much will you be paid?

In the 2009–10 academic year, the maximum amount you can get for a SSG is £2,906. The amount you receive will depend on your household income and other factors, such as when you started your course.[44]

Plus, if your household income is £50,778 or less per year, you will be eligible for the full Student Loan for maintenance, no matter how much your SSG is. The money you get through a SSG won't count as income when working out if you're entitled to income-related benefits or tax credits. [45]

How do you apply for a Special Support Grant?

If possible, you should apply for a SSG before you start your course, but you can still apply up to nine months after the start of the academic year. You apply for the grant through the main application for Student Finance England.[46]

If you're applying for the 2009–10 academic year, you can apply online at www.studentfinance.direct.gov.uk, or by using a paper form.

Wales

Who can get a Special Support Grant?

You may be able to get a SSG if you:

- are a lone parent
- have a partner who is also a student, and one (or both) of you is responsible for a child or young person aged under 20, who is in full-time non-advanced education
- have a disability and qualify for the disability premium or severe disability premium
- are deaf and qualify for Disabled Student's Allowance
- have been treated as incapable of work for at least 28 weeks in a row
- are from abroad and are entitled to an Income Support Urgent Cases Payment because you are temporarily without funds for a period of up to six weeks, or
- are waiting to go back to a course, having taken agreed time out because of an illness or caring responsibility that has now ended.[47]

How much will you be paid?

In the 2009–10 academic year, the maximum amount you can get for a

SSG is £2,906. The amount you receive will depend on your household income. Your SSG will not reduce the amount of your Student Loan for maintenance, if you have one.

If you are claiming income-related benefits, Jobcentre Plus or your local authority's Housing Benefit section will not count your SSG as income when assessing your claim.[48]

How do you apply for a Special Support Grant?

To apply, print off the application letter for a SSG from www. cyllidmyfyrwyrcymru.co.uk. Send the letter to your local authority, along with evidence. You can find your local authority's address on the same website.

You may need to send the following types of evidence:

- a passport or birth certificate, to prove your age
- a letter from your college or university
- a copy of your tax credit award
- a copy of a letter from the Department for Work and Pensions, to show you get benefits as a lone parent, and
- a letter (printed on company paper) from a professional person who knows your circumstances and can confirm that you are a lone parent (a professional person can be a doctor, lawyer, teacher, police officer or minister of religion).[49]

Northern Ireland

Who can get a Special Support Grant?

You could get a SSG if you are a new full-time student and you:

- are a lone parent
- have a partner who is also a student, and one (or both) of you is responsible for a person aged under 20 who is in full-time education below higher education level
- have a disability, and qualify for the disability premium or severe disability premium

- are deaf and qualify for Disabled Student's Allowances
- have been treated as incapable of work for at least 28 weeks in a row
- are from abroad and entitled to an Income Support urgent cases payment because you are temporarily without funds for a period of up to six weeks, or
- are waiting to go back to a course after taking agreed time out because of an illness or caring responsibility that has now come to an end.[50]

How much will you be paid?

The maximum amount you can get for a SSG is £3,406 per year. Your local Education and Library Board will work out the amount of your grant, based on your household income. As a rough guide, you can expect to receive:

- the full amount of the grant if your household income is £18,820 or less per year, or
- a partial grant if your household income is between £18,821 and £40,238 per year.[51]

How do you apply for a Special Support Grant?

To apply for a SSG, you should contact your local Education and Library Board as soon as possible after applying for your course. Don't wait until you have a firm offer of a place. Your local Education and Library Board will tell you what to do to get help in time for the start of your course.[52]

Fee Grant

What is a Fee Grant?

Fee Grants are payments that help students with the cost of higher education fees. The money is paid directly to your university or college, and you do not have to repay a Fee Grant. Your eligibility for a Fee Grant will depend on your course and household income. In England and Northern Ireland, the grant is only open to part-time students, but in Wales, full-time and part-time students can get a Fee Grant. If you are a part-time student and you already have a degree, you cannot normally apply for this support.

England[53]

Who can get a Fee Grant?

To apply for a Fee Grant, your part-time course must:

- last for at least one year
- lead to a higher education qualification, and
- not take more than twice as long to complete as the equivalent full-time course.

You will not be able to apply for a Fee Grant if you are studying more than one part-time course at a time, or if you are doing a part-time Initial Teacher Training course.

How much will you be paid?

The amount of your Fee Grant will depend on the intensity of your course and your household income. You can get the maximum Fee Grant for your course's intensity if you're receiving:

- Income Support
- Housing Benefit
- Income Related Employment and Support Allowance
- Council Tax Benefit
- Income-Based Jobseeker's Allowance, or
- New Deal Allowance.

If you aren't receiving one of the benefits listed above, the amount of your Fee Grant will be based on your household income. As a general guide, if your household income is less than £16,510 per year, you will get the full grant of:

- £805, if your course intensity is between 50 and 59 per cent of a full-time course

- £970, if your course intensity is between 60 and 74 per cent of a full-time course, or
- £1,210, if your course intensity is 75 per cent or more of a full-time course.

As the amount of household income increases, the amount of the Fee Grant is scaled down. If your household income is £24,916 per year or more, you will not be able to get a Fee Grant.

How do you apply for a Fee Grant?

You can apply for a Fee Grant when you do your main application for Student Finance England. You can do the application online or on paper. For help with your application, contact Student Finance England on 0845 300 5090.

Wales[54]

Who can get a Fee Grant?

You can get a Fee Grant if you normally live in Wales and you study at a higher education institution in Wales. Fee Grants are available no matter what the amount of your household income is.

If you are a part-time university student, and your study is equal to at least 50 per cent of a full-time course, you could be entitled to receive a Fee Grant. Your eligibility will depend on your household income. Your college or university should be able to tell you whether your course qualifies for a Fee Grant, and your local authority will work out how much support you can get.

How much will you be paid?

If you are a full-time student, the maximum amount you can get is £1,940. If you are a part-time student, there are three different rates you could get, depending on how intensive your course is. The maximum amounts you can get are:

- £635, if your study is between 50 per cent and 59 per cent of a full-time course, or

- £765, if your study is between 60 per cent and 74 per cent of a full-time course, or
- £955, if your study is 75 per cent or more of a full-time course.

How do you apply for a Fee Grant?

You apply for a Fee Grant when you do your main application to Student Finance Wales. You can apply for support online at www.studentfinancewales.co.uk, or you can print out forms from the website. If you do your application on paper, you will have to return the forms to your local authority, along with certain pieces of evidence. If you apply online, you will also have to send evidence to your local authority.[55]

For help with your application, you can contact your local authority or phone Student Finance Wales on 0845 602 8845.

Northern Ireland[56]

Who can get a Fee Grant?

You may be able to get a Fee Grant if you are a part-time higher education student and studying at least 50 per cent of a full-time course. Your eligibility will depend on your household income. Your college or university should be able to tell you whether your course qualifies for a Fee Grant, and your local Education and Library Board will work out how much support you can get. There is no age limit for this support.

How much will you be paid?

There are three different rates you could get, depending on how intensive your course is. The maximum amounts you can get in 2008–09 are:

- £785, if your study is between 50 per cent and 59 per cent of a full-time course, or
- £945, if your study is between 60 per cent and 74 per cent of a full-time course, or
- £1,180, if your study is 75 per cent or more of a full-time course.

How do you apply for a Fee Grant? [57]

You can get an application form (PTG1) for a Fee Grant from your university, college or Education and Library Board. Or you can download a form from www.studentfinanceni.co.uk. You should send your application to your Education and Library Board. If you attend the Open University, there is a different application form for Fee Grants. For information about applying to the Open University, e-mail general-enquiries@open.ac.uk, or phone 0845 300 6090.

Course Grant

If you're a part-time student, you can apply for a Course Grant to help with course-related costs. The amount of your grant will depend on your household income.

England[58]

You will get the full Course Grant of £260 if you are receiving:

- Income Support
- Housing Benefit
- Income-Related Employment and Support Allowance
- Council Tax Benefit
- Income-Based Jobseeker's Allowance, or
- New Deal Allowance.

If you are not receiving one of the benefits listed above, the amount of your Course Grant will depend on your household income. You will get the full Course Grant of £260 if your household income is £25,509 per year or less. You will get a partial grant if your household income is between £25,510 and £27,505 per year, and you will not get a grant if your household income is £27,506 per year or more.

You can apply for a Course Grant when you do your main application for Student Finance England. You can do the application online or on paper. For help with your application, contact Student Finance England on 0845 300 5090.

Wales[59]

The maximum amount you can get for a Course Grant is £1,075. Students who already have a degree cannot normally apply for this support.

You apply for a Course Grant when you do your main application for Student Finance Wales. You can apply for support online at www. studentfinancewales.co.uk, or you can print out forms from the website. If you do your application on paper, you will have to return the forms to your local authority, along with certain pieces of evidence. If you apply online, you will also have to send evidence to your local authority.[60]

For help with your application, you can contact your local authority or phone Student Finance Wales on 0845 602 8845.

Northern Ireland[61]

In 2008–09, the maximum amount you can get for a Course Grant is £255. The amount does not depend on how intensive your course is.

You can get an application form (PTG1) for a Course Grant from your university, college or Education and Library Board. Or you can download a form from www.studentfinanceni.co.uk. You should send your application to your Education and Library Board. If you attend the Open University, there is a different application form for Course Grants. For information about applying to the Open University, e-mail general-enquiries@open.ac.uk, or phone 0845 300 6090.

Childcare Grant

If you're a full-time student in higher education, and you have dependent children, you could get help with the cost of childcare through a Childcare Grant. The amount of your grant depends on your household income and covers up to 85 per cent of your actual childcare costs.

England[62]

You can apply for a Childcare Grant if your children are:

- aged under 15 and in registered or approved childcare, or

- aged under 17 with special needs, and in registered or approved childcare.

If you (or your spouse or partner) get the childcare element of Working Tax Credit, you won't be able to get the Childcare Grant as well.

The Childcare Grant can cover up to 85 per cent of your childcare costs during term-time and holidays. The amount you get depends on your household income and the actual cost of your childcare. You can get a maximum of £148.75 per week if you have one child, or £255 per week if you have two or more children.

Visit www.direct.gov.uk to find out if your childcare provider is a registered or approved provider. The rules your provider needs to meet are different according to where you are studying.

Apply for a Childcare Grant by filling out the relevant sections on your main application for student finance, and by also completing the Childcare Grant application form (CCG1). You can apply online or on paper. Together with your childcare provider, you will need to fill out and submit a 'confirmation of childcare payments' form (CCG2) three times each year.

Wales[63] **W**

The maximum amount you can get for a Childcare Grant is £161.50 per week if you have one child, and £274.55 per week if you have two or more children. If you are studying part-time, the amount of your grant will be scaled to match the intensity of your study. The grant is paid at the beginning of each term and does not have to be repaid.

Apply for a Childcare Grant when you do your main application for Student Finance Wales. You can apply for support online at www. studentfinancewales.co.uk, or you can print out forms from the website. If you do your application on paper, you will have to return the forms to your local authority, along with certain pieces of evidence. If you apply online, you will also have to send evidence to your local authority.[64]

For help with your application, you can contact your local authority or phone Student Finance Wales on 0845 602 8845.

Northern Ireland[65]

The maximum you can get for a Childcare Grant is £148.75 per week if you have one child, and £255 per week if you have two or more children. The grant can only be used for 'prescribed' childcare, and does not have to be repaid.

You can apply for a Childcare Grant before or during your course. You cannot get the grant if you or your husband, wife or partner receives the childcare element of Working Tax Credit.

Apply for a Childcare Grant when you do your main application for student support from Student Finance NI. You should apply for financial help as soon as you have applied for a place on a course, before your place is confirmed. You can apply online at www.studentfinanceni.co.uk, or you can get an application form from your Education and Library Board. If your course choice changes after you apply for financial support, tell your Education and Library Board straight away. For help with your application, contact your local Education and Library Board, or phone Student Finance NI on 0845 600 0662.[66]

Parent's Learning Allowance

If you're a student in higher education and you have children, you could get help with course-related costs through a Parent's Learning Allowance (PLA). The amount of your allowance depends on your household income, and does not have to be repaid.

England[67]

You can apply for a PLA if you're a full-time student with dependent children. The amount you get will depend on your household income, but the maximum annual amount you can receive for a PLA is £1,508, and the minimum is £50.

Apply by filling out the relevant sections on your main application for student finance. You can apply online or on paper, and you should send your completed forms to Student Finance England.

For help with your application, contact Student Finance England on 0845 300 5090.

Wales[68]

Full-time and part-time students can apply for a PLA when doing their main application to Student Finance Wales. The amount of your PLA depends on your household income, but you could receive between £50 and £1,508 per year. The allowance is paid at the beginning of each term and does not have to be repaid. If you are studying part-time, the amount of your allowance will be scaled to match the intensity of your study.

Apply for support online at www.studentfinancewales.co.uk, or apply by printing out forms from the website. If you do your application on paper, you will have to return the forms to your local authority, along with certain pieces of evidence. If you apply online, you will also have to send evidence to your local authority.[69]

For help with your application, you can contact your local authority or phone Student Finance Wales on 0845 602 8845.

Northern Ireland[70]

If you're a full-time student, you can apply for a PLA. The amount of your allowance depends on your household income, but the maximum amount for a PLA is £1,470 per year. You do not have to repay the allowance.

Apply for a PLA when you do your main application for student support from Student Finance NI. You should apply for financial help as soon as you have applied for a place on a course, before your place is confirmed. You can apply online at www.studentfinanceni.co.uk, or you can get an application form from your Education and Library Board. If your course choice changes after you apply for financial support, tell your Education and Library Board straight away. For help with your application, contact your local Education and Library Board, or phone Student Finance NI on 0845 600 0662.[71]

Help with travel costs

England

Depending on your age and where you're studying, you could get help with the cost of transport to and from your place of learning. Each local authority in England offers some kind of help with transport costs for students who need it. Your local authority has to make sure that you aren't prevented from attending college or the sixth form because there is no transport available to you, or because you can't afford the cost.

To get help with transport costs, you must be:

- aged 16 to 18, or
- doing a course that you started before you turned 18.

You must also be attending:

- a school sixth form
- a sixth form college, or
- a further education college.

Your local authority may take a number of things into account when deciding whether to offer you support, including your household income and how far you live from your college. To find out what support is available in your area, contact your local authority or search www.direct.gov.uk for information.

Scotland[72]

If you are a full-time student, you can apply to the Student Awards Agency for Scotland for help with the cost of daily travel to your college or university. If you are living away from home, each year you can claim three return journeys home from where you live during term-time, as well as travel to and from your college or university during term-time.

The amount you can get is limited, and you must pay the first £155 of the total cost of travel for the year. The agency will only cover the cheapest fares available for the type of transport you use. For example, if the cheapest fares are offered under the Student Railcard or Bus Pass schemes, you will be paid the amount for travel at the cheapest rate, plus the cost of the railcard or bus pass.

Northern Ireland[73]

You can get a grant to pay reasonable travel costs related to your course if:

- you are attending clinical training as part of your medical or dental course in the UK or Republic of Ireland, at a place other than your normal place of attendance, or
- you are attending an educational institution outside the UK, as part of your UK course, for at least 50 per cent of an academic quarter (an academic quarter is normally equal to one term).

The amount of help you receive will depend on your income. Generally, you will have to pay the first £295 of your travel costs, and the grant will cover the rest, provided the cost is reasonable. Your Education and Library Board will decide whether the costs you have to pay are reasonable.

If you are studying at an institution outside the UK for at least 50 per cent of an academic quarter, and you have to take out medical insurance, you can also get help to cover the cost of the insurance.

Apply for help with travel costs when you do your main application for student support from Student Finance NI. You should apply for financial help as soon as you have applied for a place on a course, before your place is confirmed. You can apply online at www.studentfinanceni. co.uk, or you can get an application form from your Education and Library Board. If your course choice changes after you apply for financial support, tell your Education and Library Board straight away. For help with your application, contact your local Education and Library Board, or phone Student Finance NI on 0845 600 0662.[74]

Maintenance Grant

What is a Maintenance Grant?

Maintenance Grants help you to meet the costs of accommodation and living while you're doing a full-time higher education course. You do not have to repay the grants. If you qualify for a Maintenance Grant, this could reduce the amount of your Student Loan for maintenance.

Your Maintenance Grant will usually be paid straight into your bank account at the start of each term.[75]

England

Who can get a Maintenance Grant?

You can get a full Maintenance Grant if you:

- are doing a full-time higher education course, and
- your household income is £25,000 or less per year.

You can get a partial grant if your household income is £50,020 or less per year. See www.direct.gov.uk for more detailed information about the amount you are eligible to receive.[76]

How much will you be paid?

In the 2009–10 academic year, the maximum amount you can get for a Maintenance Grant is £2,906. The amount you receive will depend on your household income and other factors, such as when you started your course. You'll get at least a partial grant if your household income is £50,020 or less per year.[77]

How do you apply for a Maintenance Grant?

If possible, you should apply for a Maintenance Grant before you start your course, but you can still apply up to nine months after the start of the academic year. Apply for the grant through your main application form for Student Finance England.[78]

If you're applying for the 2009–10 academic year, you can apply online at www.studentfinance.direct.gov.uk, or by using a paper form.

Northern Ireland

Who can get a Maintenance Grant?

Maintenance Grants are available to new full-time students from lower income households.[79] Contact your local Education and Library Board for more information about eligibility rules.

How much will you be paid?

The maximum amount you can get for a Maintenance Grant is £3,406 per year. Your local Education and Library Board will work out the amount of your grant, based on your household income. As a rough guide, you can expect to receive:

- the full amount of the grant if your household income is £18,820 or less per year, or
- a partial grant if your household income is between £18,821 and £40,238 per year.

Up to £1,792 of your Maintenance Grant will replace your Student Loan for maintenance.[80]

If you are a continuing student, you could get a Higher Education Bursary of up to £2,000 instead of a Maintenance Grant.[81]

How do you apply for a Maintenance Grant?

To apply for a Maintenance Grant, you should contact your local Education and Library Board as soon as possible after applying for your course. Don't wait until you have a firm offer of a place. Your local Education and Library Board will tell you what to do to get help in time for the start of your course.[82]

Help with tuition fees for higher education in Scotland[103] S

If you are Scottish or from the European Union, and you are studying full-time at a publicly funded higher education institution in Scotland, you could be entitled to free tuition, so long as you meet certain residency rules. If you are studying part-time, you will have to meet certain income rules as well as residency rules.

If you meet all of the necessary rules, then the Student Awards Agency for Scotland will pay your tuition fees. You do not have to pay anything back. The agency will only pay for one year of your course tuition at a time, so you have to apply to the agency each year to get help with your fees. You will usually have to apply for help before the closing date, which is around the end of June (the June before you start your course, not after). Check www.saas.gov.uk for details of the closing date and application process each year. When you apply, you can ask the agency to pay the money directly to your institution.

You will not be eligible to receive a Bursary (see page 239) or an Additional Loan from the agency unless they are paying for your tuition fees.

Normally, you cannot get help with your tuition fees if you have received support from public funds for a full-time higher education course in the past, or if you are repeating a course of study.

Residency rules

To qualify for a fee-waiver, you must:

- have been ordinarily resident in the UK and Islands for three years immediately before the first day of the first academic year of your course, and
- be ordinarily resident in Scotland on the first day of the first academic year of your course.[104]

'Ordinarily resident' means that you live in a place year after year by choice.[105] If your main reason for living in Scotland is to study, and you would otherwise be living in a different country, you will not count as being ordinarily resident.

Income rules

If you are studying an eligible course part-time, you could qualify for free tuition if you meet at least one of the following conditions:

- You receive:
  - Severe Disablement Allowance
  - Disability Living Allowance
  - Incapacity Benefit
  - Employment and Support Allowance
  - Carer's Allowance (if you gave up the allowance, but you have

underlying entitlement to it, you could still qualify for free tuition), or
- Attendance Allowance
- Your family receives:
  - Income Support
  - Working Tax Credit
  - Pension Credit
  - Housing Benefit, or
  - Income-based Jobseeker's Allowance
- Your only family income is benefits
- You are a registered jobseeker and have been for at least six weeks in a row before you apply for your course
- Your family's net income is less than the level for receiving Income Support

If you would like to find out more about the fee-waiver scheme and eligibility rules, you should contact your college or university.

Are your fees paid in full?

The Student Awards Agency for Scotland will pay the 'standard rate' of fees for you. The standard rate depends on where you are studying and when you enter your course. The following is a general guide to how much will be paid:

- If you started your course in the 2006–07 academic year or later, or you are returning to study after a break of at least a year, the agency will pay:
  - £1,285 per year for a Higher National Certificate, Higher National Diploma, or equivalent
  - £1,820 per year for a degree or equivalent, or
  - £2,895 per year for a medicine course.
- If you started your course in the 2005–06 academic year or earlier, and you are studying a Higher National Certificate, Higher National Diploma, degree or equivalent, your fees will be paid at the standard rate of £1,285.

The cut-off date

Your fees will be paid only if you're still attending your course on or after a specific cut-off date. If you withdraw from your course before the cut-off date, the Student Awards Agency for Scotland will not pay your fees.

The cut-off dates for the 2009–10 academic year are:

- 1 December 2009 for courses which start between 1 August 2009 and 31 December 2009
- 1 March 2010 for courses which start between 1 January 2010 and 31 March 2010, and
- 1 June 2010 for courses which start between 1 April 2010 and 30 June 2010.

If you transfer to another course or institution, the agency will pay the fee for the course and institution you are attending on the cut-off date.

Can you get help with tuition fees if you study at a non-publicly funded institution?

The fees for non-publicly funded institutions are generally higher than the standard rate. If you're studying at a non-publicly funded institution in Scotland, you can get help with the fees, but the Student Awards Agency for Scotland will not pay the full cost. The agency will pay £1,205 towards your fees, if you are doing a course which the government has chosen for support. You will be responsible for paying the difference.

Help with tuition fees for further education in Scotland

If you are Scottish and you are in further education, you may not have to pay tuition fees for your course, so long as you meet certain residency rules. If you are in part-time further education, you will have to meet residency and income rules to avoid paying fees.

If you meet all of the necessary rules for a further education fee-waiver, you will not have to pay tuition fees for the following courses at a college:

- academic courses up to Higher level
- courses that do not lead to formal qualifications (such as independent living skills courses)
- basic skills courses, such as literacy and numeracy
- work-related courses (such as Scottish Vocational Qualifications)

Residency rules

If you have lived in Scotland all your life and you have no restrictions on staying there, it is very likely that you will qualify for a fee-waiver. In general, the residency rules for a further education fee-waiver are:

- You must be ordinarily resident in Scotland on the first day of the first academic year of your course. For further education courses, this will be the date your course starts.
- If you are a UK national, you must have lived in the UK, the Channel Islands or the Isle of Man for the three years immediately before your course starts.[106]

'Ordinarily resident' means that you live in a place year after year by choice.[107] If your main reason for living in Scotland is to study, and you would otherwise be living in a different country, you will not count as being ordinarily resident.

There may be more specific residency rules you have to meet in addition to the general rules above. To find out what these rules are, check with your college.[108]

There are special rules for some EU citizens, EEA migrant workers, refugees or asylum seekers, to make sure that they meet the residency requirements for free tuition.[109] You may qualify for free tuition on the basis of being:

- a registered jobseeker
- an asylum seeker living in Scotland (or you could qualify if your spouse or parent is an asylum seeker living in Scotland), or
- in the care of a local authority and living in a foster home or children's home.

Income rules[110]

If you are in part-time further education, you will have to meet some income rules in order to qualify for a fee-waiver. You may be able to get a fee-waiver if one of the following applies to you:

- You or your family receive:
  - Income Support
  - Working Tax Credit
  - Pension Credit
  - Income-Based Jobseeker's Allowance, or
  - Housing Benefit
- You receive:
  - Carer's Allowance (if you gave up the allowance, but you have underlying entitlement to it, you could still qualify for free tuition)
  - Employment and Support Allowance
  - Disability Living Allowance
  - Severe Disablement Allowance
  - Attendance Allowance, or
  - Incapacity Benefit

If you are not getting any of the benefits listed above, you may still qualify for a fee-waiver if your household's taxable income for the last tax year is less than:

- £7,937, if you are the only person in the household
- £11,878, if you are in a couple household with no children
- £18,173, if you are in a household with dependant children.

If your income in the current tax year is much lower than your income in the last tax year, you may be able to use your current income for assessment.

How do you apply for a fee-waiver?

Often, fee-waivers will be automatically processed when you apply for a course. Your college should give you an application form if it requires any further information from you (particularly if you are a part-time student). Most courses will be eligible for a fee-waiver, but your college should make it clear in its recruitment material if your course does not qualify.[111]

Young Student's Bursary

What is a Young Student's Bursary?

A Young Student's Bursary (YSB) is a grant that helps students in higher education to pay the cost of living. YSBs are administered by the Student Awards Agency for Scotland, and do not have to be repaid. The amount of your bursary depends on your household income. Payments will be made monthly, straight into your bank account. You do not need to take out a Student Loan in order to get a YSB. However, if you do take out a loan and get a YSB, the YSB can replace part of your Student Loan for maintenance, reducing the amount you need to borrow and repay.

Who can get a Young Student's Bursary?

You will be eligible for a YSB if you meet all of the following rules:

- you are eligible for help with the full standard rate of your tuition fees (£1,820) (see page 240)
- your course started in the 2001–02 academic year or later, or you returned to your studies in the 2001–02 academic year or later, after having a break for at least one year
- you are studying in Scotland
- you are doing a full-time higher education course (such as a Higher National Certificate, Higher National Diploma, or degree), or you are doing a PGDE or PGDipCE course
- you are (or were) aged under 25 before the first day of the first academic year of your course

You may not be eligible for a YSB if you are:

- married
- in a civil partnership
- live with a partner, or
- have supported yourself from earnings or benefits outside full-time education for any three years before the first day of the first academic year of your course.

Contact the Student Awards Agency for Scotland if you are not sure about your eligibility.

How much will you be paid?

The amount of your bursary depends on your household income. As a rough guide, you will get:

- the highest amount of £2,640 if your household income is £19,310 or less per year
- £2,163 if your household income is £22,000 per year
- £1,631 if your household income is £25,000 per year, or
- zero if your household income is over £34,195 per year.

How do you apply for a Young Student's Bursary?

You can apply for a YSB online at www.saas.gov.uk, with your main application for funding from Student Awards Agency for Scotland. The agency prefers online applications, but if you would like to do a paper application instead, you can phone them on 0845 111 1711 to ask for a form.

Student's Outside Scotland Bursary[113]

What is a Student's Outside Scotland Bursary?

A Student's Outside Scotland Bursary (SOSB) is a grant that helps Scottish people who are studying outside Scotland to pay the cost of living. To get a SOSB, you have to be on a full-time higher education course at a UK institution. SOSBs are administered by the Student Awards Agency for Scotland, and the amount you are paid depends on your family income. You do not have to repay the grant, and you do not have to take out a Student Loan in order to get a SOSB. However, if you have a loan, the SOSB will replace part of your loan, reducing the amount of money you have to borrow and repay.

Who can get a Student's Outside Scotland Bursary?

You can apply for a SOSB if:

- you are eligible for help with your tuition fees
- your course started in the 2006–07 academic year or later, or you returned to your studies in the 2006–07 academic year or later after a break of at least one year
- you are studying at a UK institution outside Scotland, and
- you are doing a full-time higher education course (such as a Higher National Certificate, Higher National Diploma, or degree), or you're doing a PGDE or PGDipCE course.

You may not be able to apply for a SOSB if you have received support from UK public funds for a higher education course before, or if you have to repeat a year of your course. If you will be doing a period of paid placement for your course, you will not be able to claim the SOSB during this time.

How much are you paid?

The amount you are paid depends on your household income. As a rough guide, you will get:

- the maximum amount of £2,150 per year if your household income is £21,760 or less per year
- £1,761 per year if your household income is £22,000 per year
- £1,328 per year if your household income is £25,000 per year, or
- zero if your household income is over £34,195 per year.

Young students who get a SOSB may also qualify for an additional loan of up to £605.

How do you apply for a Student's Outside Scotland Bursary?

You can apply for a SOSB online at www.saas.gov.uk, with your main application for funding from Student Awards Agency for Scotland. The agency prefers online applications, but if you would like to do a paper application instead, you can phone them on 0845 111 1711 to ask for a form.

Dependant's Allowance[114]

If you are in full-time further education and you are financially or legally responsible for an adult (this includes caring for an adult), then you may be able to apply for Dependant's Allowance. The amount of the allowance depends on your income, your dependant's income and your family circumstances. The maximum amount you can get is £49.48 per week.

Childcare Fund[115]

If you are studying at a university or further education college, your institution should have a Childcare Fund to help students pay for registered childcare. If you are a lone parent, part-time or mature student, you will have priority for help. However, other students can still apply for support. Your university or college will decide whether or not you are eligible.

You will get Childcare Fund payments on top of any bursary you receive, and you must use the money to pay for registered childcare only. Some colleges may offer different kinds of support, such as on-site nurseries or childcare vouchers. Contact your university or college for more information.

Lone Parent's Grant and Additional Childcare Grant for Lone Parents[116]

If you are a student in full-time higher education, and you are widowed, divorced, separated or single, and you are bringing up children, you could get extra support through a Lone Parent's Grant. If you have at least one dependent child, you can claim a grant of £1,270.

If you receive the Lone Parent's Grant, you could also get the Additional Childcare Grant for Lone Parents. This provides extra help of up to £1,185 per year to pay for formal childcare costs. 'Formal childcare' includes childminders, after-school clubs, day care and education. If your children are aged eight or under, your grant can only be used for childcare providers who are registered with the local authority.

Additional Support Needs for Learning Allowance[117]

If you are in full-time further education and you have to pay extra costs because of your disability, you can apply for an Additional Support Needs for Learning Allowance (ASNLA). This allowance is not based on your income, and provides help with your travel and study costs. It is paid on top of any other disability grants and benefits you might receive.

Vacation Grant for care-leavers[118]

If you are a full-time student and you used to be in care, you may be able to get a grant of up to £100 per week to help pay your accommodation costs. You can qualify for this grant if you were in care immediately before you started your course, or were in care when you finished school (at the legal school leaving age).

All-Ireland Scholarships[119]

What are All-Ireland Scholarships?

All-Ireland Scholarships (AIS) provide financial support to high-achieving students who come from a low-income household. The AIS scheme is funded by the JP McManus Charitable Foundation. The scholarships support the top 25 students who attend a grant-aided post-primary school or a further education college in Northern Ireland. Nineteen scholarships will be available through the school sector and six through further education colleges. At least two scholarships will be offered in each county.

Who can apply for an All-Ireland Scholarship?

To apply for an AIS, you must:

- be getting Education Maintenance Allowance

- achieve high marks in your Council for Curriculum Examinations and Assessment (CCEA) A2 A-level exams, and
- intend to go to university in the UK or Republic of Ireland to study a full-time degree course.

The CCEA will check the academic performance of those students who have applied for an AIS, and give a list of the top students to the Department for Employment and Learning. The CCEA will make sure that this list offers at least two scholarships per county, and that scholarships are split appropriately between schools and further education colleges.

How much will you be paid?

The AIS scheme offers financial support of £5,500 per year. You will get information about the payment time and method once you win a scholarship.

An AIS will not affect your entitlement to other student support grants.

How do you apply for an All-Ireland Scholarship?

To apply for an AIS, download a self-nomination form from www.delni. gov.uk. You will have to fill out the form and ask the principal of your school or college to sign it as well. You should send the form to the CCEA at 29 Clarendon Road, Clarendon Dock, Belfast.

The Department for Employment and Learning will tell you that your name has been forwarded to the JP McManus Trustees, and the Trustees will then be responsible for telling you if you have won a scholarship.

Students from Northern Ireland who study in the Republic of Ireland[120]

If you are from Northern Ireland and you plan to study at a publicly funded college in the Republic of Ireland, you will not pay tuition fees. Instead, the Irish Government will pay your fees. However, your college will make an extra charge for registration, usually about €900. Your local Education and Library Board will pay this registration fee, if you apply to them.

Financial support for work-based learning

Pre-employment programmes

If you're taking part in a pre-employment programme, there is a range of financial support you could get. Most courses pay a training allowance, and some also help with costs such as travel and childcare.

Entry to Employment

If you join Entry to Employment (e2e), you can get the maximum Education Maintenance Allowance of £30 per week, regardless of your household income. See page 221 for detailed information on how to apply for Education Maintenance Allowance and Income Support for those in learning.

While you're taking part in e2e, you can get help with your travel expenses to and from your programme. Plus, if you need help with paying for childcare, you can apply to Care to Learn for support. See page 230 for information on Care to Learn.

Skill Build

Training Allowance

If you are aged 16 to 18, and you are taking part in Skill Build, you will get a training allowance of at least £50 per week.[121] To get this funding, you must be 'endorsed' at Level 1 or below by Careers Wales. You will get the weekly allowance for the whole length of your endorsement, even if you pass the age of 18 before the endorsement ends.[122]

Help with travel costs

If you are a non-employed learner, and you pay more than £5 per week for travel, you may be able to get help with these expenses. You can claim for necessary, reasonable travel expenses you incur when going to and from your place of learning. You will be expected to take the most economical route and method of transport.[123]

Help with accommodation costs

If you are a non-employed learner, you may be able to get some help with accommodation costs, where your particular accommodation is essential for you to access learning.[124]

Help with childcare costs

You can get help with childcare costs if you are a non-employed learner and a lone parent. You can get help with the cost of registered or accredited childcare, up to £29.75 per day (or £148.75 per week) for one child, or up to £51 per day (or £255 per week) for two or more children. To get funding, your childcare provider must be registered by the Care Standards Inspectorate for Wales or approved by an accredited organisation's Quality Assurance Scheme.[125]

Get Ready for Work

Training Allowance

If you're taking part in Get Ready for Work (GRFW) full-time, you will usually be able to claim a Training Allowance. This is a payment of around £55 per week, depending on your programme provider. Full-time attendance means that you do your programme for more than 25 hours per week, spread over five days and not counting meal breaks. You will get the full Training Allowance so long as you have full attendance or you are absent only for authorised reasons. Your Training Allowance will be reduced for each day of unauthorised absence.[126]

Travel costs

Your programme provider should help you with reasonable travel costs. If you are getting a Training Allowance, you will have to cover the first £3 of your travel costs per week. If you are getting Incapacity Benefit, you can get help with the full cost of travel.[127]

Training for Work

Training Allowance[128]

While you are taking part in Training for Work (TfW), you can get a training allowance which is equal to the amount of your benefits plus £10 per week, except in the following cases:

- If you are getting Incapacity Benefit, you will not be eligible for the extra £10 per week.[129]
- If you have 'employed status', you cannot get the Training Allowance because you already receive a wage from your employer.[130]

If you are taking part in self-employment training, the Training Allowance you receive during your test trading will be treated as part of your business profits. This means it is taxable income. Jobcentre Plus should tell you this at your Pre-entry Interview.[131]

If you get a job out of the TfW programme, you will be paid the usual rate for the job.

Help with costs[132]

You may be able to get some help with travel, meal and childcare costs. Skills Development Scotland and your TfW provider will decide the support you can get. You should be able to get advice from Jobcentre Plus.

Skillseekers

Employed Skillseekers

If you are taking part in Skillseekers as an employed trainee, you will be paid your usual wage by your employer. You should not be financially worse off than a non-employed Skillseeker who is getting an allowance and help with travel costs.[133]

Non-employed Skillseekers

If you are a non-employed Skillseeker, you will get an allowance of at least £55 per week.[134]

You can also get some help with reasonable travel costs. You will have to pay the first £3 per week towards travel, but your programme provider will pay the rest, based on the cost of using public transport. If no public transport is available, you will be paid 20 pence per mile for private transport.

If you have to live away from home to do training because there is no other local training available, you can get help paying for your accommodation. You can get up to £20 per day, but each case will be considered separately.

Your programme provider should pay for any protective clothing, books or equipment you need to do your training.[135]

Training for Success

If you join Training for Success (TfS), you will be able to get an Educational Maintenance Allowance (EMA) of £40 per week. You will get this allowance until you finish the TfS programme, or until you start a Level 2 or 3 apprenticeship.[136]

Under certain circumstances, you may be able to get support from the Social Security Agency in addition to your EMA. This could be the case if you are disabled, a lone parent, a carer, or estranged from your family and facing severe hardship. In this situation, you should contact your local Social Security office to talk about making a claim for Income Support.

If your parents or carers are getting Income Support, Income-based Jobseeker's Allowance or Housing Benefit, your EMA will not affect their benefit.[137] Your parents or carers may also be able to claim Child Benefit or Child Tax Credit while you are taking part in the programme (see page 45).[138]

You can also get some help with travel costs. You will have to pay the first £3 of your travel costs per week, but your TfS provider should cover the rest.[139]

Bridge to Employment **NI**

Benefits

If you are getting a benefit payment, you will continue to receive this while you do Bridge to Employment (BTE). You should tell your local Social Security office that you are taking part in BTE.

Travel costs **NI**

While you are taking part in BTE, you will get help with your travel costs. This support is worked out based on the cheapest cost of public transport available to you. If you cannot use public transport, you will be paid 25 pence per mile for private transport costs.

Childcare **NI**

If you are a lone parent or guardian of a child aged 15 or under, you may be able to claim childcare payments. You can get a maximum of £95 per week for one child and £140 per week for two or more children. If your children only need after-school care, you can get a maximum of £55 per week for one child, and £85 per week for two or more children. This money is paid to a registered childminder.

If a relative provides childcare for your children, you can get a maximum of £55 per week for one child, and £85 per week for two or more children. If a relative only provides after-school care for your children, you can get a maximum of £35 per week for one child, and £55 per week for two or more children.

Lodging allowance **NI**

Depending on where you live, you may be able to get a lodging allowance. For more information, you can call Training Services on 028 9044 1885 during the week.

Steps to Work NI

Training premium

If you are on Step Two of Steps to Work (StW), and you are receiving benefits, you can get a training premium of £15.38 per week. This will not affect the amount of your benefit payments.

If you do the Essential Skills training on Step Two, you will get an extra £10 per week on top of your premium. When you achieve your qualification, you will get a £100 bonus.[140]

Childcare NI

While you are on StW, you can get help with childcare if you are:

- a lone parent, or
- a partner of a benefit claimant.

If your child is in registered care, you can get a maximum of £130 per week for one child, and a maximum of £240 per week for two or more children. 'Registered care' is care provided by:

- registered childminders, nurseries or play schemes registered with a Health and Social Services Board
- out-of-hours clubs run by schools on school premises, and
- childcare schemes run on Crown or government property.

If your child is looked after by a relative, you can get a maximum of £70 per week for one child, and a maximum of £100 per week for two or more children. To get funding, the relative must be aged over 18 and be the grandparent, brother, sister, aunt or uncle of your child.[141]

Other costs NI

You may also be able to get help with interview travel costs, or with paying for goods and services which will help you to find work. Speak to your adviser for more information.[142]

Apprenticeships

If you are working towards an apprenticeship, you will usually be entitled to a wage. See pages 191 to 207 to find out the wage entitlements for apprentices in your part of the UK.

Career Development Loans

What is a Career Development Loan?[143]

A Career Development Loan (CDL) is a bank loan which helps you pay for work-related learning. If you're aged 18 or over, you can use a CDL to fund up to two years of learning (or three years in some cases), whether you are employed, self-employed or unemployed. The loan scheme is run by the Learning and Skills Council together with three high street banks. A CDL is a personal loan between you and the bank, and you are responsible for making repayments, so check how much your monthly repayments will be before you take out the loan. The Learning and Skills Council will pay the interest on your loan while you're learning, and for one month after you've stopped training. You will then have to start paying the loan back.

You can use a CDL to cover three kinds of costs:

- course fees (the CDL will cover 80 per cent of your course fees, or 100 per cent if you have been out of work for three months or more at the time you apply for the loan)
- other course costs, including books, equipment, tools, childcare, travel expenses and some disability-related costs, and
- living expenses, such as food, ordinary clothing or footwear, household fuel, rent, housing costs and council tax.

Your loan can be used for just one type of cost, or for all three types. However, to use the loan for living expenses, your costs must not be covered by any other grant or state benefit, and you cannot work for more than 30 hours per week.

What learning courses can you do with a Career Development Loan?[144]

CDLs cover a wide range of learning courses that will help you to improve your job skills, including full-time, part-time or distance learning courses. You can use a CDL to achieve many different qualifications, from National Vocational Qualifications or Scottish Vocational Qualifications, to Open University and postgraduate qualifications. In some circumstances, you can also use your CDL to pay for qualification assessments.

Some courses are not eligible for CDL funding, or have restrictions. These include:

- careers counselling courses (you can't use a CDL to fund any course that solely provides you with careers information, advice and guidance, but you can use a CDL to fund a course which leads to a professional qualification in career guidance)
- franchise courses (you can use a CDL only to cover the initial learning costs, but you cannot use a CDL to pay for the franchise or to buy a licence from the franchiser), and
- Foundation courses (you can use a CDL to fund a stand-alone Foundation course, but if you're doing a Foundation course as the first step towards a degree course, you cannot use a CDL).

Who can apply for a Career Development Loan?[145]

To qualify for a CDL, you must be:

- aged 18 or over
- ordinarily resident in England, Scotland or Wales, with an unlimited right to remain in the UK
- unable to pay for the course yourself, and
- intending to work in the European Union (or Iceland, Norway or Liechtenstein) once you have finished your course.

You cannot apply for a CDL if:

- you have a job and your employer will receive a grant for your learning

- you are entitled to some other types of financial help (for example, a mandatory grant or a Student Loan), or
- you are getting a NHS non-means-tested bursary.

You can't use a CDL to pay for anything that is already being covered by another source of public funding.

How much can you borrow?

You can borrow anything between £300 and £8,000 for your CDL. The loan will help you fund up to two years of learning, or up to three years if your course includes one year of relevant practical work experience. If your course lasts longer than this, you may still be able to use a CDL to pay for part of it.

You can apply for a CDL with Barclays, the Co-operative Bank or the Royal Bank of Scotland. If your loan is approved, you and your learning provider will complete a 'Start Certificate' and give it to your bank, who will release the funds. The bank cannot release any funds until your learning provider has confirmed that you have started your course. Your bank will pay your course fees directly to your learning provider, and money for other expenses directly into your own bank account. If your course lasts for one year or longer, the bank may pay money for living expenses in stages throughout each year of your course.[146]

You will repay the loan to the bank over an agreed period at a fixed rate of interest, starting from one month after you finish training. The Learning and Skills Council will pay the interest on your loan while you're learning, and for the first month after you stop training.[147]

Making repayments

If you can't afford the repayments and you want to postpone them, you must reach an agreement with your bank before the repayments are due to start. You may be able to postpone your repayments for up to 17 months if you:

- are unemployed and claiming benefits
- are employed and you or your partner are getting:

- – Income Support
- – Housing Benefit
- – Council Tax Benefit
- – Working Tax Credit, or
- – Pension Credit
- are receiving a Training Allowance, or
- have to extend your course (due to ill health or other special circumstances).

If you fail to complete your course, you will still be responsible for repaying the full amount of your loan to the bank. This also applies if your learning provider stops trading, or if you are unhappy with the course for any reason.[148]

How do you apply for a Career Development Loan?

The first step in applying for a CDL is choosing a bank. CDLs are provided by Barclays, the Co-operative Bank and the Royal Bank of Scotland, and the interest rates and processing time may vary from bank to bank. Once you have chosen a bank, you will have to ask the bank for a CDL application form. You should apply well in advance of your course, so that you have time to apply to another bank if the first bank refuses your application. Barclays and the Royal Bank of Scotland accept applications three months before your course start date, and the Co-operative Bank accepts applications six weeks before the start date. You can only apply to one bank at a time.

All of the bank application forms ask you to work out your monthly living expenses. Knowing your expenses will help you to work out an appropriate repayment rate and schedule. Remember to take all expenses into account, such as books and materials, travel, childcare and any disability-related costs. You may also need to send supporting evidence with your application, such as copies of bank statements or a bill as proof of your address.

The bank will let you know whether or not your application is successful. If the bank grants you a CDL, it will send you a credit agreement that you need to sign and return. You may have to wait two to three weeks for an answer from the bank.[149]

If you need advice, you can:

- call the CDL Help Line on 0800 585 505
- book a call-back at a time which suits you, or
- email a CDL adviser through www.direct.gov.uk.

Endnotes

1 ema.direct.gov.uk/ Accessed on 17 March 2009

2 www.support4learning.org.uk/money/financial_support_for_further_education_
students/education_maintenance_allowance.cfm Accessed on 5 February 2009

3 www.cyllidmyfyrwyrcymru.co.uk/portal/page?_pageid=56,1835661&_
dad=portal&_schema=PORTAL and www.cyllidmyfyrwyrcymru.co.uk/portal/page?_
pageid=56,1835710&_dad=portal&_schema=PORTAL Accessed on 9 April 2009

4 www.cyllidmyfyrwyrcymru.co.uk/portal/page?_pageid=56,1835717&_
dad=portal&_schema=PORTAL Accessed on 9 April 2009

5 www.emascotland.com/newemasandme.htm Accessed on 9 April 2009

6 www.emascotland.com/newthela.htm Accessed on 9 April 2009

7 www.emascotland.com/newemasandme.htm Accessed on 9 April 2009

8 www.emascotland.com/newfaqs.htm Accessed on 9 April 2009

9 www.delni.gov.uk/index/further-and-higher-education/further-education/fe-
financial-help/ema-educational-maintenance-allowance Accessed on 9 April 2009

10 www.delni.gov.uk/index/further-and-higher-education/ema-educational-
maintenance-allowance/ema-entitlement.htm Accessed on 9 April 2009

11 www.delni.gov.uk/index/further-and-higher-education/ema-educational-
maintenance-allowance/ema-how-to-apply.htm Accessed on 9 April 2009

12 www.direct.gov.uk/en/EducationAndLearning/AdultLearning/
FinancialHelpForAdultLearners/DG_10033131 Accessed on 17 March 2009

13 www.studentfinancewales.co.uk/portal/page?_pageid=56,1275515&_
dad=portal&_schema=PORTAL Accessed on 9 April 2009

14 www.saas.gov.uk/student_support/other_funding.htm#discretionary Accessed on
9 April 2009

15 www.saas.gov.uk/student_support/other_funding.htm#discretionary Accessed on
9 April 2009

16 www.studentfinanceni.co.uk/portal/page?_pageid=54,1266398&_dad=portal&_
schema=PORTAL Accessed on 16 April 2009

17 www.studentfinanceni.co.uk/portal/page?_pageid=54,1266398&_dad=portal&_
schema=PORTAL Accessed on 16 April 2009

18 www.direct.gov.uk/en/EducationAndLearning/UniversityAndHigherEducation/
StudentFinance/Applyingforthefirsttime/DG_171571 Accessed on 16 April 2009

19 www.studentfinancewales.co.uk/portal/page?_pageid=56,1277564&_
dad=portal&_schema=PORTAL Accessed on 16 April 2009

[20] www.studentfinancewales.co.uk/portal/page?_pageid=56,1277616&_dad=portal&_schema=PORTAL and www.studentfinancewales.co.uk/portal/page?_pageid=56,1277595&_dad=portal&_schema=PORTAL Accessed on 16 April 2009

[21] www.studentfinancewales.co.uk/portal/page?_pageid=56,1277564&_dad=portal&_schema=PORTAL Accessed on 16 April 2009

[22] www.sfc.ac.uk/information/information_funding/student_support/bursary_support_2007_08.html Accessed on 16 April 2009

[23] www.sfc.ac.uk/information/information_funding/student_support/bursary_support_2007_08.html Accessed on 16 April 2009

[24] www.sfc.ac.uk/information/information_funding/student_support/bursary_support_2007_08.html Accessed on 16 April 2009

[25] www.studentfinanceni.co.uk/portal/page?_pageid=54,1266217&_dad=portal&_schema=PORTAL#4 Accessed on 17 April 2009

[26] www.studentfinanceni.co.uk/portal/page?_pageid=54,1266217&_dad=portal&_schema=PORTAL#4 Accessed on 17 April 2009

[27] www.delni.gov.uk/index/further-and-higher-education/higher-education/studentfinance.htm Accessed on 16 April 2009

[28] www.direct.gov.uk/ Accessed on 2 June 2009

[29] www.studentfinancewales.co.uk/portal/page?_pageid=56,1276150&_dad=portal&_schema=PORTAL Accessed on 17 April 2009

[30] www.studentfinancewales.co.uk/portal/page?_pageid=56,1275486&_dad=portal&_schema=PORTAL Accessed on 17 April 2009

[31] Learndirect Scotland (2008) *Helping you meet the costs of learning: Your guide to funding 2008-09*, p.28

[32] www.saas.gov.uk/student_support/special_circumstances/dsa_eligibility.htm Accessed on 3 June 2009

[33] Student Finance NI (2008) *A Guide to Financial Support for Higher Education Students 2008-09*, pp.16–17

[34] Student Finance NI (2008) *A Guide to Financial Support for Higher Education Students 2008-09*, p.7

[35] Student Finance Direct (2008–09) *Childcare Grant and other support for full-time student parents in higher education*, p.12

[36] www.studentfinancewales.co.uk/portal/page?_pageid=56,1276150&_dad=portal&_schema=PORTAL Accessed on 17 April 2009

[37] www.studentfinancewales.co.uk/portal/page?_pageid=56,1275486&_dad=portal&_schema=PORTAL Accessed on 17 April 2009

38 Learndirect Scotland (2008) *Helping you meet the costs of learning: Your guide to funding 2008-09*, p.27

39 www.saas.gov.uk/student_support/supplimentary_grants.htm Accessed on 3 June 2009

40 Student Finance NI (2008) *A Guide to Financial Support for Higher Education Students 2008-09*, p.15

41 Student Finance NI (2008) A Guide to Financial Support for Higher Education Students 2008/09, p.7

42 www.direct.gov.uk/en/EducationAndLearning/UniversityAndHigherEducation/StudentFinance/Applyingforthefirsttime/DG_171557 Accessed on 16 April 2009

43 www.direct.gov.uk/en/EducationAndLearning/UniversityAndHigherEducation/StudentFinance/Applyingforthefirsttime/DG_171557 Accessed on 16 April 2009

44 www.direct.gov.uk/en/EducationAndLearning/UniversityAndHigherEducation/StudentFinance/Applyingforthefirsttime/DG_171557 Accessed on 16 April 2009

45 www.direct.gov.uk/en/EducationAndLearning/UniversityAndHigherEducation/StudentFinance/Applyingforthefirsttime/DG_174046 Accessed on 16 April 2009

46 www.direct.gov.uk/en/EducationAndLearning/UniversityAndHigherEducation/StudentFinance/Applyingforthefirsttime/DG_171557 Accessed on 16 April 2009

47 www.cyllidmyfyrwyrcymru.co.uk/portal/page?_pageid=56,1862080&_dad=portal&_schema=PORTAL Accessed on 16 April 2009

48 www.cyllidmyfyrwyrcymru.co.uk/portal/page?_pageid=56,1862080&_dad=portal&_schema=PORTAL Accessed on 16 April 2009

49 www.cyllidmyfyrwyrcymru.co.uk/portal/page?_pageid=56,1862080&_dad=portal&_schema=PORTAL Accessed on 16 April 2009

50 Student Finance NI (2008) A Guide to Financial Support for Higher Education Students 2008/09, p.12

51 www.studentfinanceni.co.uk/portal/page?_pageid=54,1266217&_dad=portal&_schema=PORTAL#4 Accessed on 17 April 2009

52 www.delni.gov.uk/index/further-and-higher-education/higher-education/studentfinance/applying-for-financial-help.htm Accessed on 17 April 2009

53 www.direct.gov.uk/ Accessed on 2 June 2009

54 www.studentfinancewales.co.uk/portal/page?_pageid=56,1275515&_dad=portal&_schema=PORTAL Accessed on 17 April 2009

55 www.studentfinancewales.co.uk/portal/page?_pageid=56,1275486&_dad=portal&_schema=PORTAL Accessed on 17 April 2009

56 Student Finance NI (2008) *A Guide to Financial Support for Higher Education Students 2008-09*, p.25

57 Student Finance NI (2008) *A Guide to Financial Support for Higher Education Students 2008-09*, p.25

58 www.direct.gov.uk/ Accessed on 2 June 2009

59 www.studentfinancewales.co.uk/portal/page?_pageid=56,1275996&_dad=portal&_schema=PORTAL Accessed on 17 April 2009

60 www.studentfinancewales.co.uk/portal/page?_pageid=56,1275486&_dad=portal&_schema=PORTAL Accessed on 17 April 2009

61 Student Finance NI (2008) *A Guide to Financial Support for Higher Education Students 2008-09*, p.25

62 www.direct.gov.uk/ Accessed on 2 June 2009

63 www.studentfinancewales.co.uk/portal/page?_pageid=56,1276150&_dad=portal&_schema=PORTAL Accessed on 17 April 2009

64 www.studentfinancewales.co.uk/portal/page?_pageid=56,1275486&_dad=portal&_schema=PORTAL Accessed on 17 April 2009

65 Student Finance NI (2008) *A Guide to Financial Support for Higher Education Students 2008-09*, p.14

66 Student Finance NI (2008) *A Guide to Financial Support for Higher Education Students 2008-09*, p.7

67 www.direct.gov.uk/ Accessed on 2 June 2009

68 www.studentfinancewales.co.uk/portal/page?_pageid=56,1276150&_dad=portal&_schema=PORTAL Accessed on 17 April 2009

69 www.studentfinancewales.co.uk/portal/page?_pageid=56,1275486&_dad=portal&_schema=PORTAL Accessed on 17 April 2009

70 Student Finance NI (2008) *A Guide to Financial Support for Higher Education Students 2008-09*, p.15

71 Student Finance NI (2008) *A Guide to Financial Support for Higher Education Students 2008-09*, p.7

72 Learndirect Scotland (2008) *Helping you meet the costs of learning: Your guide to funding 2008-09*, p.27

73 Student Finance NI (2008) *A Guide to Financial Support for Higher Education Students 2008-09*, p.16

74 Student Finance NI (2008) *A Guide to Financial Support for Higher Education Students 2008-09*, p.7

75 www.direct.gov.uk/en/EducationAndLearning/UniversityAndHigherEducation/StudentFinance/Applyingforthefirsttime/DG_171557 Accessed on 16 April 2009

76 www.direct.gov.uk/en/EducationAndLearning/UniversityAndHigherEducation/ StudentFinance/Applyingforthefirsttime/DG_174046 Accessed on 16 April 2009

77 www.direct.gov.uk/en/EducationAndLearning/UniversityAndHigherEducation/ StudentFinance/Applyingforthefirsttime/DG_174046 Accessed on 16 April 2009

78 www.direct.gov.uk/en/EducationAndLearning/UniversityAndHigherEducation/ StudentFinance/Applyingforthefirsttime/DG_171557 Accessed on 16 April 2009

79 www.delni.gov.uk/index/further-and-higher-education/higher-education/ studentfinance.htm Accessed on 16 April 2009

80 www.studentfinanceni.co.uk/portal/page?_pageid=54,1266217&_dad=portal&_ schema=PORTAL#4 Accessed on 17 April 2009

81 www.delni.gov.uk/index/further-and-higher-education/higher-education/ studentfinance.htm Accessed on 16 April 2009

82 www.delni.gov.uk/index/further-and-higher-education/higher-education/ studentfinance/applying-for-financial-help.htm Accessed on 17 April 2009

83 www.ilawales.co.uk/MainPage.aspx?section=DoIQualify&lang=e Accessed on 9 April 2009

84 www.ilawales.co.uk/MainPage.aspx?section=DoIQualify&lang=e Accessed on 9 April 2009

85 www.ilawales.co.uk/MainPage.aspx?section=Applying&lang=e Accessed on 9 April 2009

86 www.ilascotland.org.uk/What+is+ILA+Scotland/Eligibility.htm Accessed on 9 April 2009

87 www.ilascotland.org.uk/ILA+Homepage.htm Accessed on 9 April 2009

88 www.direct.gov.uk/en/EducationAndLearning/AdultLearning/ FinancialHelpForAdultLearners/Adultlearninggrant/DG_068343 Accessed on 9 April 2009

89 www.direct.gov.uk/en/EducationAndLearning/AdultLearning/ FinancialHelpForAdultLearners/Adultlearninggrant/DG_068348 Accessed on 9 April 2009

90 www.direct.gov.uk/en/EducationAndLearning/AdultLearning/ FinancialHelpForAdultLearners/Adultlearninggrant/DG_068346 Accessed on 9 April 2009

91 www.direct.gov.uk/en/EducationAndLearning/AdultLearning/ FinancialHelpForAdultLearners/Adultlearninggrant/DG_068346 Accessed on 9 April 2009

92 www.direct.gov.uk/en/EducationAndLearning/AdultLearning/ FinancialHelpForAdultLearners/Adultlearninggrant/DG_068348 Accessed on 9 April 2009

[93] www.direct.gov.uk/en/EducationAndLearning/AdultLearning/ FinancialHelpForAdultLearners/Adultlearninggrant/DG_068350 Accessed on 9 April 2009

[94] www.direct.gov.uk/en/EducationAndLearning/14To19/MoneyToLearn/ Caretolearn/DG_066971 Accessed on 17 March 2009

[95] caretolearn.lsc.gov.uk/whatiscaretolearn/ Accessed on 17 March 2009

[96] www.direct.gov.uk/en/EducationAndLearning/14To19/MoneyToLearn/ Caretolearn/DG_066973 Accessed on 17 March 2009

[97] caretolearn.lsc.gov.uk/apply Accessed on 17 March 2009

[98] www.ukperformingarts.co.uk/funding/dada.asp Accessed on 18 March 2009

[99] www.direct.gov.uk/en/EducationAndLearning/14To19/MoneyToLearn/ DanceandDrama/DG_066987 Accessed on18 March 2009

[100] www.direct.gov.uk/en/EducationAndLearning/14To19/MoneyToLearn/ DanceandDrama/DG_10027090 Accessed on 18 March 2009

[101] www.studentfinancewales.co.uk/portal/page?_pageid=56,1835674&_ dad=portal&_schema=PORTAL Accessed on 9 April 2009

[102] www.studentfinancewales.co.uk/portal/page?_pageid=56,1835749&_ dad=portal&_schema=PORTAL Accessed on 9 April 2009

[103] www.saas.gov.uk/student_support/fees.htm Accessed on 20 April 2009

[104] www.learndirectscotland.com/NR/rdonlyres/F21C4903-41E2-48AB-9655- E247A9172CEB/0/IAG060408V3FullTimeHigherEducation.pdf Accessed on 3 June 2009

[105] Learndirect Scotland (2008) *Helping you meet the costs of learning: Your guide to funding 2008-09*, p.9

[106] Learndirect Scotland (2008) *Helping you meet the costs of learning: Your guide to funding 2008-09*, p.8

[107] Learndirect Scotland (2008) *Helping you meet the costs of learning: Your guide to funding 2008-09*, p.9

[108] www.scotland.gov.uk/Topics/Education/Funding-Support-Grants/FFL/FE Accessed on 20 April 2009

[109] www.learndirectscotland.com/NR/rdonlyres/F32ADB19-10E9-4919-9644- 53B7D76879C4/0/IAG100508V4FurtherEducationFeeWaivers.pdf Accessed on 3 June 2009

[110] www.learndirectscotland.com/NR/rdonlyres/F32ADB19-10E9-4919-9644- 53B7D76879C4/0/IAG100508V4FurtherEducationFeeWaivers.pdf Accessed on 3 June 2009

[111] www.learndirectscotland.com/NR/rdonlyres/F32ADB19-10E9-4919-9644-53B7D76879C4/0/IAG100508V4FurtherEducationFeeWaivers.pdf Accessed on 3 June 2009

[112] www.saas.gov.uk/student_support/scottish_inside/ysb.htm Accessed on 17 April 2009

[113] www.saas.gov.uk/student_support/scottish_outside/2006-2007/sosb.htm and www.saas.gov.uk/faqs_bursary.htm#how_pay Accessed on 20 April 2009

[114] Learndirect Scotland (2008) *Helping you meet the costs of learning: Your guide to funding 2008-09*, p.16

[115] Learndirect Scotland (2008) *Helping you meet the costs of learning: Your guide to funding 2008-09*, p.16 and p.27

[116] Learndirect Scotland (2008) *Helping you meet the costs of learning: Your guide to funding 2008-09*, p.27

[117] Learndirect Scotland (2008) *Helping you meet the costs of learning: Your guide to funding 2008-09*, p.16

[118] Learndirect Scotland (2008) *Helping you meet the costs of learning: Your guide to funding 2008-09*, p.29

[119] www.delni.gov.uk/allirelandscholarships Accessed on 20 April 2009

[120] www.delni.gov.uk/index/further-and-higher-education/higher-education/studentfinance/applying-for-financial-help.htm Accessed on 20 April 2009

[121] www.careerswales.com Accessed on 1 April 2009

[122] Welsh Assembly Government, *Programme Specification for Welsh Assembly Government Work Based Learning Programmes 1 August 2007 – 31 July 2010*, para. 5.1

[123] Welsh Assembly Government, *Programme Specification for Welsh Assembly Government Work Based Learning Programmes 1 August 2007 – 31 July 2010*, para.7.1 and 7.6

[124] Welsh Assembly Government, *Programme Specification for Welsh Assembly Government Work Based Learning Programmes 1 August 2007 – 31 July 2010*, para. 7.13.

[125] Welsh Assembly Government, *Programme Specification for Welsh Assembly Government Work Based Learning Programmes 1 August 2007 – 31 July 2010*, para. 8.1–8.2.

[126] Skills Development Scotland, *Programme Rules for Get Ready for Work 2009–10*, para. 9

[127] Skills Development Scotland, *Programme Rules for Get Ready for Work 2009–10*, para. 18.1.6

[128] www.hie.co.uk/trainingforwork.htm Accessed on 20 March 2009

[129] DWP, *Provider Led Pathways to Work Guidance*, Section 13, Part 2, para. 9

[130] DWP, *Provider Led Pathways to Work Guidance*, Section 13, Part 2, para. 17

[131] DWP, *Provider Led Pathways to Work Guidance*, Section 13, Part 2, para.19

[132] DWP, *Provider Led Pathways to Work Guidance*, Section 13, Part 2, para. 38

[133] Scottish Enterprise (2007) *Programme Rules for Skillseekers and Modern Apprenticeships 2007-08*, para. 15

[134] www.careers-scotland.org.uk/Education/Training/Skillseekers.asp Accessed on 7 April 2009

[135] Scottish Enterprise (2007) *Programme Rules for Skillseekers and Modern Apprenticeships 2007-08*, para. 14.3–14.4

[136] Department for Employment and Learning (2008) *Training for Success 2008 Operational Guidelines*, para. 3.1

[137] www.delni.gov.uk Accessed on 3 April 2009

[138] Department for Employment and Learning (2008) *Training for Success 2008 Operational Guidelines*, para. 3.2

[139] Department for Employment and Learning (2008) *Training for Success 2008 Operational Guidelines,* para. 3.5

[140] www.delni.gov.uk/index/finding-employment-finding-staff/fe-fs-help-to-find-employment/stepstowork/stw-steptwo.htm Accessed on 7 April 2009

[141] www.delni.gov.uk/index/finding-employment-finding-staff/fe-fs-help-to-find-employment/stepstowork/stw-childcare.htm Accessed on 7 April 2009

[142] www.delni.gov.uk/index/finding-employment-finding-staff/fe-fs-help-to-find-employment/stepstowork/stw-help-and-information.htm Accessed on 7 April 2009

[143] www.direct.gov.uk/en/EducationAndLearning/AdultLearning/FinancialHelpForAdultLearners/CareerDevelopmentLoans/DG_10033237 Accessed on 21 April 2009

[144] www.direct.gov.uk/en/EducationAndLearning/AdultLearning/FinancialHelpForAdultLearners/CareerDevelopmentLoans/DG_10033241 Accessed on 21 April 2009

[145] www.direct.gov.uk/en/EducationAndLearning/AdultLearning/FinancialHelpForAdultLearners/CareerDevelopmentLoans/DG_10033240 Accessed on 21 April 2009

[146] www.direct.gov.uk/en/EducationAndLearning/AdultLearning/FinancialHelpForAdultLearners/CareerDevelopmentLoans/DG_10033242 Accessed on 21 April 2009

[147] www.direct.gov.uk/en/EducationAndLearning/AdultLearning/
FinancialHelpForAdultLearners/CareerDevelopmentLoans/DG_10033237
Accessed on 21 April 2009

[148] www.direct.gov.uk/en/EducationAndLearning/AdultLearning/
FinancialHelpForAdultLearners/CareerDevelopmentLoans/DG_10033240
Accessed on 21 April 2009

[149] www.direct.gov.uk/en/EducationAndLearning/AdultLearning/
FinancialHelpForAdultLearners/CareerDevelopmentLoans/DG_10033242
Accessed on 21 April 2009

6 Financial Support for Young People in Particular Circumstances

Benefits for young people from abroad and those who are subject to immigration control UK

This book assumes that you will not have problems claiming benefits because of your residence or immigration status, or because you have recently arrived in the UK.

However, people from abroad often have limited rights to receive benefits and tax credits. Immigration is a complex area and it is easy to make mistakes, so it is vital to get specialist independent help. This chapter is just a general introduction to some of the issues involved.

There are links between the Home Office and the Department for Work and Pensions. If your stay in the UK is subject to immigration control, you should not even ask an official body about your benefit rights without first getting skilled, independent advice and help. Even an enquiry may count as a criminal offence and you could be removed from the UK or refused permission to enter or remain in the UK in the future.

If you cannot (or should not) claim benefits, you may still be able to ask your local council for help, especially if you are a young person or you are vulnerable in some other way (for example, you are in poor health or you are a parent). This help is normally given to young people in England and Wales under section 17 of The Children Act 1989 (different law applies in Scotland and Northern Ireland). Again, get advice before asking your council for help.

Further information is available in the Child Poverty Action Group's Welfare Benefits and Tax Credits Handbook and Migration and Social Security Handbook.

Benefits for young people with a disability or a long-term health problem

If you have a health problem or disability, you may be able to claim certain benefits. Unlike Jobseeker's Allowance (JSA), your right to disability and ill-health benefits is not limited by your age or because you are in care or a care-leaver.

You can still receive some benefits even if you are in work, education or training.

Who can claim?

If you are aged 16 or older, you can claim these benefits in your own right. If your parent or carer (your 'appointee') receives Disability Living Allowance for you, when you turn 16 you can revoke the appointeeship (or the appointee can write to DWP and 'resign'). You will then get the benefit in your own right, even if your disability means that you have trouble coping with or understanding the benefits system.

Appointees must spend benefits on behalf of the person they receive them for.[1]

Disability Living Allowance

You can claim Disability Living Allowance (DLA) if you either need extra care or support, or you have trouble getting around. Eligibility is not based on your income or savings. DLA is tax-free and can be paid on top of other benefits – it can even increase some benefits (such as

Income Support or Employment and Support Allowance). There is no list of illnesses or disabilities which qualify, and it's not just people who have very obvious disabilities who qualify. People with moderate learning disabilities, substance misuse problems, anorexia, severe behavioural problems and mental health difficulties, as well as people with more obvious physical disabilities and health problems, can qualify.

DLA is paid even if you don't have a carer and it does not matter whether you live with parents or on your own. If you live in, or spend time in, residential care or hospital, get advice because you may only be entitled to DLA for the days you spend at home.

There are two parts (components) to DLA: a care component and a mobility component. The care component is paid at three rates, and the mobility component is paid at two rates. You can qualify for both components, or for one component on its own, but you will only be paid one of the rates.

Who qualifies for Disability Living Allowance?

The care component

The rate you get for the care component depends on the amount of help you need and whether or not you need help during either day or night, or both day and night. For all rates, you don't need to show that you receive the help you need, you just need to show that the help is 'reasonably required'.

The low rate [2]

To get the low rate, you must need help with bodily functions (that is, all the things your body does) at least once a day for a significant time (either one single period or more than one). You can also claim the low rate if you are aged at least 16 and you are unable to cook a main meal. You may qualify for the low rate if you need someone to remind you to take medication each day, or someone to watch over you to prevent self-harm, or if you need a bit of help with a daily task.

The middle rate [3]

To get the middle rate, you must need:

- frequent help with bodily functions during the day, or someone to watch over you almost all the time during the day in case you get into danger or cause danger to others, or
- frequent or prolonged help with bodily functions during the night, or someone to be awake either for a long time or at frequent intervals to look in on you during the night.

The high rate [4]

If you satisfy both one of the day and one of the night conditions for the middle rate, or if you have a terminal illness, you will qualify for the high rate of the care component.

The mobility component

Again, the rate you get for the mobility component depends on how much trouble you have getting around. Your ability to walk is assessed taking account of any equipment you use such as a stick or artificial limb.

The lower rate [5]

You will qualify for the lower rate if you need someone to guide or supervise you most of the time when you are in unfamiliar outdoor places. For the lower rate, your disability can be physical or mental.

The higher rate [6]

There are six different ways to qualify for the higher rate. To claim this rate, your trouble with walking outdoors must have a physical cause. You will qualify if:

- you are unable to walk, or
- you are virtually unable to walk because of a combination of factors (for example, you can only walk a short distance, or at a slow speed,

or walking takes a long time, or you can only walk in an unusual manner, or you have pain or severe discomfort when you walk), or

- the effort of walking could endanger your health (for example, because of cardiac or breathing problems), or
- you have no legs or feet, or
- you are both deaf and blind, or
- you qualify for the higher-rate care component and you have a severe mental impairment which means your behaviour is both disruptive and dangerous.

Before you can claim DLA, you must meet the rules of entitlement for at least three months (unless you are terminally ill). You will also be expected to satisfy the rules for another six months after you claim.[7]

How to claim Disability Living Allowance

You can get a claim form from the DWP on 0845 712 3456. If you phone to make a claim, the DWP will send you a date-stamped claim form and you then have six weeks to complete and return the whole form.[8] The date-stamp is a way to make sure that your claim begins from the date of your phone call. If you make a claim online, this will be dated from when you register.

You may also claim by printing a claim form from the DWP website (www. dwp.gov.uk/eservice/) or by picking up a claim form from a local advice agency. However, your claim will then be dated from the date the DWP receives your completed claim form.

It is important to take time to complete the form and to fully explain your needs and how much help you require. Use the extra spaces on the form to show how and why you need help each day, and the type of help you need. Also describe how your disability or health problem affects you and why this means that you need help from others. There is space on the form for a carer and someone who knows you in a professional capacity to add information. It is best to ask someone who knows your needs well to fill out this part, rather than someone who has the most qualifications.

It is also a good idea to keep a diary showing what help you need hour by hour on a normal day. Include this with the claim form as evidence. It may be helpful to seek advice on completing the claim from a welfare rights or disability advice service

DLA is given for any period of time from six months to an indefinite period. If the decision maker decides they need more information before they can make a decision, the DWP may ask you to have an examination with a doctor contracted to work for them. You can have someone with you during this examination to help you make your case. You may also be asked to have a medical examination if the DWP decides to look at your claim again in the future, or if they feel that your health has changed.

If you are unhappy with the amount you have been given (or if your claim has been turned down), you can ask the DWP to look at its decision again. If you are still unhappy with the decision, you can appeal to an independent tribunal. Normally, you must appeal within one month of being sent the decision. You may wish to seek independent advice before deciding whether to make an appeal.

If you live in certain types of accommodation[9]

If you stay in accommodation which is funded in whole or in part by the NHS or Social Services, your DLA care component will be suspended after 28 days.

This applies if your accommodation is paid under:

- Part III National Assistance Act 1948
- Part IV Social Work (Scotland) Act 1968
- the Mental Health (Care and Treatment) (Scotland) Act 2003
- the Community Care and Health (Scotland) Act 2002
- the Mental Health Act 1983, or
- any other enactment relating to persons under disability, to young persons or to education or training.

This rule could apply if you live in a children's home, a residential school, or a residential care home. If you stay in funded accommodation for short periods which are separated by less than 28 days, these periods can be added together to push you over the 28-day suspension time limit. If you are receiving free in-patient NHS treatment during your stays, your mobility component will be suspended as well.

This rule does not affect the following kinds of accommodation:[10]

- accommodation or personal care in a private dwelling
- foster-parent accommodation
- respite care with a family who are paid by Social Services or the Social Work Department to look after you
- accommodation where you pay rent
- housing for homeless people.

It is important to tell the DWP if you move into any type of accommodation which will affect your benefits. It is also important to tell them as soon as you know you will leave the accommodation. If you live in accommodation where you can't normally receive DLA, you can still receive it for any time you spend away (for example, weekends with parents).

Incapacity Benefit UK

Incapacity Benefit is for people who cannot work because of physical or mental ill health or disability. It has not been possible to make a new claim for this benefit since 27 October 2008 unless you can link a new claim back to a past Incapacity Benefit claim. If you currently receive Incapacity Benefit, please refer to the third edition of the Young Person's Handbook.

People who currently receive Incapacity Benefit will continue to get it unless they leave the benefit for 12 or more weeks (if you leave the benefit because of paid work or training, you may have up to 104 weeks to re-claim it in certain situations), or until the government decides when to change existing Incapacity Benefit payments to Employment and Support Allowance over the next few years.

Employment and Support Allowance

There are two ways to qualify for Employment and Support Allowance (ESA): either as a result of paying National Insurance Contributions, or as a result of having a low income.

Who qualifies for Employment and Support Allowance?

To qualify for ESA, you must be aged 16 or older, have 'limited capability for work', and you must not be otherwise entitled to Jobseeker's Allowance, Statutory Sick Pay, or Income Support (for example, as a carer).

National Insurance contribution rules UK

You must have paid enough National Insurance contributions in order to qualify for ESA through the contributions route. However, people under the age of 20 (or 25 in some cases) can qualify without having paid National Insurance contributions.[11]

You may qualify for ESA in Youth if you are:[12]

- aged under 20
- aged under 19 and not in education
- aged under 19 and in education for less than 21 hours per week (not counting education which is unsuitable for someone of your age who does not have a disability), or
- aged 20 to 24 and:
  - have been on a course of full-time education or training in the three months before you turned 20 (that is, training of an occupational or vocational nature or which is government-sponsored via the Learning and Skills Council), and
  - no longer attend the course, and
  - stopped attending some time after the last two tax years before the calendar year when you claim ESA.

Once awarded, ESA in Youth may be paid beyond the age of 25.

The Assessment Phase[13]

The first 13 weeks of your claim is called the Assessment Phase (AP) and during this time you are paid the basic rate of ESA. To receive ESA, you must show that you have Limited Capability for Work (LCW), and for the first 13 weeks, you will show this through medical certificates.

The AP ends when the Department for Work and Pensions (DWP) decides that you either:

- do not have LCW, or
- have LCW and qualify for the Support Component of ESA, or
- have LCW and qualify for ESA with the proviso that you do work-related activity.

You must have one Work-Focused Interview (normally in the eighth week of your claim), unless the interview is deferred. You must attend the interview and you must participate by giving details of your qualifications, education, plans for work, and so on.

During the AP, you will have a Work Capability Assessment (WCA) with a health professional chosen by the DWP (this may not be a doctor), unless there is enough evidence to show that a WCA is not needed.

The AP ends when the WCA is complete. If the WCA has not been completed within 13 weeks (for example, because of DWP delay or non-attendance by you), then your AP may continue beyond 13 weeks.

Your AP can also end when the DWP has enough evidence to decide that you qualify for the Support Component of ESA.

The Limited Capability for Work Assessment [14]

The WCA uses a points system to decide whether or not you have LCW. To count as having LCW, you must score at least 15 points on the WCA.

The points system is at page 368.

The WCA is used when it is not clear to a DWP Decision Maker that you have LCW. You will usually have to fill in form ESA50 (which asks questions based on the WCA). The answers on the form may show that you have LCW, but if there is doubt, you will have a medical examination by a health care professional.

It is very important to fill in the ESA50 form carefully, and preferably with independent help.

The following people are automatically treated as having LCW and will not have a WCA: [15]

- hospital inpatients
- people suffering from a progressive disease where death within six months can reasonably be expected
- people being treated by intravenous, intraperitoneal or intrathecal chemotherapy (there are other forms of delivering chemotherapy which do not qualify)
- people refraining from work because they carry, or have been in contact with, an infectious disease
- pregnant women where there is a serious risk to the health of the mother or the child if the woman does not refrain from work, and
- women who are pregnant or have recently given birth but are not entitled to maternity allowance or statutory maternity pay, from six weeks before the baby is due to two weeks after the birth.

Overall, many more people are failing the WCA compared with the old medical assessment used for Incapacity Benefit.

Exceptional circumstances

If you do not pass the WCA, you can still be treated as having LCW if the health care professional can give evidence that:

- you are suffering from a severe life-threatening disease, and there is medical evidence that the disease is uncontrollable, or uncontrolled, by a recognised therapeutic procedure (in the case of a disease that is uncontrolled, there must be a reasonable cause for the disease to be uncontrolled by a recognised therapeutic procedure), or
- you suffer from a specific disease, bodily or mental disablement, and there is a substantial risk to the mental or physical health of any person if you are found not to have LCW.

The last category is a very important safeguard for many people who fail the WCA. It takes into account the range of work you can do, along with things such as getting ready for work, travel to and from work, and the broad results of being found as not having LCW. [16] 'Substantial risk' means that there is a risk of serious harm, even though it may be unlikely to happen. [17]

More assessments: the Support Group and the Work-Related Activity Group[18] **UK**

As well as doing a WCA, you also have to do a test to decide whether you have Limited Capability for Work-Related Activity (LCWRA). The LCWRA test will apply unless you are terminally ill or you have other proof that you have LCWRA (for example, you are on the kind of chemotherapy or you have the kind of pregnancy described in the previous section). The LCWRA test has 46 descriptors, and if you satisfy at least one, you will qualify for the Support Component of ESA.

If it is clear to a Decision Maker that you have LCWRA, no test will be required. If you have LCWRA, you will get the highest rate of ESA (including the Support Component) and you will not have to participate in work-related activity. You will be in what is commonly called the 'Support Group'.

If you do not pass the LCWRA test, but you do have LCW, then you receive ESA at a lower rate (but you can add on the Work Related Activity Component to your basic rate of ESA), and you have to participate in work-related activity. You will be in what is commonly called the 'Work-Related Activity Group'.

If you are in the Work-Related Activity Group, you will also have a Work-Focused Health Related Assessment. This checks your barriers to paid work and how these might be managed or reduced. The assessment also asks for your views on your situation and your aspirations. These will go into a capability report which is given to you and your personal adviser.

Work-Related Activity Group

If you qualify for the Work-Related Activity Component because you do not have LCWRA, you will have a further five Work Focused Interviews (WFIs) with your personal adviser. The interviews will usually be held monthly, unless there is a reason for them to be deferred (you have no right to appeal a decision not to defer a WFI, though you could use the DWP's complaints procedure and take judicial review or ombudsman action).

You must attend and participate in the WFIs, which means that you must give details of your qualifications, education, plans for work, and so on, and also agree to an Action Plan. The Action Plan sums up the WFI and lists the jobsearch and training activities you are willing to do, and anything else that is relevant to finding or staying in work. This could include drawing up a CV, taking steps to improve your health, doing some voluntary work or training, and looking for suitable jobs.

Even though you have to agree to the Action Plan, at present you are not required to carry out anything specific in the Plan (though this may change in the future). The Plan must be in writing and a copy of the Plan must be given to you.

If you fail to attend or participate in a WFI, or to draw up an Action Plan, and you do not notify the DWP within five working days that you had good cause for not attending or participating, then your ESA Work Related Activity Component will be sanctioned. This means that it is reduced by 50 per cent for four weeks and then by 100 per cent until you either attend and participate in WFIs or qualify for the Support Component. As soon as you either attend and participate in WFIs or qualify for the Support Component, the sanction will be lifted but not backdated. The basic rate of ESA cannot be sanctioned.

When deciding whether or not you have good cause for not attending or participating in a WFI, the DWP must take a number of things into account.[19] You can have good cause if you:

- did not understand the need to take part in the WFI because of learning, language or literacy difficulties, or because you were given misleading information by government staff

- had transport difficulties and no reasonable alternative was available
- were attending an interview with an employer
- were following up employment opportunities as a self-employed earner
- were attending a medical or dental appointment and it was unreasonable in the circumstances to change the appointment
- were accompanying someone for whom you have caring responsibilities to a medical or dental appointment, and it was unreasonable for that person to change their appointment
- had an accident, sudden illness or relapse of a physical or mental condition, or your dependant or someone you care for had an accident, sudden illness or relapse of a physical or mental condition
- were attending the funeral of a relative or close friend on the day of your WFI
- have a physical or mental condition which made it impossible to attend at the time and place fixed for the interview, or
- the established customs and practices of your religion stopped you attending on that day or at that time.

The DWP will also take into account anything else which it deems appropriate.

The DWP has set up many safeguards to help you avoid sanctions. These include contacting you before the WFI to remind you to attend, offering alternative times, dates and venues for the WFI, visiting you at home when there has been no verbal contact before the WFI, and visiting you at home if you have a mental health problem or learning disability.

The personal advisers' work may be done by organisations under contract to DWP (including private companies). These companies do not have the power to sanction you, but they will pass on information about sanctions to DWP Decision Makers.

Employment and Support Allowance amounts

Contributory ESA and Income-Related ESA are paid at the same rate. During the Assessment Phase, ESA is paid at the same rate as Income Support and Jobseeker's Allowance.

Income-Related ESA can be increased to include premiums (for example, if you are a carer) and housing costs for owner-occupiers. There is no disability premium for Income-Related ESA because this has been subsumed into the main rates.

Income is assessed for Income-Related ESA in the same way it is assessed for Income Support (see page 53).

There is no special rate for couples who are claiming the Work Related Activity Component or the Support Component. If both members of a couple qualify for ESA, double amounts of the Work Related Activity Component or the Support Component are paid.

The ESA rates are at page 364.

Working while on Employment and Support Allowance

You can do a limited amount of work while you get ESA. The same rules about work apply to both contributory ESA and Income-Related ESA.

You are allowed to do:[20]

- work for which the earnings in any week do not exceed £20, or
- work for which the earnings in any week do not exceed £93, and which is:
    - part of a treatment programme under medical supervision, or
    - done while you are a hospital in- or out-patient, or
    - supervised by someone from a public, local authority or a voluntary body involved in providing work for people who have a disability
- work for less than 16 hours per week (on average), where your earnings in any week do not exceed £93, and where you do not do this work for more than 52 weeks (if you have done this kind of work

before while you were on ESA, and you want to do the work again, you must either wait 52 weeks from the last period of work, or stop claiming ESA for at least 12 weeks)

- work for less than 16 hours per week (on average), where your earnings in any week do not exceed £93, if you are on the ESA Support Component
- work while self-employed under an approved training programme
- voluntary or unpaid work where it is reasonable to work without pay (you can be paid out-of-pocket expenses)
- work on an unpaid work placement approved in advance by DWP
- domestic tasks carried out for a relative or in your own home, or
- work in an emergency to protect people, property or livestock.

If you do any other work (paid or unpaid), or if you exceed the average earnings limit or the working hours limit in any week, you will be disqualified for ESA because you will not count as having LCW.[21]

If you have a partner who is in paid work for 24 or more hours per week, you cannot get Income-Related ESA.

If you earn more than £20 per week and you also get Housing Benefit, this can be affected (but this will change in April 2010).

People on work-based training

Trainees who are employed will normally qualify for Statutory Sick Pay. Those who are not employees will usually qualify for ESA.

Switching from Jobseeker's Allowance to Employment and Support Allowance during illness

If you are claiming Jobseeker's Allowance and you are sick for more than two weeks, or if you expect your sickness to last for more than two weeks, you will have to make a claim for ESA instead.

You should notify Jobcentre Plus as soon as you are sick because you can continue to claim Jobseeker's Allowance for up to two weeks, despite being unfit for work.[i] If you are unable to visit Jobcentre Plus to sign on because of your sickness, you should also tell them straight away so that your payments aren't disrupted. The Jobcentre should then send you a form so that you can notify them about your sickness. You must complete and return this form to safeguard your benefit. You can receive Jobseeker's Allowance while sick for up to two fortnights out of every 12 months that you claim the benefit.

If you fail to sign on at Jobcentre Plus on the right day, you have five working days to sign a written declaration stating that you had good cause for not signing-on on your normal day. Good cause might include a few days of sickness. Your Jobseeker's Allowance claim should not be stopped because you could not sign on due to sickness (but payment of your benefit will be delayed).[ii]

[i] Reg 55 Jobseeker's Allowance Regulations 1996 [ii] Reg 24 Jobseeker's Allowance Regulations 1996

Accidents or diseases which are related to work or training **UK**

If you have an accident or contract a 'prescribed disease' in the course of your work or work-based learning, and 15 weeks later you are still suffering some disability because of the accident or disease, you may qualify for Industrial Injuries Disablement Benefit (IIDB). (You can see the full list of prescribed diseases in the Child Poverty Action Group's Welfare Benefits and Tax Credits Handbook and Disability Rights Handbook, and there is some information in DWP leaflet SD 6, 'Ill or Disabled because of a disease or deafness caused by work?' You can also find information at www.jobcentreplus.gov.uk.)

Employed learners can make a claim for IIDB through Jobcentre Plus. Unwaged learners or trainees can make a claim for IIDB through the Analogous Industrial Injuries Scheme.

The Analogous Industrial Injuries Scheme (AIIS) is a discretionary scheme which uses the same guidance, doctors and benefit rates as Jobcentre Plus. It covers non-employed learners on work-based learning that is either funded by the Learning and Skills Council, and its equivalent groups in Scotland and Wales, or by the DWP. The scheme does not cover work experience placements, or any non-employed status learning that might be arranged privately, through schools or further education colleges.

How to claim

If you have an accident or contract a prescribed disease because of your work, you should tell your employer and learning provider as soon as possible. Your learning provider must send a report to the Learning and Skills Council.

If you do not have employed status, the Learning and Skills Council will send the report to the AIIS team. The AIIS team will write to you with information about the scheme and invite you to start the claims process.

If you have employed status, it is up to you to start the claims process by contacting your local Jobcentre Plus office, or you can download a form from the Jobcentre Plus website.

Making a claim to Disablement Benefit does not mean that you cannot take legal action against your employer or training provider. However, if you are awarded compensation by the court, this may be reduced to take the benefits you receive into account. DWP booklet GL27, 'Compensation and social security benefits', has more details.

You can contact the AIIS at: Analogous Industrial Injuries Scheme, Jobcentre Plus, Castleford IIDB Centre, Leodis Way, Leeds, LS88 8AQ, or you can phone them on 01977 464094.

What happens next?

Depending on your employment status, a Decision Maker from either Jobcentre Plus or the AIIS team will decide if your accident counts as an industrial accident and send you a copy of the decision. If your accident is accepted, you can make a claim for the benefit.

If you have contracted a prescribed disease, a decision will not normally be made until you have a medical examination.

If the doctor decides that your disability is at least 14 per cent, the rate of IIDB you receive will depend on the extent of your disability. You don't need to show that you are permanently disabled, because awards can range from a few months to a lifetime. You can receive IIDB 15 weeks after the date of your accident, or the date you contracted the prescribed disease. (Even if you continued with your training during these 15 weeks, you can still apply for IIDB.) IIDB does not depend on National Insurance contributions.

If you are awarded IIDB at 100 per cent and you need daily care and attention, you may be able to claim Constant Attendance Allowance.

If you have received a means-tested benefit (for example, Income Support, Income-Based JSA, or Income-Related ESA) since your accident, you may not be able to claim some or any arrears of disablement benefits. IIDB counts as income for income-based benefits, so if you are getting a means-tested benefit now, this benefit may be reduced by the amount of IIDB you receive. IIDB is not affected by Incapacity Benefit, Statutory Sick Pay, Training Allowance or earnings.

Appeals UK

To appeal against a Decision Maker's decision, you should follow the advice on the decision letter. Take note of any time limits for making an appeal. You may have to attend a medical examination to make sure the decision on your claim is fair.

Financial support for young people who are looked after by local authorities or who have left care E W S

If you are looked after by a local authority (in local care), or if you have been looked after in the past and you are currently under 18, you may be barred from claiming some benefits. But you may be entitled to receive extra help and support from the local authority which was legally responsible for you, or even from the council where you currently live.

The Social Services Department (in Scotland, the Social Work Department) is the part of the local authority which may have a duty of care to help you. This department may also be known as Children's Service or Children and Families Service.

The Children (Leaving Care) Act 2000

This law which sets out the support a care leaver should get came into force in England and Wales in October 2001. A similar law came into force in Scotland in April 2004. The law applies to most (but not all) young people who are in, or who have just left, local authority care. Your social worker will be able to tell you if it applies to you.

This legislation amended the Children Act 1989, but it only applies to young people who leave care after October 2001. From April 2004, the Children (Scotland) Act 1995 was also amended along the same lines. A young person who left the care of a Scottish local authority before 1 April 2004 is not included.

You are covered by this legislation in England and Wales if you are an 'eligible', 'relevant' or 'former relevant' young person. There are also 'qualifying' young people who are covered.

In Scotland there are groups of young people who are classed as 'compulsorily supported', 'currently looked after' or 'discretionarily supported' under the law.[24]

If you are looked after by a local authority for at least 13 weeks after your 14th birthday, including a period when you are aged 16, the local authority should tell you which category you fall into.[25] In Scotland, if you are looked after by a local authority within three months of becoming compulsorily supported, or within three months of asking for help, the local authority should tell you which category you fall into.

If you are classed as a relevant or eligible young person according to the law (or the equivalent in Scotland), the local authority must assess your current and future needs within three months of your 16th birthday. The assessment should consider your training, education and employment needs, your need for financial support, your accommodation and other matters.[26] The local authority will then make a Pathway Plan which explains how your needs will be met.[27]

The Pathway Plan explains the support you will get after leaving care. It also states who your leaving-care personal adviser is. The Pathway Plan must be reviewed at least every six months (or sooner, if you ask for a review, or if your personal adviser feels it should be reviewed). If you are not happy with the Pathway Plan, you can make a formal complaint as well as asking for a review.

Eligible young people

You are eligible if you are 16 or 17, are currently looked after by a local authority and you have been looked after by a local authority for at least 13 weeks since the age of 14. The 13 weeks don't have to be continuous. However, if you spent regular, short periods in care and you returned to live with your parents afterwards (for example because you have a disability and go into respite care), these periods do not count towards the 13 weeks.

Relevant young people

You are relevant if you are 16 or 17 and have been looked after by a local authority for at least 13 weeks since you were 14 years old, but you are no longer looked after. You are also relevant if you have been looked after for at least 13 weeks since you were 14 years old, but when you turned 16, you were in custody or hospital.

Former relevant young people

You are classed as a former relevant young person if you were either a relevant or eligible young person, and you are now aged 18, 19 or 20. There is no equivalent in Scotland.

Qualifying young person

You are a qualifying young person (or a compulsorily supported person in Scotland) if you:

- are currently under 18, and
- were in care at the age of 16, and
- have been in care for less than 13 weeks since you turned 14.

You are still a qualifying young person even if you are not currently in care.

A discretionarily supported person

You are a discretionarily supported young person if you are aged 19 or 20, have been looked after at any time since the age of 16, but are not a compulsorily supported person.

Child in need

You may get help with accommodation, finances and other things if you are classed as a child in need because of special needs, poverty, poor housing, ill-health, family or other difficulties.[28] This help is known as Section 17 Payment and Support in England and Wales and Section 22 in Scotland. All payments under this legislation do not count as income for benefits, but may be taken into account if they are meeting a need which you claim a Social Fund crisis loan for, or if you are claiming Jobseeker's Allowance on the grounds of severe hardship.

Under Section 17 (Section 22 in Scotland), a local authority cannot have blanket rules to restrict who it will help or how it will help them.[29] Acting unreasonably or failing to act reasonably can leave a local authority open to legal challenge.[30]

If you are a child in need, and you are getting help under Section 17 (Section 22 in Scotland), there are no restrictions on the benefits you can claim, other than the restrictions that apply to all those aged 16 to 17.

However, if you get help with accommodation or money on an ongoing basis under Section 17 or Section 22, Jobcentre Plus staff might refuse you benefits on the grounds that you are actually an eligible, relevant or former relevant young person.[31] Your benefits should not be refused if you received support for accommodation under Section 17 or Section 22 after 7 November 2002, because from this date the law was amended so people who were provided only with accommodation under Section 17 or Section 22 do not count as being 'looked after'.

According to case law,[32] if you are supported after the age of 16 under Section 17 or Section 22, and you are given accommodation and lots of help, then your local authority may be required to give you the same kind of support that care-leavers receive. However, you may need legal advice to make sure that Social Services or the Social Work Department gives you support in these circumstances.

The DWP set out guidance in 2003,[33] but it isn't very clear about support for a child in need. You might find that your rights to benefits are limited. Currently, this aspect of the law is not settled, and it would be worthwhile to challenge any decisions that are not made in your favour.

Benefits for young people in care and care-leavers

If you are an eligible or relevant young person in England or Wales, or you are compulsorily supported or currently looked after in Scotland, you can't receive Housing Benefit or Jobseeker's Allowance at all.[34] You can only receive Income Support, if you are:

- a lone parent (including those still in education), or
- a single foster parent, or
- sick or disabled, and you have been getting Income Support since before October 2008, when ESA was introduced.

If you have a child in care you can still access all other benefits (Child Benefit, Child Tax Credits, Health in Pregnancy Grant, Healthy Start Vouchers and maternity grant after the child is born).

If you have a Limited Capacity for Work (see the section on ESA) you may be able to claim ESA while you are an eligible or relevant young person (or the Scottish equivalent). This applies even if you are still in education.

Your right to benefits is only restricted until you are 18. If you are an 18 year old care-leaver and you are still in full-time non-advanced education you may be entitled to Income Support on the grounds of 'estrangement' until you turn 21. This is the case whether you are living on your own or with former foster-carers, but not if you return home to parents. If you go back home to live with parents or other adults, you will be barred from claiming Jobseeker's Allowance for six months, or until you turn 18, whichever comes first. You could get Income Support or ESA during those six months if you are in any of the categories described above.[35] Your parents may also be able to re-qualify for Child Benefit and Child Tax Credit if you are still in non-advanced education.

If you are a relevant or eligible young person (or the equivalent in Scotland), you can claim all other benefits besides Jobseeker's Allowance and Housing Benefit – for example, you can claim Disability Living Allowance, Carer's Allowance and Child Benefit if you meet the rules for those benefits. But even if you can claim Income Support or ESA, you are still barred from claiming Housing Benefit until you are 18.

If you are a qualifying young person, you can claim any benefit, as long as you meet the rules of entitlement, including the rules of entitlement for those aged 16 and 17 to receive Jobseeker's Allowance (see page 42).

Sometimes there is confusion about which benefits you can claim when you turn 18 and remain living with your former foster carers. At that point, you can claim Jobseeker's Allowance in your own right without restriction, or Income Support on the grounds that you are in education and estranged from your parents (if you have not already been eligible to claim Income Support or ESA when you were 16 or 17). You can also claim Housing Benefit if your former foster carers charge you rent. [36]

Rights to financial support from Social Services (or the Social Work Department in Scotland)

If you are an eligible, relevant, or former relevant young person (or, for Scotland, if you are looked after, or were looked after for at least 13 weeks since the age of 14, or are a compulsorily supported person), you have rights to financial and other support from the local authority which last looked after you. Qualifying young people (and, in Scotland, discretionarily supported people) can get help on a discretionary basis.

Pathway Plan

If you are a relevant, eligible, or former relevant young person, your Pathway Plan will set out the support you need and what you can expect to receive. Specifically the Plan must include information about the following:[37]

* Personal support accommodation

- Education or training
- Employment or other activity or occupation
- Family and social relationships
- Practical and other skills for independent living
- Financial support
- Health needs
- Back-up plans in case the Pathway Plan breaks down

Pathway Plans should build on any education plans and intentions you already have, and they must show how Social Services will help you to stay in or move into education, training or employment.

Relevant and eligible young people

Social Services must have clear criteria for the financial support they will give relevant and eligible young people. They must keep a list of what they will normally give financial help for, and how they will treat any income you may have.[38]

Things which should be a priority for financial support are:

- travel costs (for example, for education)
- educational materials or special equipment
- other educational costs
- costs linked to special needs (such as a disability or pregnancy)
- the cost of childcare
- clothing
- contact with family or other significant people
- cultural or religious needs
- counselling or therapeutic needs, and
- hobbies or holidays.

Your rights to financial support must be fully explained to you. The above list is not a complete list of costs that can be met, and there is no set amount of money which Social Services should provide, because their support is meant to reflect an individual's needs. Social Services may decide to apply sanctions (such as taking away your privileges), but not so much that you don't have enough to live on. Either with or without a sanction, you must get at least the amount of help that you would receive through the benefit system.[39]

Some local councils are more generous than the benefit system. They may pay rewards for attending training or finding a job. If you get an Education Maintenance Allowance, the council may decide that this acts as your reward for staying in education. But if you have an income from work or training, the council can ask you to contribute to the cost of your care, rent, and so on. However, they must take your personal circumstances into account, and not just apply blanket rules about how much you should contribute. If you are aged 16 or 17, you are looked after and getting Income Support (or your level of income is equal to Income Support), you cannot be asked to contribute to the cost of your care. If you are working or have an income from training, the council can ask you to contribute to the cost of your care, but they have to ask you properly, using a contribution notice.

If you are unhappy with either the financial support you receive, or the amount you have to contribute to the cost of your care, you should make a formal complaint and think about taking further action against Social Services. In Scotland this is known as 'an appeal'.[40]

Former relevant young people

If you are a former relevant young person aged under 21, Social Services must provide you with:

- a leaving-care grant (this should be enough to set up home, and the grant may need to cover more than one attempt to set up home)
- enough financial support for you to finish education (even if this takes you beyond the age of 21), including travel, accommodation, maintenance, tuition and vacation time accommodation
- financial help so that you can take part in, or look for, training or employment if you are under 24, and
- discretionary financial help if needed for your welfare.[41]

Qualifying young people

If you are a qualifying young person under the age of 21, Social Services must:[42]

- advise and befriend you
- when needed, provide help in kind (or discretionary help in cash in exceptional circumstances)
- give financial help with education, training or employment (which may continue beyond 21), and
- help you if other needs arise.

Social Services must also give care leavers practical help and support to claim benefits.

Payments made to care leavers under the Children Act (and equivalent Scottish and Northern Ireland legislation) do not count as income and capital for all means-tested benefits and tax credits, unless you are involved in a trade dispute.[43]

Housing Benefit

The Shared Room Rate restriction is the rule which restricts your Housing Benefit for rent in the private unregulated sector to the average rent for a one bedroom property with shared facilities.[44] If you are under 22, and were looked after by a local authority for any length of time at all (even just one night) after you were 16, the Shared Room Rate restriction doesn't apply. Because Housing Benefit claim forms do not usually ask about your care-leaver status, it is important to make sure you are exempt from the restriction and also tell the local authority that you are claiming Housing Benefit.

However, you may still be restricted under the Housing Benefit rules for private tenants (see page 324).

If you are in care, or you are a care-leaver with restricted access to benefits, you can't get Housing Benefit until you are aged 18. This is the case even if you are in one of the groups which qualify for Income Support or ESA.

Leaving Care Grant

When you leave care at age 18, the local authority may give you a grant to help to set you up in a place of your own. You may also get this grant some time after you have turned 18, if you don't need the money until later on. When you're setting up your own home, you might qualify for a Social Fund grant, too (see page 91).

Young people who need support with housing costs

Housing Benefit

What is Housing Benefit?

Housing Benefit (HB) can help you pay some or all of your rent. HB is handled by your local council.

Who can claim Housing Benefit?

You can claim HB if you have to pay rent (or other payments) to live somewhere (including a hostel, flat, house or room). There is no lower age limit for HB. However, you can't get HB for rent you pay to your parents or other close relatives if you live with them at the same address. 'Close relatives' include brothers and sisters, but not aunts, uncles, cousins or grandparents. However, if the council think that you have set up a tenancy with a relative (or anyone else) just to misuse the HB scheme, they can refuse to pay it. This applies whether or not you are living at the same address as the person who gives you a tenancy.

To claim HB, you must have less than £16,000 in savings or capital and you must also be on a low income. The amount of HB you get depends on your income and family circumstances.

You do not need to receive Income Support (IS), Income-Based Jobseeker's Allowance (JSA (IB)) or Income-Related Employment and Support Allowance (ESA (IR)) in order to claim HB, but if you do (or if your income is at the same level as these benefits), you will qualify for the maximum amount of HB.

Even if you pay rent, you can't get HB if you are:

- a student, unless you are in a group which qualifies for IS, ESA (IR) or JSA (IB), or you are aged under 19 and not in higher education (university degree or above), or you are a lone parent, disabled, or have consent to be absent from your course because of illness or caring responsibilities[45], or

- not renting on a commercial basis.[46]

If you are told you are excluded from getting HB for any reason, you should get advice then think about whether you want to and submit an appeal to a tribunal if you disagree with that decision.

How much is Housing Benefit?

Your HB can be reduced because of where you live or the type of accommodation you live in (for example, if your accommodation is too large for you). This reduction depends on who provides your accommodation and what age you are. If you rent your home from a local authority or housing association, then most of these restrictions usually don't apply. However, if your accommodation is too large for you (for example, a two-bedroom flat for a single person), then your HB may be cut to the rate of a one-bedroom flat.

If you rent from a private landlord (not including a housing association), then the amount of rent you can claim for HB will be restricted to the Local Housing Allowance (LHA) rate for the area you live in, for the type of accommodation you have, and for your family size and make-up. Staff at the Valuation Office Agency (previously the Rent Service), which is independent from the local authority, sets the figures for the LHA.

You can find out the LHA rate for your area at www.voa.gov.uk/LHADirect/index.htm

If your rent is more than the LHA, you will have to pay the shortfall. If your rent is less than the LHA, you can keep up to £15 extra per week and this won't affect your other benefits.

Your age

If you are under 25 and have a private landlord, your LHA is set at the 'shared room rate'. This is the amount for a one bedroom property with shared facilities. [48]

You won't be affected by the Shared Room Rate rule if you:

• have a child or a 'non-dependant' living with you, or
• are severely disabled and get a severe disability premium with your HB, IS, ESA (IR) or JSA, or
• were accommodated by social services or were in care, and the court order still applied to you after you were 16 (you will not be affected by the rule until you turn 21). [49]

Most young people aged 16 or 17 who are, or were, in care will not be able to claim HB until they reach 18 (see the rules about who can claim HB after being in care on page 323).

Even if you are exempt from the Shared Room Rate rule, the LHA can still affect you. Many people renting in the private sector find that their HB does not cover all of their rent because the LHA is too low. If this applies to you, see the information about Discretionary Housing Payments on page 331.

How Housing Benefit is calculated

People on Income Support, Income-Based Jobseeker's Allowance or Income-Related Employment and Support Allowance

If you get IS, JSA (IB), or ESA (IR), your HB will cover your maximum eligible rent. However, as explained in the last section, your eligible rent is not the same as the amount of rent you actually have to pay.

Other people who are on a low income

If you claim other benefits besides HB, or if you are on a low income or training allowance, then the local authority has to calculate your HB by first working out how much of your income is above the fixed amounts (set out in Appendix 2), and then deducting 65 per cent of that excess income from your eligible rent. The fixed amounts are called 'Applicable

Amounts' and they are made up of personal allowances and premiums (set out in Appendix 2). If you think that you are entitled to more benefit than you are getting, you should ask the local authority to explain their calculation.

The 65 per cent of excess income is called a 'taper' because as your excess income goes up, your benefit tapers down. If you have too much excess income, you will not qualify for HB.

Non-dependants

A non-dependant is someone aged 18 or over who is not part of your benefit claim. They must be normally living with you in order to be classed as a non-dependant.

Some non-dependants are ignored – for example, other tenants or lodgers, or your landlord (if you live with your landlord and pay them rent, or if the landlord receives Attendance Allowance or the Disability Living Allowance care component).[50]

Your HB is reduced for every non-dependant who lives with you (unless you are in a couple). The law assumes that non-dependants will contribute towards your rent, whether or not they actually do so. The amount the law expects non-dependants to contribute depends on their income.[51] It is important to check that your HB is being reduced by the right amount, and to also tell the local authority if the non-dependant's income changes.

Your HB should not be reduced if you are registered as blind or if you get the Disability Living Allowance care component (see page 299).[52]

If you are 18 or over and you normally live with someone who gets either HB, or help from IS or JSA (IB) towards their mortgage interest, you will count as a non-dependant. This means you will have to pay the person you live with to make up the cut in their benefit. This can be quite high – from £7.40 per week (if you are 18 and getting JSA based on your National Insurance contributions) up to £47.75 per week (if you earn more than £382 per week). If you are aged under 18 (or aged under 25 and getting your own means-tested benefit), the HB of the person you live with should not be reduced because you live with them.

Occupying the home **UK**

You must normally live in the home for which you are claiming HB, but you can live away from home for up to 13 weeks without losing your benefit. The 13 weeks restart when you return home, even if you return for only one night. While you are away, you must have plans to return home, and you must not sub-let your home to someone else.[53] Your reason for being away from home will not affect your benefit. Other benefits have less generous rules if you are not living in your home, so get advice if you plan to go away.

You can get HB for your home for up to 52 weeks if you have a specific reason for living somewhere else (for example, if you are remanded in custody and you are awaiting trial or you are in hospital).

If you move from one home to another

If you move to a new home while you are claiming HB for your old home, you may be able to get HB for both homes for up to four weeks. To get this help, you must have actually moved into the new home, and your local authority must agree that you could not have reasonably avoided paying rent for both your new home and your old home at the same time. For example, you have moved because a training place or job has started unexpectedly, or you had to accept a tenancy offer straight away, before you could give your landlord enough notice. You can only get HB for both homes if you have actually moved into your new home and you started claiming HB before you moved in. You also have to claim again after you move in.[54]

If you move because you are afraid that violence may occur to you in your home, or that an ex-partner or family member may treat you violently in your home or home area, you will be able to get HB for more than one home. In cases of violence, you can get HB for both homes for up to 52 weeks, so long as you intend to return to your old home at some point, and so long as your local authority agrees that it is reasonable to pay HB for both. If you do not intend to return home, then you can only get HB for both homes for up to four weeks. There are some other circumstances when you may be able to get HB for both homes, so get advice.

How to claim Housing Benefit **UK**

You can get HB claim forms from your local council. If you claim IS, JSA (IB) or ESA (IR), you can fill out a HB claim form as part of your claim pack. Your local authority may send you more claim forms after you have given them your first form because they may need more information from you, and you must fill out these extra forms as well.

You might think that filling out the HB claim form with your IS, ESA or JSA claim is enough. However, because of the way the claim system works, you sometimes have to fill out the HB claim form twice. Recent government changes have tried to prevent the need to fill out the form twice, but if the council sends you another claim form, then you should complete it and return it as quickly as you can. You have one month to return the form from the time the council says it sent the form to you, even if they sent it some weeks before you got it.

If you can, try to get confirmation from the local council that they received your form. For example, try to get a receipt if you take the form to them. It is not always possible to get proof, but you can make your own note of when you returned the form or who you spoke to.

If you have missed out on claiming HB, you can ask for your claim to be backdated for up to six months from the date when you ask for backdating. Your claim will be backdated if you show that you have 'good cause' for claiming late.[55] 'Good cause' for a late claim is not clearly defined, but includes:

- a sickness or disability which prevented you from claiming
- difficult personal circumstances which prevented you from claiming
- problems with literacy and language
- being young and not knowing the benefit rules.

You can appeal against a refusal to backdate a HB claim.

Evidence and information for your claim [56]

The council can ask you to give evidence and information which is 'reasonably required' to assess your HB claim. If you don't provide this evidence and information, the council must decide on your right to HB, and not just shut down your claim. If the evidence does not exist or if getting the evidence is costly or risky, it is not reasonable for the council to require it, and you should insist that the council process your claim with only the evidence and information you can provide. The council should give you one month (or longer where reasonable) to provide evidence and information.

Delays

The council has a legal duty to process your claim within 14 days of receiving all the information it needs.[57] Very few councils meet this legal deadline. If you are a private tenant (including a housing association tenant), the council also has a legal duty to make a payment on account of HB 14 days after you make your claim, unless they have asked you for evidence and information and you have failed to provide it without a good reason.[58] Very few councils stick to the law and make payments on account automatically, so you should ask for a payment to be made. The council can only refuse to pay you if they have asked you for the evidence and information and you don't have a good reason for not giving it to them.

Who receives the Housing Benefit payments?

If you pay rent to the council, then your HB will be credited to your rent account. If you are renting from a private landlord, your HB will be paid to you, unless you owe eight or more weeks of rent arrears, or if you are unlikely to pay your rent.

If you rent from a housing association, your HB may be paid directly to you, or it can be paid to your landlord instead. It will be paid to your landlord if you ask for this to be done, if it is in your interests, or if you owe eight or more weeks of rent arrears and your landlord asks for the payment.

If your circumstances change, you must tell your local authority in writing. If your IS, JSA or ESA stops, this can affect your HB.

If you do not tell the council about changes of circumstances, you may have to repay any overpayment.

Start of the payment period

The usual rule is that HB will start on the Monday after the date you claim for HB. Even if the date you claimed was a Monday, HB will start the next Monday. However, if you claim for HB in the same benefit week that you move into your home and first become liable for rent, your HB should be paid from the day your liability to pay rent started.

Overpayments[59]

Overpayments are amounts of HB which you received but shouldn't have received. The council can claim overpayments back from you. However, if the overpayment was made because of an 'official error', then the council cannot claim it back unless it is reasonable for them to expect you to realise that you were overpaid.

An overpayment can only be claimed back from the person who caused the overpayment. In the past, overpayments could be claimed back from your landlord receiving HB, and this caused rent arrears. Now, overpayments can only be claimed back if the landlord knew about your circumstances and did not tell the council.[60]

Discretionary housing payments[61]

Your local council can give Discretionary Housing Payments (DHP) if they think you need extra help to meet your housing costs. Because DHPs are discretionary, you cannot insist on one. The amount of DHP and the period it is granted for are also discretionary. There are limits to the amount that can be paid to you by the council and DHPs are not a long-term solution. You cannot appeal to an independent tribunal about a discretionary decision, but you can ask the council to look at their decision again if you do not agree with it.

DHPs can be useful if you don't qualify for maximum HB, if your HB is reduced for non-dependants, or if you are a private tenant and your HB does not cover all of your rent.

Extended payments of Housing Benefit

If you have been receiving IS, JSA (IB) or ESA for at least 26 weeks and your right to benefit stops because you have started work or increased your hours of work to 16 or more per week, you can qualify for up to four weeks of maximum HB. To receive the extra HB, you should tell either Jobcentre Plus or the HB service within four weeks of starting your job or increasing your hours. If you just stop signing on as unemployed, you will not receive the extra money.

Challenging decisions – appeals and the ombudsman

Your local council must send you a written notice about any decision it makes on your HB claim. If your claim is 'stuck' (and is not being sorted out because the council are waiting for information from you or your landlord), you can insist that the council make a decision based only on the evidence that they already have. The decision may not be in your favour, but at least you can appeal and get the claim moving again. If you do not qualify for HB, the notice will give reasons. If you want to know more about how your HB was worked out, you can write to your local authority and ask for a written statement. You have the right to ask your local authority to reconsider their decision on almost all matters relating to your HB.

If you don't agree with the council's decision, you can write to them and say that you want to appeal against their decision, stating the reason why. After you appeal, the local council will consider changing their decision. If they don't, they will send your appeal to an independent tribunal who can submit their own decision on your case. The tribunal usually involves just one person, not a court. You don't have to attend the tribunal, but you stand a much better chance of winning if you do. You must appeal within one month of the first decision being sent out, but you may be able to appeal more than one month after the date of the decision if you can show good reasons for the appeal being late. If it is 13 or more months since you got the decision, you cannot appeal at all. You can get more information from www.tribunals.gov.uk. If you don't want to appeal, just write to the council and ask them to reconsider their decision.

The local government ombudsman

You can complain to the local government ombudsman if you think the council dealt with your claim unfairly or caused unreasonable delays. The ombudsman is separate from the appeal system. Get information on complaining to the ombudsman from your local library or advice centre, or by going to www.lgo.org.uk.

Endnotes

1   Reg. 33 Social Security (Claims and Payments) Regulations 1987

2   S 72 (1) (a) Social Security Contributions and Benefits Act 1992

3   S 72 (1) (b) Social Security Contributions and Benefits Act 1992

4   S 72 (4) (a) Social Security Contributions and Benefits Act 1992

5   S 73 (1) (d) Social Security Contributions and Benefits Act 1992

6   S73 (1) (a) & (2) &(3) Social Security Contributions and Benefits Act 1992

7   S 72 (2) & S 73 (9) Social Security Contributions and Benefits Act 1992

8   The six week deadline can be extended where you have a good reason for not meeting it.

9   S 72(8) Social Security Contributions and Benefits Act 1992 & Regs 9, 10 & 12A Social Security (Disability Living Allowance) Regulations 1991

10   Reg 9 Social Security (Disability Living Allowance) Regulations 1991

11   Para 4, Sch. 1 Welfare Reform Act 2007

12   Regs 8-3 Employment and Support Allowance Regulations 2008

13   Regs 4-7 Employment and Support Allowance Regulations 2008

14   Regs 19-21 Employment and Support Allowance Regulations 2008

15   Regs 32, 33 Employment and Support Allowance Regulations 2008

16   CIB/26/2004 and CSIB/33/2004

17   CIB/3519/2002

18   Regs 34-36 Employment and Support Allowance Regulations 2008

19   Reg. 61(3) Employment and Support Allowance Regulations 2008

20   Reg. 45 ESA Employment and Support Allowance Regulations 2008

21   Reg. 40 (1) Employment and Support Allowance Regulations 2008

22   Reg. 55 Jobseeker's Allowance Regulations 1996

23   Reg 24 Jobseeker's Allowance Regulations 1996

24   S 29 Children (Scotland) Act 1995

25   Reg. 7 Children (Leaving Care) Regulations & Guidance & Reg. 9 The Support and Assistance of Young people Leaving Care (Scotland) Regulations 2003

26   Reg. 7 The Children (Leaving Care) (England) Regulations 2001 & Schedule 2 The Support and Assistance of Young People Leaving Care (Scotland) Regulations 2003

27   Para 19B (4) Schedule 2 Children Act 1989 & Reg. 8 The Support and Assistance of Young People Leaving Care (Scotland) Regulations 2003

28   S 17 Children Act 1989 & S 22 Children (Scotland) Act 1995

29   Att Gen ex rel Tilley v London Borough of Wandsworth [1981] 1AER 1162

30   A v London Borough of Lambeth [2001] EWCA 1624

31   For example, see R v London Borough of Hillingdon ex p Berhe and others [2003] EWHC 2075.

32   R v London Borough of Hillingdon ex p Berhe and others

33   DMG JSA/IS 54

34   S 6 (1) Children Leaving Care Act 2000)

35   For all IS & JSA exceptions, see Reg. 2 The Children (Leaving Care) Social Security Benefits Regulations 2001 and Reg. 2(3) The Children (Leaving Care) Social Security Benefits (Scotland) Regulations 2004

36   Circular HB/CTB A30/95 para 17 iv

37   Dept of Health Guidance on Schedule 8 The Children (Leaving Care) Social Security Benefits Regulations 2001

38   Chapter 9 paras 5–6 Dept of Health Guidance on The Children (Leaving Care) Social Security Benefits Regulations 2001

39   Chapter 9 DoH Guidance ibid & Reg. 13 (3) The Support and Assistance of Young People Leaving Care (Scotland) Regulations 2003

40   Regs 16–19 The Support and Assistance of Young People Leaving Care (Scotland) Regulations 2003 and S 5B Social Work Scotland Act 1968

41   S 23C Children Act 1989 Ss. 29 & 30 Children (Scotland) Act 1995

42   S 24 Children Act 1989

43   Sch. 9 para. 28 Income Support (General) Regulations 1987, Sch 7 para. 29 Jobseeker's Allowance Regulations, Sch. 5 para. 28 Housing Benefit (General) Regulations 2006

44   Reg. 2 (1) Housing Benefit (General) Regulations 2006 – see definition of 'young individual'

45   Reg. 56 Housing Benefit (General) Regulations 2006

46   Reg. 9 Housing Benefit (General) Regulations 2006

47   Reg. 12 Housing Benefit (General) Regulations 2006

48   Reg. 2 (1) Housing Benefit Regulations 2006

49   Reg. 13 (D) Housing Benefit Regulations 2006

50   Reg. 3 (1), (2) Housing Benefit (General) Regulations 2006

Financial Support for Young People in Particular Circumstances

[51] Reg. 3 Housing Benefit (General) Regulations 2006

[52] Reg. 74 Housing Benefit (General) Regulations 2006

[53] Reg. 7 Housing Benefit (General) Regulations 2006

[54] Reg. 7 Housing Benefit (General) Regulations 2006

[55] Reg. 83 (12) Housing Benefit (General) Regulations 2006

[56] Reg. 86 Housing Benefit (General) Regulations 2006

[57] Regs 89 (2), 90(1) & 91 (3) Housing Benefit (General) Regulations 2006

[58] Reg. 93 Housing Benefit (General) Regulations 2006

[59] Reg. 99 Housing Benefit (General) Regulations 2006

[60] Reg. 101 (2) Housing Benefit (General) Regulations 2006

[61] The Discretionary Financial Assistance Regulations 2001

[61] S 182 Housing Act 1996

[61] The Homelessness (Priority Need for Accommodation) (England) Order 2002 SI no. 2051

[61] Allocation of Housing and Homelessness (Eligibility) (England) Regulations 2006, SI no. 1294

[61] S 188 Housing Act 1996

[61] S 202 of the Housing Act 1996

[61] If you are 16 or 17 and leave home without your parents' agreement, in theory they could ask for you to be made a Ward of Court. This means that no important decisions can be made about you unless the Court agrees. However, this very rarely happens. Your parents could also report you as missing to the police. However, if you are living somewhere, doing some type of education and you seem to be safe, the police may be reluctant to get involved.

[61] Ss 175–177 Housing Act 1996

[61] Ss 191(1), 191(2) and S 191(3) and Ss 196(1) and 196(2) and S 196(3) Housing Act 1996.

[61] Ss 17 and S 20 of the Children Act 1989

[61] R v Barnet LBC ex parte G: R v Lambeth LBC ex parte W: R v Lambeth ex parte A [2003] UKHL 57

[61] S 23B(8) Children Act 1989 as amended by S 2 Children (Leaving Care) Act 2000

[61] LA has a legal duty to assess a relevant child's needs – Part 2 para. 19B(4), Sch.2 and S 23B(3) Children Act 1989, as amended by Ss 1 and 2 Children (Leaving Care) Act 2000

[61] Ss 23B(3) and 23E Children Act 1989, as amended by Ss 2 and 3 Children (Leaving Care) Act 2000 and S 23B(2) AND 23D Children Act 1989, as amended by Ss 2 and 3 Children (Leaving Care) Act 2000

[61] S 1(3) Law of Property Act 1925

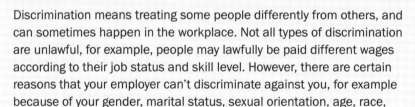

7 Moving into Work: Rights, Benefits and Equality

What is discrimination? UK

Discrimination means treating some people differently from others, and can sometimes happen in the workplace. Not all types of discrimination are unlawful, for example, people may lawfully be paid different wages according to their job status and skill level. However, there are certain reasons that your employer can't discriminate against you, for example because of your gender, marital status, sexual orientation, age, race, disability and religious beliefs.[1]

Equalities legislation UK

UK employment law gives all employees protection against discrimination in the workplace on the grounds of sex, race, age, disability, pregnancy, sexual orientation, religion and belief.

The following section provides you with some more detailed information about UK equalities legislation, the rights that these laws give you, what to do if you feel you have been the victim of discrimination and details of where you can access further information and support.

The Equality Bill[2]

The aim of the Equality Bill, which will come into force in autumn 2009, is to tackle discrimination of all kinds and in all forms, and to help make equality a reality for everyone. The Bill strengthens the law by, for example, banning age discrimination in the provision of goods, facilities or services, ensuring public bodies report on equality issues such as gender pay, and extending the period during which women-only shortlists are allowed. The Equality Bill also aims to support wider work to promote equality by, for example, ensuring the public sector has enough regard for equality when buying goods and services, and by supporting the work of the Equalities and Human Rights Commission.

The Bill brings together nine current laws relating to equality in a single Act, providing a clearer legal framework for equality and making the law easier to understand and put in place. The current laws the Equality Act will replace are:

- the Equal Pay Act 1970
- the Sex Discrimination Act 1975
- the Race Relations Act 1976
- the Disability Discrimination Act 1995
- much of the Equality Act 2006
- the Employment Equality (Religion or Belief) Regulations 2003
- the Employment Equality (Sexual Orientation) Regulations 2003
- the Employment Equality (Age) Regulations 2006
- the Equality Act (Sexual Orientation) Regulations 2007,

and other laws relating to equality.[3]

The Equality Bill was announced in the Queen's Speech in December 2008. It was published in April 2009 and is expected to come into force from autumn 2009.

The laws discussed in the following sections are those in place at the time of publication. The forthcoming Equality Act will replace all of these laws once it is in place.

The Equality Act 2006[4] 🇺🇰

The Equality Act 2006, which came into effect in the United Kingdom in April 2007, can be seen as a preview to the new Equality Bill in the way it simplifies the law on equality and discrimination. It was a big step forward in fighting unfair discrimination in the UK. The main steps of the Equality Act 2006 include:

- creating the Commission for Equality and Human Rights and defining its purpose and functions
- making it unlawful to discriminate against anyone on the grounds of religion or belief when providing goods, facilities and services, education, the use of premises, and the exercise of public functions
- allowing the government to introduce laws against discrimination on the grounds of sexual orientation when providing goods, facilities and services, education, the use of premises and the exercise of public functions, and
- creating a duty on public authorities to promote equality of opportunity between women and men, and prohibit sex discrimination and harassment in the exercise of public functions.

Sexual orientation, religion and belief 🇺🇰

The introduction of the Employment Equality (Sexual Orientation) Regulations 2003 and the Employment Equality (Religion or Belief) Regulations 2003 was a major step forward in tackling unfair discrimination in the UK. The Regulations implement parts of the European Employment Directive (Council Directive 2000/78/EC), and establish a general framework for equal treatment in employment.

The Employment Equality (Sexual Orientation) Regulations 2003 make it unlawful to discriminate against workers because of sexual orientation. These Regulations apply to vocational training and all aspects of employment, including recruitment, promotions, dismissals and training.[5]

The Employment Equality (Religion or Belief) Regulations 2003 make it unlawful to discriminate against workers because of religious or similar belief. Again, these regulations apply to vocational training and all aspects of employment, including recruitment, promotions, dismissals and training.[6]

Age discrimination 🆄🅺

Age discrimination is when someone is unfairly treated differently from others because of their age, and it can happen in all parts of the employment process, including recruitment, promotion, training and dismissal. Although age discrimination is something usually associated with older people, it can take place against young people too.

Age discrimination laws are in place to make sure that you are not denied a job, an equal chance of training or a promotion because of your age. They are also there to protect you from victimisation or harassment because of your age.[7]

The Employment Equality (Age) Regulations 2006

Legislation bans employers from discriminating on the grounds of age when:

- deciding whom to employ
- offering the terms of employment, and
- providing opportunities for promotion, training, transfer or any other benefit.[9]

The rights and responsibilities associated with these regulations apply to all employers.

Exceptions to the law

There are some important exceptions in this legislation. The following exceptions may be relevant to you.

National Minimum Wage

It is not unlawful for employees to receive different levels of pay based on their age if these differences are in line with the National Minimum

Wage rates for young workers.[10] This means, for example, that those aged 22 or over are legally entitled to earn more than those aged 21 or under.

The rates from 1 October 2008 are:

Population	Rate per hour (October 2008)
Workers over the age of 22	£5.73
Workers aged 18 to 21	£4.77
Workers aged 16 to 17	£3.53

These rates are usually updated in October of each year. You can find out the current National Minimum Wage by visiting www.hmrc.gov.uk/nmw.

These regulations are enforced by Her Majesty's Revenue and Customs (HMRC). If you would like more information or advice or would like to make a complaint you can call the National Minimum Wage helpline on 0845 600 0678.

Positive action

The term 'positive action' refers to a variety of measures designed to prevent discrimination, or to overcome the effects of past discrimination. Positive action is not about giving some people more favourable treatment than others in the recruitment process. Positive action initiatives are designed so that employers can encourage people from certain groups who are under-represented in the workplace to apply for jobs and promotions. While information and sometimes additional training can be given to under-represented applicants, final selection for job positions must always be made on merit.

Certain positive action initiatives are permitted by law, specifically:

- Sections 47 and 48 of the Sex Discrimination Act 1975
- Sections 37 and 38 of the Race Relations Act 1976

- Employment Equality Regulations for Religion and Belief and Sexual Orientation
- The Disability Discrimination Act
- The Government Two Ticks Scheme, introduced to support the employment of people with disabilities in a similar way.[11]

Positive action can also be taken against age-related discrimination. It is legal for employers to offer training, facilities or general encouragement to people from a particular age group if doing so is intended to compensate for employment disadvantages associated with people of that particular age group.[12]

One of the ways the Equality Bill aims to strengthen existing laws is by extending the scope for positive action to give employers a chance to make their workforce more diverse when choosing between two job candidates of equal merit (for example, by allowing a firm to choose a female candidate over a male candidate, if they are both of equal merit and women are under-represented in the firm).[13]

Exception for provision of certain benefits based on length of service

Employers are allowed to provide employees with benefits linked to their length of service.[14] This could mean that someone who has been working for your employer longer than you might be entitled to receive extra benefits, like higher pension contributions.

Employment rights 🆄🅺

Employment contract 🆄🅺

You are legally entitled to a contract from your employer within two months of starting a new job. This contract sets out the nature of your job and any terms and conditions associated with it. Your contract should include the following information:

- your name and the name of your employer
- the date employment started
- your rate of pay

- your hours of work and holiday entitlement
- the title and description of your job and your place of work
- your notice period
- details of your employer's grievance and disciplinary procedure
- if the employment is not permanent, the period for which it is expected to continue or, if it is fixed, the date on which it is to end[15]

Pay

Under the National Minimum Wage regulations, all workers are entitled to be paid at least the National Minimum Wage rate for each hour that they work (see page 341).[16]

The right to time off for study or training

No matter where you live, you have the right to paid time off work to study or train for approved qualifications (see page 107) if you:

- are an employee
- are aged 16 or 17
- are not in full-time education
- have no (or few) qualifications.

Working time regulations

Working time regulations for young workers

If you are aged 16 or 17, there are special rules to protect you from working too much daily and weekly. You may not ordinarily work more than:

- eight hours per day
- 40 hours per week.

These working hours cannot be averaged out and there is no opt-out available.

You may work longer hours where this is necessary either to:

- maintain continuity of service or production, or
- respond to a surge in demand for a service or product

and provided that:

- there is no adult available to perform the task
- your training needs are not adversely affected.

Young workers who are employed on ships or as part of the armed forces are excluded from these working time limits under the Working Time Regulations.[17]

Opting out

If you are aged over 18, your employer may ask you to opt out of these working time regulations. This means signing a form which says you are happy to work longer hours. However, an employer cannot legally force you to opt out: it should be your free choice. If you do opt out, you can also change your mind at any time and request to be covered by working time regulations again.

Your employer is breaking the law if they treat you unfairly or sack you because you refuse to opt out. If you think your employer has treated you unfairly you might be able to take them to an employment tribunal. You can find out more about your rights and the steps you can take if you have been unfairly treated by visiting the TUC website at www.tuc.org.uk.

Time off: special rules for young workers

Daily rest

If you are aged 16 or 17, you are entitled to 12 uninterrupted hours in each 24-hour period in which you work. The other 12 hours may be interrupted if periods of work are split up over the day or do not last long.

Your entitlement to daily rest can be reduced or excluded in exceptional circumstances only. Where this occurs, you should receive compensatory rest within three weeks.

Weekly rest

If you are aged 16 or 17, you are entitled to two days off each week. This cannot be averaged over a two-week period, and should normally be two days in a row.

If the nature of the job makes it unavoidable, your weekly time off can be reduced to 36 hours, as long as you receive compensatory rest.

Rest breaks at work: special rules for young workers

If you are aged 16 or 17 and you are required to work for more than four and a half hours at a stretch, you are entitled to a rest break of 30 minutes.

If you are working for more than one employer, your work for each one should be added together to see if you are entitled to a rest break.

Your entitlement to breaks can be reduced or excluded in exceptional circumstances only. Where this occurs, you should receive compensatory rest within three weeks.[18]

Statutory Sick Pay UK

If you have to take more than four days off work because of illness, you may be entitled to sick pay. The government sets a minimum amount of sick pay you should receive. This is called Statutory Sick Pay (SSP).

You are entitled to get SSP for up to 28 weeks.

In order to get Statutory Sick Pay, you must be aged 16 or over and be earning enough to pay National Insurance contributions (an average of £95 per week before tax and National Insurance). If you meet these criteria, then you will get the standard SSP rate of £79.15 per week for the period for which you are absent from work because of sickness.[19]

Some employers are generous and pay more than this minimum amount. You should check your contract or ask your trade union to see if this is the case.

Holiday entitlement **UK**

Currently, under the Working Time Regulations, all full-time employees are legally entitled to a minimum of 28 days' paid holiday (including Bank Holidays) a year.[20]

For each week of holiday, you should get as many days off as you work in a normal working week. This means that the actual amount of paid holiday entitlement you receive depends on how many days you work. You should get 5.6 times your normal working week in holiday entitlement.

You should always check your contract or employment handbook to see if your employer offers more generous holiday entitlements.

The Citizens Advice Bureau website, www.citizensadvice.org.uk, has lots of useful information on your employment rights. You can find a more detailed explanation of holiday pay entitlements there.

Antenatal Care **UK**

If you are pregnant you are entitled to a reasonable amount of paid time off work for antenatal care. This has to be negotiated with your employer.

Maternity leave **UK**

Any pregnant employee has the right to 26 weeks of Ordinary Maternity leave (OML). New mothers can also ask for a further 26 weeks of Additional Maternity Leave (AML), making one year in total.

This right belongs to all pregnant employees. It does not matter how long you have been with your employer, how many hours you work or how much you are paid, so long as you can meet the 15-week notification requirement outlined below.

You should tell your employer that you are pregnant and intend to take maternity leave at least 15 weeks before the beginning of the week your baby is due.

You will need to tell your employer that you are pregnant, when the baby is due and when you want to start your maternity leave.

You can start OML any time from 11 weeks before the beginning of the week when your baby is due.[21]

AML starts at the end of OML and lasts for 26 weeks. To be eligible for AML, employees have to have worked for 26 weeks once they reach the 15th week before the week their baby is due.

Statutory Maternity Pay

From 1 April 2008, you are entitled to Statutory Maternity Pay, so long as:

- once you reach the 15th week before your baby is due, you have been employed by the same employer without a break for at least 26 weeks, and
- you are earning more than £95 per week.

Statutory Maternity Pay is 90 per cent of your average weekly earnings for the first six weeks of your maternity leave. For the following 33 weeks, you are entitled to receive either £123.06 or 90 per cent of your average earnings – whichever is less.

This is usually paid to you by your employer in the same way as your normal wages.[23]

Some employers have their own maternity leave arrangements which may be more generous. You can find out if this is the case by looking at your employment contract.

Other benefits

If you do not qualify to receive SMP you may be able to claim Maternity Allowance through Jobcentre Plus. Maternity Allowance is paid at the same rate as SMP.

There are a number of other benefits which expectant and new mothers may be entitled to receive. These include Child Trust Funds, the Sure Start Maternity Grant, the Health in Pregnancy Grant, Child Benefit, free prescriptions and dental treatment, and Tax Credits.

Paternity leave 🆄🅺

You are entitled to paid paternity leave if you meet the following criteria:

- you are the biological father of the baby and/or you are the mother's husband, civil partner or partner
- you have worked continuously for the same employer for 26 weeks by the 25th week of pregnancy and will continue to do so up to the birth of the child
- you earn at least the lower earnings limit of £90 per week for National Insurance contributions (if you earn less, you are entitled to two weeks' unpaid leave).

If you meet these criteria, you are entitled to up to two weeks' paternity leave, which must be taken within 56 days of the baby being born. This time off must be taken in one go. It cannot be taken as odd days or as two separate weeks.

If you would like to take paternity leave, you will need to tell your employer before the end of the 25th week of pregnancy.

Statutory Paternity Pay

While you are on paternity leave you may be entitled to Statutory Paternity Pay (SPP) of £123.06 per week, or 90 per cent of your average weekly earnings – whichever is less.

To claim SPP you must be earning over £95 per week.[24] You must also notify your employer that you would like to be paid SPP at least 28 days before you begin paternity leave.[25]

Other benefits

If you do not qualify for SPP because you are not earning more than £95 per week you may be entitled to receive other benefits. These include Income Support, Housing Benefit, Council Tax Benefit and Tax Credits.

Tax Credits and young people UK

You may be entitled to claim Tax Credits. There are two types of Tax Credit: Child Tax Credit (CTC) and Working Tax Credit (WTC) and the main features of the credits are:

- You must be at least 16 to claim them.
- The Tax Credits are administered by Her Majesty's Revenue and Customs (HMRC) rather than the Department for Work and Pensions.
- Entitlement is based on your gross annual income rather than net weekly income.
- There is no capital limit but any income above £300 per year from taxable savings counts as income.
- If you have children and you make a new claim for Income Support or Income-Based Jobseeker's Allowance or Income-Related Employment and Support Allowance you will need to claim CTC for your children. Your benefit will be calculated on the amounts for adults only. Any elements for adults and housing costs (such as mortgages) will still be met by IS/JSA (IB)/ESA (IR). Existing IS/JSA (IB) claimants with children may be transferred onto CTC at some date during 2010-11.
- Tax Credits are paid on top of other benefits, but they count as income for Housing Benefit and Council Tax Benefit, unless you also receive Income Support, Income-Based Jobseeker's Allowance or Income-Related Employment and Support Allowance.
- If you get maximum Child Tax Credits, you might get passported benefits such as free school meals, prescriptions and dental care. If you are working, you may get help with up to 80 per cent of your childcare costs.
- A claim for Tax Credits by a lone parent will not trigger Child Support Agency involvement.
- Any maintenance you receive is completely ignored as income.
- Couples must make a joint claim. If you separate, you must claim as single people.
- Certain other types of income are ignored – for example, maintenance, training allowances, Disability Living Allowance,

Housing Benefit, Child Benefit, Guardian's Allowance, Income Support, Income-Based Jobseeker's Allowance or Income-Related Employment and Support Allowance, reimbursement of expenses 'wholly exclusively and necessarily' involved in your employment, the first £100 of Statutory Maternity Pay and Maternity Allowance, Statutory Sick Pay.

Child Tax Credit (UK)

Child Tax Credit is designed to provide additional support for families with children. Depending on individual circumstances it is payable for children and for young people aged 16 to 19 who are still living with their families, provided they are in full-time non-advanced education. It is based on family income.

You can receive CTC in your own right if:

- you have main responsibility for a child under 16 years old (or one under 20 who is in full time non-advanced education if they normally live with you)
- you are present and ordinarily resident in Great Britain
- you are not a 'person subject to immigration control'.

Child Tax Credit is payable to the person who has the main caring responsibility for at least one child or qualifying young person. To get Child Tax Credit you do not need to be the parent of the child you are responsible for. It is awarded until the end of the tax year unless there are significant changes in your circumstances.

Tax Credits your parents claim for you

See pages 42-52

Working Tax Credit

Working Tax Credit (WTC) is paid by HMRC to people with or without families who are on a low income.

You can receive WTC if:

- you (or your partner if you have one) are responsible for a child and one of you is employed for at least 16 hours a week
- you have a physical or mental disability which means that you are disadvantaged in finding or keeping work and you either receive or have recently received certain disability-related benefits, and you are employed for at least 16 hours per week
- you or your partner are aged at least 25 and employed for at least 30 hours per week
- you are present and ordinarily resident in Great Britain, and
- you are not subject to immigration control'.

Childcare costs

It is possible for HMRC to include 80 per cent of your childcare costs in your WTC calculation. However, you can't receive more than £175 per week for one child and £300 per week for two or more children. You must also meet some other conditions:

- The childcare must be 'relevant' – in other words, a nursery, after-school club, breakfast club or provided by an approved childminder (but not if they are a close relative).
- If you are single, you must work for at least 16 hours per week to get help with childcare costs. If you have a partner, both of you must work for least 16 hours per week.
- If you a have a partner and only one of you works for at least 16 hours per week, you can still get help with childcare costs if the other person is:
    - in hospital or prison, or
    - 'incapacitated' (ill) and receiving a benefit because of this.
- You must tell HMRC if your childcare costs go up or down by £10 per week or more for 4 or more weeks. If you don't, they may make you pay a £300 penalty.

How much Tax Credit can you get?

You receive various elements in your Tax Credit calculation depending on your circumstances. If you have a child with a disability or you receive a benefit for disability or long-term sickness, you may qualify for higher amounts.

If your income is less than £6,420 per year and you qualify for WTC, you will receive maximum tax credits.

If your income is more than this threshold, your maximum Tax Credit amounts gradually reduces by 37p for each pound that your income is above the threshold. If you only qualify for CTC, you receive the maximum if your income is less than £16,040 per year (or if you receive IS/ JSA (IB)/ESA (IR)) and then it reduces by 37p for each pound that your income is above that level until you are left with the family element of CTC of £545 per year. You keep the family element unless your income reaches £50,000 when it then reduces by 6.67p for each pound that your income is above that level.

The calculation also takes into account your 'relevant period'. Normally this will be a full year, but if you go onto tax credits later in the year, your relevant period will be reduced to take account of this. Also, if your childcare costs or household composition changes, HMRC works out a new relevant period to adjust your Tax Credit entitlement.

If you receive WTC, you will still be able to get it for four weeks if you stop work.

Overpayments

Because tax credits are based on annual income, some people may find that they are paid too much tax credit. This might be because their income rises, their entitlement reduces (for example, childcare costs decrease by more than £10 per week for more than 4 weeks) or their couple status has changed and HMRC has not been informed.

An overpayment will usually be clawed back from your ongoing tax credit entitlement.

If your income increases by up to £25,000 per year, HMRC will ignore this and only count any increase above £25,000 per year.

If you do find that you have been overpaid, the law gives HMRC a general discretion to waive recovery of an overpayment.[26] They will also not recover the overpayment if it was their fault and you couldn't be reasonably expected to realise this or if repaying an overpayment would cause you hardship.[27]

HMRC will not consider waiving recovery unless you ask them to. If they refuse to waive recovery, you can complain to the HMRC adjudicator (www.adjudicatorsoffice.gov.uk) and you can ask your MP to complain to the Parliamentary Ombudsman. Sometimes it may be possible to take a form of legal action known as judicial review.

To prevent an overpayment, it is important to tell HMRC if you start or stop being a couple, have children, a child leaves your household or if your childcare costs decrease by £10 per week for four or more weeks.

How to claim

You can get a tax credit claim form (TC600) at Jobcentre Plus if you are entering work after being out of work (and they should help you to complete it if you ask), or by phoning HMRC on 0845 300 3900.

Your claim can be backdated for up to three months before you claimed if you were entitled, you do not need to show any special reasons and you should also apply for backdating if you think you missed out.

Healthy Start scheme

This provides vouchers worth £3 per week per child towards a range of healthier foods including fresh milk, infant formula milk and fresh fruit and vegetables. The vouchers may be used in a wide range of shops, including supermarkets, chemists, grocers and markets.

You are eligible for Healthy Start vouchers if you are pregnant or have a child under the age of four, and if you also:

- are pregnant and aged under 18 (in this case, you do not have to be receiving any benefit to qualify)
- receive Income Support, Income-Based Jobseeker's Allowance or Income Related Employment and Support Allowance, or
- receive Child Tax Credit (but not Working Tax Credit) and have an annual family income of below £16,040.

Endnotes

1 www.direct.gov.uk/en/Employment/DiscriminationatWork/DG_10026557
   Accessed on 16 March 2009

2 www.equalities.gov.uk/pdf/Equality%20Bill%20fact%20sheet.pdf Accessed on 16
   March 2009

3 www.equalities.gov.uk/media/press_releases/equality_bill_confirmed.aspx
   Accessed on 16 March 2009

4 www.opsi.gov.uk/acts/acts2006/ukpga_20060003_en_1 Accessed on
   16 March 2009

5 www.lluk.org/documents/FS_-_The_Employment_Equality__Sexual_Orientation__
   Regulations_2003.pdf Accessed on 16 March 2009

6 www.lluk.org/documents/FS_-The_Employmnt_Equality__Religion_or_Belief__
   Regs_03_.pdf Accessed on 16 March 2009

7 www.direct.gov.uk/en/Employment/DiscriminationAtWork/DG_10026429
   Accessed on 17 March 2009

8 www.laterlife.com/laterlife-age-discrimination-legislation-employers.htm Accessed
   on 10 February 2009

9 Reg. 7.1&7.2 Employment Equality (Age) Regulations 2006

10 Reg. 31 Employment Equality (Age) Regulations 2006

11 www.lluk.org/documents/FS-_Positive_Action.pdf Accessed on 16 March 2009

12 Reg. 29 Employment Equality (Age) Regulations 2006

13 www.equalities.gov.uk/pdf/Equality%20Bill%20fact%20sheet.pdf Accessed on
    16 March 2009

14 Reg. 32 Employment Equality (Age) Regulations 2006

15 Employment Rights Act 1996 (S 1). Available online, www.opsi.gov.uk/acts/
    acts1996/1996018.htm Accessed on 10 February 2009

16 The National Minimum Wage Regulations 1999. Available online, www.opsi.gov.
    uk/acts/acts1996/1996018.htm Accessed on 10 February 2009

17 www.tuc.org.uk/tuc/youngpeople.pdf Accessed on 17 March 2009

18 The Working Time (Amendment) Regulations 2002. Available online, www.opsi.
    gov.uk/si/si2002/20023128.htm Accessed on 10 February 2009

19 www.businesslink.gov.uk/bdotg/action/detail?type=RESOURCES&itemId=107379
    2637 Accessed on 17 March 2009. See also www.dwp.gov.uk/lifeevent/benefits/
    statutory_sick_pay.asp Accessed on 17 March 2009

[20] Working Time Regulations 1998 (s 13). Available online, www.opsi.gov.uk/si/ si1998/19981833.htm Accessed on 10/02/2009. See also www.direct.gov.uk/ en/Employment/Employees/WorkingHoursAndTimeOff/DG_10029788 Accessed on 10 February 2009

[21] www.direct.gov.uk/en/Parents/Moneyandworkentitlements/WorkAndFamilies/ index.htm Accessed on 10 February 2009

[22] www.hmrc.gov.uk/employers/stat-pymnt-rates09-10.htm Accessed on 16 March 2009

[23] www.direct.gov.uk/en/Bfsl1/BenefitsAndFinancialSupport/DG_10018741 Accessed on 10 February 2009

[24] www.hmrc.gov.uk/employers/stat-pymnt-rates09-10.htm Accessed on 16 March 2009

[25] www.direct.gov.uk/en/Parents/Moneyandworkentitlements/WorkAndFamilies/ index.htm Accessed on 10 February 2009

[26] S 28 & 29 Tax Credits Act 2002.

[27] HMRC leaflet COP 26: What happens if we have paid you too much tax credit

Appendix 1
Standard Letter

Standard letter to support Income Support estrangement and Jobseeker's Allowance severe hardship claims. Reproduced from www.neilbateman.co.uk with permission

TO BE USED ON HEADED PAPER

To Jobcentre Plus	
Address	
Postcode	

Dear Sir or Madam

Re: [Full name]

[Address]

[NINo]

[DOB]

The above named young person has made a claim for

a) Jobseeker's Allowance because of severe hardship and is aged 16 or 17
b) Income Support while in full time non-advanced education, aged from 16 to 20, because of necessity they live away from and are

estranged from their parents/carers and no one is acting in their place
c) Jobseeker's Allowance during the Child Benefit Extension Period,
and aged 16 or 17, because of necessity they are living away from their
parents or anyone acting in their place and they are estranged from their
parents/carers [Delete which sentences do not apply]. I enclose a copy
of their consent for us to act for them.

[To be used for IS estrangement cases and JSA CBEP only] In law,
'estrangement' implies emotional disharmony, where there is no desire
to have any prolonged contact with the parents or they feel similarly
towards the young person. It is possible to be estranged even though
parents are providing some financial support or the young person still
has some contact with them (based on Commissioner's decision R(SB)
2/87. Also see R(IS) 5/05.

As can be seen from this case law, it is sufficient for only one party to
feel estranged. Please also refer to CIS/4096/2005. Estrangement
may also occur even when peoples' relationships are amicable – see
CH/117/2005 and CH/3777/2007.

The following is confirmation of the young person's estrangement/
emotional disharmony/being alienated in affection with parents/carers:

[Give examples/evidence]

Parents/carers should not be contacted by DWP staff for verification
because claimants' statements do not require corroboration unless their
evidence is inherently improbable or self-contradictory (please refer to
R(SB) 33/85 and R(I) 2/51). This is set out in internal DWP Guidance
in IS Bulletin 04-07 'Estranged Young People aged 16-19 Claiming
Income Support' and also in DWP Guidance 'Making a Severe Hardship
Decision' (available on the Jobcentre Plus Intranet). These two guidance
documents state that: 'The young person should be believed unless their
statement is self-contradictory or inherently improbable...There is no rule
in law that corroboration of the customer's own evidence is necessary
and it is seldom safe to reject evidence solely because the customer's
demeanour does not inspire confidence in their truthfulness'.

In addition, I wish to inform you of the following risks associated with contacting parents: [Give reasons why contact is inappropriate or delete above sentence if this is not relevant]

[Use only for JSA severe hardship payment claims]. This person will experience severe hardship for the following reasons: [Give details and delete those which are not relevant]

Lack of financial resources:

Risk to health:

Has insecure accommodation:

Possible loss of accommodation:

Has debts:

Carer/parent has financial pressures:

Carer/parent unable/unwilling to adequately support financially:

The young person or a member of their family would be vulnerable without payment:

The young person is pregnant:

Others:

Please send me a copy of your decision and please also direct any further enquires via me.

Yours faithfully

[Name and job title]

8

Appendix 2
Benefit rates

Social security and tax credit rates for young people in 2009-10

Means-tested benefits

Income Support and Income-Based Jobseeker's Allowance (weekly rates)

Personal Allowances

Single person, under 18	50.95
Single person, 18 to 24	50.95
Single person, 25+	64.30
Lone parent, under 18	50.95
Lone parent, 18+	64.30
Couple, both under 18	50.95 or 76.90
Couple, one under 18 (both qualify)	76.90
Couple, one under 18, one 25+	64.30
Couple, both 18+	100.95

Premiums

Carer	29.50
Disability, single	27.50
Disability, couple	39.15
Enhanced disability, single person or lone parent	13.40

Enhanced Disability, couple	19.30
Severe Disability, per qualifying person	52.85

Housing Benefit and Council Tax Benefit (weekly rates)

The same as for Income Support, Income-Based Jobseeker's Allowance or Pension Credit, except for:

Personal Allowances

Single person, 16 to 24 (n/a for Council Tax Benefit if under 18)	50.95
Lone parent, under 18 (n/a for Council Tax Benefit)	50.95
Couple, both under 18 (n/a for Council Tax Benefit)	76.90
Couple, one or both 18+	100.95
Child	56.11

Premiums

Family	17.30
Family, baby rate	10.50

Entitled to Employment and Support Allowance components

Work-related activity	25.50
Support	30.8

Working Tax Credit

Annual rates

Basic element	1,890
Couple or lone parent	1,860
30 hours element	775
Disability element	2,530
Severe disability element	1,075

Weekly rates

Childcare costs, one child (80 per cent up to)	175
Childcare costs, two children (80 per cent up to)	300

Child Tax Credit (annual rates)

Family element	545
Baby addition	545
Child element	2,235
Disabled child	2,670
Severely disabled child	1,075

Non-means-tested benefits

Carer's Allowance (weekly rates)

Carer's Allowance	53.10
Adult dependant	31.70

Child Benefit (weekly rates)

Only or eldest child	20.00
Each additional child	13.20

Disability Living Allowance (weekly rates)

Care component	Low rate	18.65
	Middle rate	47.10
	High rate	70.35
Mobility Component	Low rate	18.65
	High rate	49.10

Employment and Support Allowance (weekly rates)

Personal Allowances

Under 25	50.95
25 or over	64.30
Lone parent under 18	50.95
18 or over	64.30
Couple	
both under 18	50.95

both under 18 with child	76.90
both under 18 (main phase)	64.30
both under 18 with child (main phase)	100.95
one 18+, one under 18	100.95
both over 18	100.95
claimant under 25, partner under 18	50.95
claimant 25+, partner under 18	64.30
claimant (main phase), partner under	64.30

Premiums

Enhanced disability

Single	13.40
Couple	19.30

Severe disability

Single		52.85
Couple	(lower rate)	52.85
Couple	(higher rate)	105.70
Carer		29.50

Components

Work-related Activity	25.50
Support	30.85

Industrial Injuries Disablement Benefit and Analogous Industrial Injuries Scheme (weekly rates)

(Varies depending on percentage of disablement)

Under 18	17.61-88.05
Under 18 with dependants	28.70-143.60
18+	28.70-143.60

Contribution-Based Jobseeker's Allowance (weekly rates)

Aged 16 to 24	50.95
Aged 25+	64.30

Maternity Allowance (weekly rates)

Standard rate	123.06
Adult Dependant	41.35

Statutory Maternity, Paternity and Adoption Pay

Standard rate	123.08
Earnings threshold	95.00

Statutory Sick Pay (weekly rate)	79.15
Earnings threshold	95.00

National Minimum Wage (hourly rate)

From October 2008

Aged 22+	£5.73
Aged 18 to 21 or in approved training	£4.77
Aged 16 to 17	£3.53

9

Appendix 3
Employment and Support Allowance Tests

Test for whether you have Limited Capability for Work

This is the scoring system for Employment and Support Allowance. Choose the highest descriptor for each activity, and add up the points to get your overall score. You must score at least 15 points to have Limited Capability for Work. Or, you must be in an exempt group, or count as having Limited Capability for Work because of exceptional circumstances.

Part One: Physical disabilities

Activity	Descriptors		Points
1. Walking with a walking stick or other aid, if such aid is normally used	1 (a)	Cannot walk at all	15
	1 (b)	Cannot walk more than 50 metres on level ground without repeatedly stopping or feeling severe discomfort	15
	1 (c)	Cannot walk up or down two steps, even with the support of a handrail	15
	1 (d)	Cannot walk more than 100 metres on level ground without stopping or feeling severe discomfort	9

Activity	Descriptors		Points
	1 (e)	Cannot walk more than 200 metres on level ground without stopping or feeling severe discomfort	6
	1 (f)	None of the above apply	0
2. Standing and sitting	2 (a)	Cannot stand for more than 10 minutes without help from another person (even if you are free to move around) before needing to sit down	15
	2 (b)	Cannot sit in a chair with a high back and no arms for more than 10 minutes before needing to move from the chair because the degree of discomfort makes it impossible to continue sitting	15
	2 (c)	Cannot rise to standing from sitting in an upright chair without physical help from another person	15
	2 (d)	Cannot move between two seated positions located next to one another without physical help from another person	15
	2 (e)	Cannot stand for more than 30 minutes (even if free to move around) before needing to sit down	6

Activity		Descriptors	Points
	2 (f)	Cannot sit in a chair with a high back and no arms for more than 30 minutes without needing to move from the chair because the degree of discomfort makes it impossible to continue sitting	6
	2 (g)	None of the above apply	0
3. Bending or kneeling	3 (a)	Cannot bend to touch knees and straighten up again	15
	3 (b)	Cannot bend, kneel or squat to pick up a light object (such as a piece of paper) placed 15cm from the floor on a low shelf, then move that object and straighten up again, without the help of another person	9
	3 (c)	Cannot bend, kneel or squat to pick up a light object on the floor and straighten up again without the help of another person	6
	3 (d)	None of the above apply	0
4. Reaching	4 (a)	Cannot raise either arm to put something in the top pocket of a coat or jacket	15
	4 (b)	Cannot put either arm behind your back to put on a coat or jacket	15

Activity	Descriptors		Points
	4 (c)	Cannot raise either arm to the top of your head to put on a hat	9
	4 (d)	Cannot raise either arm above your head height, as if to reach for something	6
	4 (e)	None of the above apply	0
5. Picking things up and moving or transferring them by using your upper body and arms (excluding all other activities named in Part 1 of this Schedule)	5 (a)	Cannot pick up and move a 0.5-litre carton full of liquid with either hand	15
	5 (b)	Cannot pick up and move a one-litre carton full of liquid with either hand	9
	5 (c)	Cannot pick up and move a light but bulky object (such as an empty cardboard box) requiring the use of both hands together	6
	5 (d)	None of the above apply	0
6. Manual dexterity	6 (a)	Cannot turn a 'star-headed' sink tap with either hand	15
	6 (b)	Cannot pick up a £1 coin (or equivalent) with either hand	15
	6 (c)	Cannot turn the pages of a book with either hand.	15
	6 (d)	Cannot physically use a pen or pencil	9
	6 (e)	Cannot physically use a conventional keyboard or mouse	9

Activity	Descriptors		Points
	6 (f)	Cannot do up or undo small buttons (such as shirt or blouse buttons)	9
	6 (g)	Cannot turn a 'star-headed' sink tap with one hand, but can turn it with the other	6
	6 (h)	Cannot pick up a £1 coin (or equivalent) with one hand, but can pick it up with the other	6
	6 (i)	Cannot pour from an open 0.5-litre carton full of liquid	6
	6 (j)	None of the above apply	0
7. Speech	7 (a)	Cannot speak at all	15
	7 (b)	Speech cannot be understood by strangers	15
	7 (c)	Strangers have great difficulty understanding speech	9
	7 (d)	Strangers have some difficulty understanding speech	6
	7 (e)	None of the above apply	0

Activity	Descriptors		Points
8. Hearing with a hearing aid or other aid, if normally worn	8 (a)	Cannot hear at all	15
	8 (b)	Cannot hear someone talking in a loud voice in a quiet room well enough to distinguish the words being spoken	15
	8 (c)	Cannot hear someone talking in a normal voice in a quiet room well enough to distinguish the words being spoken	9
	8 (d)	Cannot hear someone talking in a loud voice in a busy street well enough to distinguish the words being spoken	6
	8 (e)	None of the above apply	0
9. Vision including visual acuity and visual fields, in normal daylight or bright electric light, with glasses or other aid to vision, if such aid is normally worn	9 (a)	Cannot see at all	15
	9 (b)	Cannot see well enough to read 16-point print at a distance greater than 20cm	15
	9 (c)	Have 50 per cent or greater reduction of visual fields	15
	9 (d)	Cannot see well enough to recognise a friend at a distance of a least five metres	9
	9 (e)	Have at least 25 per cent, but less than 50 per cent, reduction of visual fields	6
	9 (f)	Cannot see well enough to recognise a friend at a distance of at least 15 metres	6
	9 (g)	None of the above apply	0

Activity	Descriptors		Points
10 (a) Continence other than enuresis (bed-wetting) where the claimant does not have an artificial stoma or urinary collecting device	10 (a) (i)	Has no voluntary control over the evacuation of the bowel	15
	10 (a) (ii)	Has no voluntary control over the voiding of the bladder	15
	10 (a) (iii)	At least once a month loses control of bowels so that the claimant cannot control the full evacuation of the bowel	15
	10 (a) (iv)	At least once a week loses control of bladder so that the claimant cannot control the full voiding of the bladder	15
	10 (a) (v)	Occasionally loses control of bowels so that the claimant cannot control the full evacuation of the bowel	9
	10 (a)(vi)	At least once a month loses control of bladder so that the claimant cannot control the full voiding of the bladder	6
	10 (a) (vii)	Risks losing control of bowels or bladder so that the claimant cannot control the full evacuation of the bowel or the full voiding of the bladder if not able to reach a toilet quickly	6
	10 (a) (viii)	None of the above apply	0

Activity	Descriptors		Points
10 (b) Continence where the claimant uses a urinary collecting device, worn for the majority of the time, including an indwelling urethral or suprapubic catheter	10 (b) (i)	Is unable to affix, remove or empty the catheter bag or other collecting device without physical help from another person	15
	10 (b) (ii)	Is unable to affix, remove or empty the catheter bag or other collecting device without causing leakage of contents	15
	10 (b) (iii)	Has no voluntary control over the evacuation of the bowel	15
	10 (b) (iv)	At least once a month, loses control of bowels so that the claimant cannot control the full evacuation of the bowel	15
	10 (b) (v)	Occasionally loses control of bowels so that the claimant cannot control the full evacuation of the bowel	9
	10 (b) (vi)	Risks losing control of bowels so that the claimant cannot control the full evacuation of the bowel if not able to reach a toilet quickly	6
	10 (b) (vii)	None of the above apply	0

Activity	Descriptors		Points
10 (c) Continence other than enuresis (bed wetting) where the claimant has an artificial stoma	10 (c) (i)	Is unable to affix, remove or empty stoma appliance without physical help from another person	15
	10 (c) (ii)	Is unable to affix, remove or empty stoma appliance without causing leakage of contents	15
	10 (c) (iii)	Where the claimant's artificial stoma relates solely to the evacuation of the bowel, at least once a week loses control of bladder so that the claimant cannot control the full voiding of the bladder	15
	10 (c) (iv)	Where the claimant's artificial stoma relates solely to the evacuation of the bowel, at last once a month loses control of bladder so that the claimant cannot control the full voiding of the bladder	9
	10 (c) (v)	Where the claimant's artificial stoma relates solely to the evacuation of the bowel, risks losing control of the bladder so that the claimant cannot control the full voiding of the bladder if not able to reach a toilet quickly	6
	10 (c) (vi)	None of the above apply	0

Activity	Descriptors		Points
11. Remaining conscious during waking moments	11 (a)	At least once a week, has an involuntary episode of lost or altered consciousness, resulting in significantly disrupted awareness or concentration	15
	11 (b)	At least once a month, has an involuntary episode of lost or altered consciousness, resulting in significantly disrupted awareness or concentration	9
	11 (c)	At least twice in the six months immediately preceding the assessment, has had an involuntary episode of lost or altered consciousness, resulting in significantly disrupted awareness or concentration	6
	11 (d)	None of the above apply	0

Part Two: Mental, cognitive and intellectual function

Activity	Descriptors	Points
12. Learning or comprehension in the completion of tasks	12 (a) Cannot learn or understand how to successfully complete a simple task (such as setting an alarm clock) at all	15
	12 (b) Needs to witness a demonstration, given more than once on the same occasion, of how to carry out a simple task before the claimant is able to learn or understand how to complete the task successfully, and would be unable to successfully complete the task the next day without a further demonstration of how to complete it	15
	12 (c) Needs to witness a demonstration of how to carry out a simple task, before the claimant is able to learn or understand how to complete the task successfully, and would be unable to successfully complete the task the next day without a verbal prompt from another person	9
	12 (d) Needs to witness a demonstration of how to carry out a moderately complex task (such as the steps involved in operating a washing machine to correctly clean clothes) before the claimant is able to learn or understand how to complete the task successfully, and would be unable to successfully complete the task the next day without a verbal prompt from another person	9

Activity	Descriptors		Points
	12 (e)	Needs verbal instructions as to how to carry out a simple task before the claimant is able to learn or understand how to complete the task successfully, and would be unable, within a period of less than one week, to successfully complete the task the next day without a verbal prompt from another person	6
	12 (f)	None of the above apply	0
13. Awareness of hazard	13 (a)	Reduced awareness of the risks of everyday hazards (such as boiling water or sharp objects) would lead to daily instances of or to near-avoidance of:	15
	13 (a) (i)	injury to self or others, or	
	13 (a) (ii)	significant damage to property or possessionsto such an extent that overall day-to-day life cannot successfully be managed	
	13 (b)	Reduced awareness of the risks of everyday hazards would lead for the majority of the time to instances of, or to near-avoidance of:	9
	13 (b) (i)	injury to self or others, or	
	13 (b) (ii)	significant damage to property or possessions to such an extent that overall day-to-day life cannot successfully be managed without supervision from another person	
	13 (c)	Reduced awareness of the risks of everyday hazards has led, or would lead, to frequent instances of, or to near-avoidance of:	6

Activity	Descriptors	Points
	13 (c) (i) injury to self or others, or	
	13 (c) (ii) significant damage to property or possessions but not to such an extent that overall day-to-day life cannot be managed when such incidents occur	
	13 (d) None of the above apply	0
14. Memory and concentration	14 (a) On a daily basis, forgets or loses concentration to such an extent that overall day-to-day life cannot be successfully managed without verbal prompting from someone else in the claimant's presence	15
	14 (b) For the majority of the time, forgets or loses concentration to such an extent that overall day-to-day life cannot be successfully managed without verbal prompting from someone else in the claimant's presence	9
	14 (c) Frequently forgets or loses concentration to such an extent that overall day-to-day life can only be successfully managed with pre-planning, such as making a daily written list of all tasks forming part of daily life that are to be completed	6
	14 (d) None of the above apply	0

Activity	Descriptors	Points
15. Execution of tasks	15 (a) Is unable to successfully complete any everyday task	15
	15 (b) Takes more than twice the length of time it would take a person without any form of mental disablement to successfully complete an everyday task with which the claimant is familiar	15
	15 (c) Takes more than one and a half times, but no more than twice, the length of time it would take a person without any form of mental disablement to successfully complete an everyday task with which the claimant is familiar	9
	15 (d) Takes one and a half times the length of time it would take a person without any form of mental disablement to successfully complete an everyday task with which the claimant is familiar	6
	15 (e) None of the above apply	0
16. Initiating and sustaining personal action	16 (a) Cannot, due to cognitive impairment or a severe disorder of mood or behaviour, initiate or sustain any personal action (which means planning, organisation, problem solving, prioritising or switching tasks)	15
	16 (b) Cannot, due to cognitive impairment or a severe disorder of mood or behaviour, initiate or sustain personal action without verbal prompting from another person in the claimant's presence for the majority of the time	15

Activity	Descriptors	Points
	16 (c) Cannot, due to cognitive impairment or a severe disorder of mood or behaviour, initiate or sustain personal action without verbal prompting from another person in the claimant's presence for the majority of the time	9
	16 (d) Cannot, due to cognitive impairment or a severe disorder of mood or behaviour, initiate or sustain personal action without frequent verbal prompting from another person in the claimant's presence	6
	16 (e) None of the above apply	0
17. Coping with change	17 (a) Cannot cope with very minor, expected changes in routine, to the extent that overall day-to-day life cannot be managed	15
	17 (b) Cannot cope with expected changes in routine (such as a pre-arranged permanent change to the routine time scheduled for a lunch break), to the extent that overall day-to-day life is made significantly more difficult	9
	17 (c) Cannot cope with minor, unforeseen changes in routine (such as an unexpected change of the timing of an appointment on the day it is due to occur), to the extent that overall day-to-day life is made significantly more difficult	6
	17 (d) None of the above apply	0

Activity	Descriptors	Points
18. Getting about	18 (a) Cannot get to any specified place with which the claimant is, or would be, familiar	15
	18 (b) Is unable to get to a specified place with which the claimant is familiar without being accompanied by another person on each occasion	15
	18 (c) For the majority of the time is unable to get to a specified place with which the claimant is familiar without being accompanied by another person	9
	18 (d) Is frequently unable to get to a specified place with which the claimant is familiar without being accompanied by another person	6
	18 (e) None of the above apply	0
19. Coping with social situations	19 (a) Normal activities (for example, visiting new places or engaging in social contact) are precluded because of overwhelming fear or anxiety	15
	19 (b) Normal activities (for example, visiting new places or engaging in social contact) are precluded for the majority of the time due to overwhelming fear or anxiety	
	19 (c) Normal activities (for example, visiting new places or engaging in social contact) are frequently precluded due to overwhelming fear or anxiety	6
	19 (d) None of the above apply	0

Activity	Descriptors		Points
20. Propriety of behaviour with other people	20 (a)	Has unpredictable outbursts of aggressive, disinhibited, or bizarre behaviour, being either:	15
	20 (a) (i)	sufficient to cause disruption to others on a daily basis, or	
	20 (a) (ii)	of such severity that although occurring less frequently than on a daily basis, no reasonable person would be expected to tolerate them	
	20 (b)	Has a completely disproportionate reaction to minor events or to criticism to the extent that the claimant has an extreme violent outburst leading to threatening behaviour or actual physical violence	15
	20 (c)	Has unpredictable outbursts of aggressive, disinhibited or bizarre behaviour, sufficient in severity and frequency to cause disruption for the majority of the time	9
	20 (d)	Has a strongly disproportionate reaction to minor events or to criticism, to the extent that the claimant cannot manage overall day to day life when such events or criticism occur	9
	20 (e)	Has unpredictable outbursts of aggressive, disinhibited or bizarre behaviour, sufficient to cause frequent disruption	6

Activity	Descriptors		Points
	20 (f)	Frequently demonstrates a moderately disproportionate reaction to minor events or to criticism but not to such an extent that the claimant cannot manage overall day to day life when such events or criticism occur	6
	20 (g)	None of the above apply	0
21. Dealing with other people	21 (a)	Is unaware of impact of own behaviour to the extent that:	15
	21 (a) (i)	has difficulty relating to others even for brief periods, such as a few hours, or	
	21 (a) (ii)	causes distress to others on a daily basis	
	21 (b)	The claimant misinterprets verbal or non-verbal communication to the extent of causing himself or herself significant distress on a daily basis	15
	21 (c)	Is unaware of impact of own behaviour to the extent that:	9
	21 (c) (i)	has difficulty relating to others for longer periods, such as a day or two, or	
	21 (c) (ii)	causes distress to others for the majority of the time	
	21 (d)	The claimant misinterprets verbal or non-verbal communication to the extent of causing himself or herself significant distress for the majority of the time	9
	21 (e)	Is unaware of impact of own behaviour to the extent that:	6

Activity	Descriptors		Points
	21 (e) (i)	has difficulty relating to others for prolonged periods, such as a week, or	
	21 (e) (ii)	frequently causes distress to others	
	21 (f)	The claimant misinterprets verbal or non-verbal communication to the extent of causing himself or herself significant distress on a frequent basis	6
	21 (g)	None of the above apply	0

Test for whether you have Limited Capability for Work-Related Activity

You will not have to do work-related activity if you can satisfy at least one of the following:

Activity	Descriptors	
1. Walking or moving on level ground	Cannot:	
	1 (a)	walk with a walking stick or other aid, if such aid is normally used
	1 (b)	move with the aid of crutches, if crutches are normally used, or
	1 (c)	manually propel the claimant's wheelchair more than 30 metres without repeatedly stopping, experiencing breathlessness or severe discomfort

2. Rising from sitting and transferring from one seated position to another	Cannot complete both of the following:
	2 (a) rise to standing from sitting in an upright chair without physical help from someone else, and
	2 (b) move between two seated positions next to one another without physical help from someone else
3. Picking up and moving or transferring by the use of the upper body and arms (excluding standing, sitting, bending or kneeling and all other activities specified in this Schedule)	Cannot pick up and move 0.5-litre carton full of liquid with either hand
4. Reaching	Cannot raise either arm as if to put something in the top pocket of a coat or jacket
5. Manual dexterity	Cannot:
	5 (a) turn a 'star-headed' sink tap with either hand, or
	5 (b) pick up a £1 coin or equivalent with either hand
6. Continence	6 (a) Continence other than enuresis (bed-wetting) where the claimant does not have an artificial stoma or urinary collecting device
	6 (a) (i) Has no voluntary control over the evacuation of the bowel

	6 (a) (ii)	Has no voluntary control over the voiding of the bladder
	6 (a) (iii)	At least once a week, loses control of bowels so that the claimant cannot control the full evacuation of the bowel
	6 (a) (iv)	At least once a week, loses control of bladder so that the claimant cannot control the full voiding of the bladder
	6 (a) (v)	At least once a week, fails to control full evacuation of the bowel, owing to a severe disorder of mood or behaviour, or
	6 (a) (vi)	At least once a week, fails to control full voiding of the bladder, owing to a severe disorder of mood or behaviour
	6 (b)	Continence where the claimant uses a urinary collecting device, worn for the majority of the time, including an indwelling urethral or suprapubic catheter
	6 (b) (i)	Is unable to affix, remove or empty the catheter bag or other collecting device without physical help from another person
	6 (b) (ii)	Is unable to affix, remove or empty the catheter bag or other collecting device without causing leakage of contents
	6 (b) (iii)	Has no voluntary control over the evacuation of the bowel

6 (b) (iv)	At least once a week, loses control of bowels so that the claimant cannot control the full evacuation of the bowel, or
6 (b) (v)	At least once a week, fails to control full evacuation of the bowel, owing to a severe disorder of mood or behaviour
6 (c)	Continence other than enuresis (bed-wetting) where the claimant has an artificial stoma appliance
6 (c) (i)	Is unable to affix, remove or empty stoma appliance without physical help from another person
6 (c) (ii)	Is unable to affix, remove or empty stoma without causing leakage of contents
6 (c) (iii)	Where the claimant's artificial stoma relates solely to the evacuation of the bowel, has no voluntary control over voiding of bladder
6 (c) (iv)	Where the claimant's artificial stoma relates solely to the evacuation of the bowel, at least once a week, loses control of the bladder so that the claimant cannot control the full voiding of the bladder, or
6 (c) (v)	Where the claimant's artificial stoma relates solely to the evacuation of the bowel, at least once a week, fails to control the full voiding of the bladder, owing to a severe disorder of mood or behaviour

7. Maintaining personal hygiene	7 (a)	Cannot clean own torso (excluding own back) without physical help from someone else
	7 (b)	Cannot clean own torso (excluding back) without repeatedly stopping, experiencing breathlessness or severe discomfort
	7 (c)	Cannot clean own torso (excluding back) without regular prompting from someone else in the claimant's presence, or
	7 (d)	Owing to a severe disorder of mood or behaviour, fails to clean own torso (excluding own back) without:
	7 (d) (i)	physical help from someone else, or
	7 (d) (ii)	regular prompting from someone else in the claimant's presence
8. Eating and drinking	8 (a)	Conveying food or drink to the mouth
	8 (a)	Cannot convey food or drink to the claimant's own mouth without physical help from someone else
	8 (b)	Cannot convey food or drink to the claimant's own mouth without repeatedly stopping, experiencing breathlessness or severe discomfort
	8 (c)	Cannot convey food or drink to the claimant's own mouth without regular prompting from someone else in the claimant's physical presence, or

	8 (d)	Owing to a severe disorder of mood or behaviour, fails to convey food or drink to the claimant's own mouth without:
	8 (d) (i)	physical help from someone else, or
	8 (d) (ii)	regular prompting from someone else in the claimant's presence
	8 (b)	Chewing or swallowing food or drink
	8 (a)	Cannot chew or swallow food or drink
	8 (b)	Cannot chew or swallow food or drink without repeatedly stopping, experiencing breathlessness or severe discomfort
	8 (c)	Cannot chew or swallow food or drink without repeated regular prompting from someone else in the claimant's presence, or
	8 (d)	Owing to a severe disorder of mood or behaviour, fails to:
	8 (d) (i)	chew or swallow food or drink, or
	8 (d) (ii)	chew or swallow food or drink without regular prompting given by someone else in the claimant's presence

9. Learning or comprehension in the completion of tasks	9 (a)	Cannot learn or understand how to successfully complete a simple task (such as the preparation of a hot drink) at all
	9 (b)	Needs to witness a demonstration, given more than once on the same occasion, of how to carry out a simple task before the claimant is able to learn or understand how to complete the task successfully, and would be unable to successfully complete the task the next day without further demonstration of how to complete it, or
	9 (c)	Fails to do any of the matters referred to in (a) or (b), owing to a severe disorder of mood or behaviour
10. Personal action	10 (a)	Cannot initiate or sustain any personal action (which means planning, organisation, problem solving, prioritising or switching tasks)
	10 (b)	Cannot initiate or sustain personal action without requiring daily verbal prompting from someone else in the claimant's presence, or
	10 (c)	Fails to initiate or sustain basic personal action without requiring daily verbal prompting given by some else in the claimant's presence, owing to a severe disorder of mood or behaviour

11. Communication	11 (a)	None of the following forms of communication can be achieved by the claimant:
	11 (a) (i)	speaking (to a standard that may be understood by strangers)
	11 (a) (ii)	writing (to a standard that may be understood by strangers)
	11 (a) (iii)	typing (to a standard that may be understood by strangers)
	11 (a) (iv)	sign language (to a standard equivalent to Level 3 British Sign Language)
	11 (b)	None of the forms of communication referred to in (a) are achieved by the claimant, owing to a severe disorder of mood or behaviour
	11 (c)	Misinterprets verbal or non-verbal communication to the extent of causing distress to himself or herself on a daily basis, or
	11 (d)	Effectively cannot make himself or herself understood to others because of the claimant's disassociation from reality owing to a severe disorder of mood or behaviour

# 11 Useful Contacts

Careers Services

Connexions

www.connections-direct.com
Tel: 0808 001 3219

Careers Wales

www.careerswales.com
Learning and Careers Advice Helpline: 0800 100 900

Skills Development Scotland

www.skillsdevelopmentscotland.co.uk
Tel: 0141 225 6710
E-mail: info@skillsdevelopmentscotland.co.uk

Careers Service NI

www.careersserviceni.com
Tel: 028 90441 781
E-mail: cssu.account@delni.gov.uk

Benefits

Department for Work and Pensions

The Department for Work and Pensions can help with enquiries on most benefits (except for some which are handled by HM Revenue and Customs or Jobcentre Plus). Visit the DWP website to find the helpline number for the benefit that concerns you.

www.dwp.gov.uk

HM Revenue and Customs

HM Revenue and Customs deals with a number of benefits, including Child Benefit and tax credits. Visit the HMRC website to find the helpline number for the benefit that concerns you.

www.hmrc.gov.uk

Jobcentre Plus

Jobcentre Plus handles a range of benefits, including Jobseeker's Allowance, Employment and Support Allowance, Incapacity Benefit and Income Support.

Call 0800 055 6688 to make a benefit claim.
www.jobcentreplus.gov.uk

Child Support Agency

The Child Support Agency makes sure that parents who live apart contribute financially to the upkeep of their children.

www.csa.gov.uk.
Tel: 0845 713 3133
Textphone: 0845 713 8924

The Child Maintenance and Enforcement Division

The Child Maintenance and Enforcement Division makes sure that parents who live apart contribute financially to the upkeep of their children by paying child maintenance.

www.dsdni.gov.uk
Tel: 0800 028 7439

Books about benefit rights

Welfare to Work Handbook, Fourth Edition
(Centre for Economic & Social Inclusion)

Welfare Benefits and Tax Credits Handbook 2009–10
(Child Poverty Action Group)

Child Support Handbook 2009–10
(Child Poverty Action Group)

Lone Parent Handbook 2006–07
(One Parent Families)

Disability Rights Handbook, 34th Edition
(Disability Alliance)

Education and Training

Directgov

This website contains detailed information about almost all learning and training programmes in England, including A-levels, 14–19 Diplomas, BTECs, OCR Nationals, higher education qualifications, pre-employment programmes, apprenticeships, and work-based qualifications. Some information is relevant to Wales and Northern Ireland as well.

www.direct.gov.uk

Department for Business, Innovation and Skills

This new department is the result of a merger between the Department for Innovation, Universities and Skills and the Department for Business, Enterprise and Regulatory Reform. The new Department for Business, Innovation and Skills is responsible for encouraging skills development in England.

www.bis.gov.uk

Department for Children, Schools and Families

The Department for Children, Schools and Families is responsible for improving the government's policy for children and young people.

www.dcsf.gov.uk
Tel: 0870 000 2288
Textphone: 01928 794274
E-mail: info@dcsf.gsi.gov.uk

Learning and Skills Council

The Learning and Skills Council is responsible for planning and funding education and training for everyone in England other than those in universities.

www.lsc.gov.uk
Tel: 0870 900 6800
E-mail: info@lsc.gov.uk

Qualifications and Curriculum Authority

The Qualifications and Curriculum Authority website contains information on education and training in England, along with details of the National Qualifications Framework.

www.qca.org.uk
Tel: 0207 509 5555
E-mail: info@qca.org.uk

Apprenticeships

For general information on apprenticeships and the job sectors available for apprenticeships, check the Apprenticeships website.

www.apprenticeships.org.uk

Welsh Assembly Government

The Welsh Assembly Government website contains a section on education and training.

wales.gov.uk

Careers Wales

For information on pre-employment programmes and apprenticeships, contact Careers Wales.

www.careerswales.com
Learning and Careers Advice Helpline: 0800 100 900

Welsh Baccalaureate

www.wbq.org.uk
Tel: 0292 026 5010
E-mail: info@wbq.org.uk

Scottish Government (S)

The Scottish Government website contains a section on education and training.

www.scotland.gov.uk

Skills Development Scotland

For information on pre-employment programmes, training opportunities and apprenticeships, contact Skills Development Scotland.

www.skillsdevelopmentscotland.co.uk
Tel: 0141 225 6710
E-mail: info@skillsdevelopmentscotland.co.uk

Scottish Qualifications Authority

The Scottish Qualifications Authority decides the curriculum for most Scottish education programmes, including Highers, the Scottish Baccalaureate, and Scottish Vocational Qualifications, among others. The SQA website gives details of the Scottish Credit and Qualifications Framework.

www.sqa.org.uk
Tel: 0845 279 1000
E-mail: customer@sqa.org.uk

Department of Education

The Department of Education website contains information on learning and training programmes and policy for Northern Ireland.

www.deni.gov.uk
Tel: 0289 127 9279
E-mail: mail@deni.gov.uk

Department for Employment and Learning

The Department for Employment and Learning website gives information on apprenticeships and pre-employment programmes in Northern Ireland, along with higher education and further education qualifications.

www.delni.gov.uk
Tel: 0289 025 7777
E-mail: del@nics.gov.uk

Edexcel

Edexcel offers a wide range of qualifications, including BTECs, apprenticeships, National Vocational Qualifications, GCEs and GCSEs. Check the Edexcel website for the helpline number relevant to your qualification.

www.edexcel.com

City and Guilds

City and Guilds offers a range of qualifications throughout the UK, including the 14–19 Diploma and vocational qualifications.

www.cityandguilds.com
Tel: 0207 294 2800

Oxford Cambridge and RSA Examinations

OCR offers a number of qualifications in England, Wales and Northern Ireland, including OCR Nationals, A-levels, GCSEs, 14–19 Diplomas, the Welsh Baccalaureate, Key Skills and Functional Skills, and National Vocational Qualifications.

www.ocr.org.uk
Tel: 0122 355 3998 (for general 14–19 qualifications)
E-mail: general.qualifications@ocr.org.uk (for general 14–19 qualifications)
Tel: 0247 685 1509 (for vocational qualifications)
E-mail: vocational.qualifications@ocr.org.uk (for vocational qualifications)

Foundation Degrees

For general information on Foundation Degrees, or to find a degree, check the Foundation Degree website.

www.findfoundationdegree.co.uk

Funding for education and training

Student Finance England **E**

You can access Student Finance England through the Directgov website, or phone the company directly.

www.direct.gov.uk
Tel: 0845 300 5090

Directgov **E**

The Directgov website gives information on training allowances for all pre-employment, further and higher education programmes in England.

www.direct.gov.uk

Student Finance Wales **W**

For information on higher and further education funding in Wales, contact Student Finance Wales.

www.studentfinancewales.co.uk
Tel: 0845 602 8845

Careers Wales **W**

Contact Careers Wales for information on funding for pre-employment programmes and vocational qualifications.

www.careerswales.com
Learning and Careers Advice Helpline: 0800 100 900

Welsh Assembly Government **W**

The Welsh Assembly Government website contains some information on funding for education, including information on Individual Learning Accounts.

www.wales.gov.uk

Student Awards Agency for Scotland

For information on higher and further education funding in Scotland, contact the Student Awards Agency for Scotland.

www.student-support-saas.gov.uk
Tel: 0845 111 1711

Skills Development Scotland

Contact Skills Development Scotland for information on funding for pre-employment programmes and vocational qualifications.

www.skillsdevelopmentscotland.co.uk
Tel: 0141 225 6710

Scottish Government

The Scottish Government website gives information on funding for learning, including work-based learning.

www.scotland.gov.uk

ILA Scotland

For information on Individual Learning Accounts in Scotland, contact ILA Scotland.

www.ilascotland.org.uk
Tel: 0808 100 1090
E-mail: enquiries@ilascotland.org.uk

Student Finance NI

For information on higher and further education funding in Northern Ireland, contact Student Finance NI.

www.studentfinanceni.co.uk
Tel: 0845 600 0662

Department for Employment and Learning

Contact the Department for Employment and Learning to get information on funding for pre-employment programmes and vocational qualifications. You can also get information on Education Maintenance Allowance.

www.delni.gov.uk
Tel: 0289 025 7777
E-mail: del@nics.gov.uk

Employment and work relations

Jobcentre Plus

If you're looking for work, you can phone Jobseeker Direct. This helpline is available to anyone who is seeking employment, and Jobcentre Plus staff will help you to find part-time or full-time work.

Tel: 0845 606 0234
Textphone: 0845 605 5255
www.jobcentreplus.gov.uk

Careers services

Contact your local careers service for advice on employment and training. See page 16 for details.

Advisory, Conciliation and Arbitration Service

ACAS is the employment relations expert. It can offer free impartial help and information to people experiencing problems with their employment.

www.acas.org.uk

ACAS England
Helpline: 0845 747 4747

ACAS Wales
Tel: 0292 076 2636

ACAS Scotland
Helpline: 0845 747 4747

Labour Relations Agency

The Labour Relations Agency provides an impartial and confidential employment relations service in Northern Ireland, and it also resolves disputes through its conciliation, mediation and arbitration services.

www.lra.org.uk
Tel: 0289 032 1442
Email: info@lra.org.uk

Health and Safety Executive

The Health and Safety Executive makes sure that risks to health and welfare from work activities are properly controlled. The HSE has offices across the UK.

www.hse.gov.uk
Tel: 0845 345 0055

HSE Northern Ireland
www.hseni.gov.uk
Tel: 0800 032 0121
Textphone: 0289 054 6896
E-mail: hseni@detini.gov.uk

Trades Union Congress

The Trades Union Congress is the voice of Britain at work. With 71 affiliated unions representing nearly seven million working people from all walks of life, they campaign for a fair deal at work and for social justice at home and abroad.

www.tuc.org.uk
Tel: 0207 636 4030

Congress

Congress is made up of the Northern Ireland Committee and the Irish Congress of Trade Unions. It represents the interests of almost 750,000 working people, both in Northern Ireland and the Republic of Ireland.

www.ictuni.org
Tel: 0289 024 7940

Support organisations for young people

Child Poverty Action Group

The Child Poverty Action Group works to relieve poverty among children and families with children. It tries to make sure that those on low incomes get their full entitlement to welfare benefits. It publishes several books about current welfare rights and social policy issues.

www.cpag.org.uk
E-mail: staff@cpag.co.uk

Child Poverty Action Group Scotland

www.cpag.org.uk
Tel: 0141 552 0552
E-mail: staff@cpagscotland.org.uk

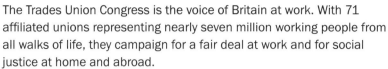

The Prince's Trust (UK)

The Prince's Trust offers a range of services and programmes to people aged 18 to 30, including educational underachievers , refugees and asylum seekers, unemployed young people and those in or leaving care.

www.princes-trust.org.uk
Tel: 0800 842 842
E-mail: info@princes-trust.org.uk

Childline (UK)

Childline is a national helpline for children and young people. If you need to talk about a problem, you can call Childline, no matter how big or small your problem is. The service is confidential and free. The Childline website also offers help and information on a range of topics relevant to young people.

www.childline.org.uk
Tel: 0800 1111

Barnardo's (UK)

Barnardo's is a charity which helps vulnerable children and young people to transform their lives and fulfil their potential. The charity works directly with children and young people across the UK, particularly those affected by drug misuse, disability, youth crime, mental health, sexual abuse, domestic violence, poverty and homelessness.

www.barnardos.org.uk
Tel: 0208 550 8822

The Who Cares? Trust (UK)

The Who Cares? Trust is a national charity which works to improve public care for children and young people who are separated from their families and living in residential or foster care.

www.thewhocarestrust.org.uk
Tel: 0207 251 3117

YoungMinds UK

YoungMinds is a national charity which works to improve the mental health of all children and young people. It provides an information service for any adult who has concerns about the mental health of a child or young person. It also produces a range of publications for young people.

www.youngminds.org.uk
Tel: 0800 018 2138

National Society for the Prevention of Cruelty to Children

The NSPCC is a national charity for child protection issues and the prevention of cruelty to children. It runs a 24-hour confidential helpline for anyone concerned about the welfare of a child or young person.

www.nspcc.org.uk
Tel: 0808 800 5000

Gingerbread and One Parent Families UK

This charity works for and with single-parent families to improve their lives. It provides help and advice to lone parent families.

www.gingerbread.org.uk
Tel: 0800 018 5026

One Parent Families Scotland

www.opfs.org.uk
Tel: 0808 801 0323

New Deal for Lone Parents Helpline

Tel: 0800 868 868
Textphone: 0845 606 2626

Equality

Commission for Equality and Human Rights

The Commission for Equality and Human Rights takes legal action on behalf of individuals who are faced with human rights issues, especially where there are strategic opportunities to push the boundaries of the law. It covers issues with race, disability, equal opportunity, age, sexual orientation and religion or belief. If the Commission can't take your case, it will offer advice through its helpline and online resources.

www.equalityhumanrights.com

England

Tel: 0845 604 6610
Textphone: 0845 604 6620

Wales

Tel: 0845 604 8810
Textphone: 0845 604 8820

Scotland

Tel: 0845 604 5510
Textphone: 0845 604 5520

Northern Ireland Human Rights Commission

The Commission has the power to conduct investigations, help individuals when they are bringing court proceedings, and to bring court proceedings itself. It welcomes enquiries from people who believe that their human rights have been violated.

www.nihrc.org
Tel: 0289 024 3987
Textphone: 0289 024 9066

Equality Commission for Northern Ireland

The Commission promotes equality of opportunity in Northern Ireland, enforcing anti-discrimination law related to age, disability, race, gender, sexual orientation (including marital and civil partner status), religious belief and political opinion.

www.equalityni.org
Tel: 0289 050 0600
Enquiry line: 0289 089 0890
Textphone: 0289 050 0589
E-mail: information@equalityni.org

Miscellaneous

Need2know

This government website provides information for young people on work, learning, housing, health and money.

www.need2know.co.uk

Citizens Advice Bureau

The Citizens Advice Bureau provides advice on a range of issues. A directory of local telephone numbers is available on its website.

www.citizensadvice.org.uk

Citizens Advice Scotland

Citizens Advice Scotland provides advice on a range of issues. A directory of local telephone numbers is available on its website, or you can lodge an enquiry online.

www.cas.org.uk

Refugee Council

If you are a migrant, seek advice from a professional. If you are an asylum seeker, have Exceptional Leave to Remain or Humanitarian Protection, you can get initial help from the Refugee Council.

www.refugeecouncil.org.uk
Tel: 0207 364 6700

Welsh Refugee Council

The Welsh Refugee Council gives practical advice and support to asylum seekers and refugees. Clients can discuss any problems they may be facing as an asylum seeker or refugee.

www.welshrefugeecouncil.org
Tel: 0292 048 9800

Scottish Refugee Council

The Scottish Refugee Council is an independent charity dedicated to providing advice, information and assistance to asylum seekers and refugees living in Scotland.

www.scottishrefugeecouncil.org.uk
Tel: 0800 085 6087

Shelter

If you need housing advice – particularly if you are without a home – Shelter will try to help.

England

www.shelter.org.uk
Tel: 0808 800 444

Shelter Cymru (Wales)

www.sheltercymru.org.uk
Tel: 0845 075 5005

Scotland

scotland.shelter.org.uk
Tel: 0808 800 4444

Housing Advice NI

Housing Advice NI aims to provide reliable independent housing advice
and information to the public in Northern Ireland. Part of its website is
dedicated to giving advice for people aged 16 to 25.

www.housingadviceni.org
Tel: 0289 024 5640 (Housing Rights Service)
Tel: 0808 800 4444 (Shelter)

Index

13